AMERICAN
VALUES IN DECLINE:
WHAT WE CAN DO

AMERICAN VALUES IN DECLINE: WHAT WE CAN DO

By

William M. Fox

ISBN: 1-58820-692-0

1stBooks - rev. 1/16/01

ACKNOWLEDGMENTS

I am particularly indebted to Dick Renner for his constructive comments and guidance. Others who helped very much were Leonard Emmel, Else Fox, Jack Hurse, Chris Jones, Don Legler, Bill Pepper, Rose Reynolds, and Jimmy Yawn.

In addition, I received useful comments and suggestions from Wayne Archer, Lou Delaney, Inge Fox-Jones, Mike Gannon, Jane Burman-Holton, Virginia Maurer, Dorie Thomas, and Perry Whydman. And I am grateful to Donna Cunningham for her assistance with word processing.

DEDICATION

To Else,

.

The best thing that ever happened to me.

CONTENTS

INTRODUCTION xv
The Power Of Values xv
Ethical Reality Can Be Complex xxvii
A Preview xxx

Chapter 1 WHY CERTAIN CORE VALUES ARE
ESSENTIAL TO OUR WELL-BEING 1
The Need To Distinguish Peripheral Values 3
Choosing Core Values 4
Our Inherited Core Values 4
    A Common Philosophy 4
    The Issue Of Slavery 7
Support For Core And Related Values Today 12
    Duty, Honesty, Integrity, And Being Responsible 12
    Being Ambitious, Hardworking, And Aspiring 18
    Emphasis On Learning 20
    Providing Equality Of Opportunity 22
Conclusion 23

Chapter 2 THE COMPATIBILITY OF OUR CORE
VALUES WITH THOSE OF VARIOUS RELIGIONS
AND OTHER SOURCES 25
Buddhism 25
Confucianism 26
Hinduism 27
Islamism 28
Judaism 29
Declaration Of The World Conference Of Religions
For Peace 30
Declaration Toward A Global Ethic 31
Declaration Of The United Nations 33
Value Orientations of Some Notables From The Past 35
Conclusion 37

Chapter 3 OUR CORE VALUES ARE BEING
SUBVERTED 39
Evidence Of Negative Change In Levels Of Honesty
And Trust 42
Evidence Of Negative Change About Regard For
Others 44
Evidence Of Negative Change In Rates Of Crime And
Violence 46
Evidence Of Negative Change In The Social
Environment 47
Evidence of Negative Change In The Maintenance Of
Healthy Family Life 49
   Decreasing Number Of Two-Parent Homes 49
   Decline In The Quality Of Family Life 51
   Increased Use Of Drugs 54
Evidence Of Negative Change In Part Of The Black
Culture 55
   Delinquency, Violence, and Crime: 56
   Illegitimacy And Broken Families: 57
   Disregard For Academic Attainment 57
   Rejection Of Positive, Black Role Models 59
   Lack Of Mutual Economic Support 60
   Unwarranted Black-Against-Black Discrimination 61
Conclusion 62

Chapter 4 HOW WE ACQUIRE VALUES 63
How A Healthy Conscience Develops 63
Further Development Through Conscious Analysis 66
The Genetic Factor 67
Conclusion 74

Chapter 5 THE ROLE OF VALUES IN CAUSING
BEHAVIOR 75
Values Influence Our Energy To Act 75
Values Influence Conscious Analysis 76
Values interact with Situational Factors 76
Values Influence Our "Can Do" Feelings 82
How These Factors Interact To Cause Behavior 82

Conclusion 83

Chapter 6 HOW TO NURTURE CORE VALUES IN
OURSELVES AND OTHERS 85
Dealing With Emotionally Charged Values 85
Dealing With The Urge For Immediate Gratification 88
   Cue Control 88
   Consequence Control 90
   What About Objections To Behavior Management?
Enhancing Feelings of Self-Efficacy 95
Encouraging Truthfulness And Full Disclosure In
Group Problem Solving 93
How The Factors Influence Ethical Behavior 97
Increasing The Likelihood For Creating Healthy And
Stable Families 98
   By Encouraging Couples To Seek Pre-marriage
   Counseling 98
   By Discouraging Inappropriate Conception 99
   By Dealing Effectively With Irresponsible Young
   Fathers 102
Improving The Quality Of Family Life 103
Reducing The Incidence Of Delinquency And Crime 105
   By Dealing Effectively With Troubled Young
   People 106
   By Dealing Effectively With The Homeless And
   The New And Long-Term Unemployed 109
   By Dealing Effectively With Hardened Criminals 117
Discouraging Fantasies About Life In Africa 117
Conclusion 120

Chapter 7 THE NEED FOR NURTURING CORE
VALUES IN OUR SCHOOLS AND HOW WE WE
CAN DO IT 121
The Erosion Of Standards And Expectations 122
   Questionable Preparation Of Teachers 124
   Lack of Parental Support 125
What Needs To Be Done 126
   Improve The Preparation Of Teachers 126

Support Successful Programs For Underachieving
Students 127
Enhance Motivation 129
Support Successful School-Reform and School-
Choice Programs 130
Support The Teaching Of Values In School 136
Reject Spurious Claims Of Unwarranted
Discrimination: 141
Show Parents Or Guardians The Evidence And Get
Them Involved 144
Prospects 145

Chapter 8 THE NEED FOR NURTURING CORE
VALUES IN POLITICAL LEADERSHIP AND HOW
WE CAN DO IT 147
The Self-Serving Culture Of Expediency,
Indifference, And Opportunism 147
The Grace Report 147
Things Have Not Gotten Better 148
The Buying And Selling Of Influence 150
What Needs To Be Done 155
Misdirections In Welfare 157
From Rationality To Rewarding Undesirable
Behavior: 158
Further Flight From Personal Responsibility 162
Resulting Decline In The Quality Of Welfare
Recipients 163
Stop Non-Productive Spending 165
Implement Governmental Specifics That Work 166
Properly Use Minimum Wages And Subsidies 169
Create Productive, 24-Hour Environments 171
Conclusion 173

Chapter 9 THE NEED FOR NURTURING CORE
VALUES IN THE ADMINISTRATION OF JUSTICE
AND HOW WE CAN DO IT 175
Diminished Personal Accountability 175
Justice For Whom? 177

Misdirections In The Rehabilitation Of Criminals.............. 177
Employers Put On The Spot.. 179
What Needs To Be Done 179

Chapter 10 THE NEED FOR NURTURING CORE
VALUES IN BUSINESS AND HOW WE CAN DO
IT 185
Inadequate Regulation.. 191
Unwarranted Compensation.. 191
Deception And Exploitation.. 193
Questionable Payoffs Abroad 196
Attempts To Justify Different Standards For Business........ 197
    The Doctrine of Laissez Faire 198
    Social Darwinism 202
    The Game Analogy 203
    Cost/Benefit Analysis.. 205
    Conclusion.. 210
Workable Programs Are Attainable 210
    Within An Organization 211
    Among Different Organizations 212
    Across Cultures 215
What Needs To Be Done 218
    Reform Boards of Directors 218
    Select The Right Leaders 221
    Ethically Empower Lower-Level Personnel 222
    Use Communication, Modeling, and Discussion 225
    Use The Principled Negotiations Approach in
    Bargaining 226
    Downsize Intelligently 228
    Reduce The Conflict Between Job and Family
    Obligations 230
    Use The Search Conference 231
    Install Gainsharing 233
    Adjust For International Operations................................. 234
    Reduce The Conflict Between Domestic And
    Foreign Work-Environment Requirements 240
Conclusion 242

OVERVIEW 243

NOTES 249

INDEX 301

INTRODUCTION

Values - the ideals, customs, and institutions of a society - deserve careful study because they define what is moral: what is right and wrong conduct. They powerfully influence the way we live and how we define ourselves.

A 1999 Wall Street Journal/NBC News poll of 2011 people found that 67 percent of Americans felt that we had experienced a moral decline.[1] Subsequent chapters will document the reality of this perception, present the values that have made us great as individuals and as a nation, and explain how we can nurture them in ourselves and others.

The Power Of Values: First, let's consider the power of values to influence behavior:

As a boy of 14, I visited the Smithsonian Institution in Washington, DC. I was startled to see a pack parachute on display, because it had been patented in 1912, and I knew that none had been issued to our allied pilots in World War I. I was even more surprised when I learned that such chutes had been issued to German pilots in the last half of 1918. Why had this happened? Why had allied pilots been denied this important protection?

I found a surprising answer through subsequent interviews and reading. Most of the pilots - and their superiors - sincerely believed that parachutes would take the edge off of their fighting resolve and possibly induce them to abandon a fight or their planes prematurely. At the same time, thousands of soldiers on the ground made frontal assaults against withering machine gun fire. Clearly, untold numbers risked their lives in the service of their values about honor and patriotism.

In this same vein, consider the unchanging behavior of British regular soldiers in America for more than 100 years. From their earliest days of fighting here, they invited numerous, unnecessary defeats and suffered thousands of needless casualties, by marching in straight lines in bright, red uniforms.

They persisted in this behavior for years, despite the many defeats they suffered due to the advantages enjoyed by a concealed and dispersed enemy. The crowning debacle, the Battle of New Orleans in 1815, lasted less than an hour. British soldiers were cut down in droves as they marched in regular columns into murderous fire from concealed and fortified American positions. Result: 192 British killed, 1265 wounded; 13 Americans killed, 13 wounded.[2]

Was this refusal to profit from disastrous experience due to simple stupidity? Hardly. Nor does it seem likely that it was the result of fearful obedience to incompetent officers, as the vastness and indifference of the colonial environment made desertion relatively safe and easy. A more likely explanation seems to be that dying by the rules and brave traditions of the professional soldier was more acceptable than surviving by the "cowardly" - though highly successful - tactics of "amateur" colonials and savages.

Such "value-power" was dramatized, also, by the behavior of Japanese kamikaze pilots in World War II. They voluntarily dived bomb-laden planes to certain death due to strongly held values about their emperor and the defense of their homeland.

And consider our Marine Corps. What has made it one of the most effective and elite fighting forces in the world? Certainly *not* high pay, perks, bonuses, or assurances of avoiding personal harm. Thomas Ricks describes Marine basic indoctrination. Recruits are denied the typical basic diversions of American youth; such as, cars, candy, video games, alcohol, drugs, and sex. They are constantly reminded that self-gratification must give way to self-discipline, and after 11 weeks, they become effective team members with those of different races and backgrounds."[3]

And what about the Mormons? They left fertile, well-developed farms in Illinois and made a long, arduous trek to the barren, undeveloped land of Utah. They only took with them the possessions they could carry and their commitment to certain values - such as integrity, hard work, and helping each other. And look what they accomplished! They carved a self-sufficient, self-respecting, and law-abiding society out of the wilderness.

Another dramatic illustration of the influence of values upon behavior is provided by the Great Depression of the 1930's. It was a period of real hardship and quiet desperation for many Americans. Twenty-five percent of the labor force was unemployed and blatant discrimination against women, blacks, Jews, and other minority groups was clearly present. Aside from "mothers' aid" payments to suitable fatherless homes, there was no unemployment insurance, social security, or food stamps, and private charity was spotty. In fact, by 1932, many states had run out of money for mothers' aid, and a third of the country's private charities had closed due to lack of funds![4]

Yet, there were relatively few burglaries and assaults, as is shown in the box below. And other crime rates were much lower in 1933 than in 1994, despite the modest amount of government assistance, the absence of sophisticated police methods and networks, and the general reduction in the standard of living - when the value of all U.S. goods and services produced had slipped from $103 billion in 1929 to $56 billion by 1933![5] Depression-era people behaved as they did due to their strong commitment to values about obeying the law, respecting the rights and property of others, and being self-sufficient. There were even individuals who starved themselves rather than "stoop to accept charity!"

	1994	1933	1994	1933	1994	1933
Average City Size	719,200	641,543	147,139	140,433	34,525	35,290
# of Cities	N=65	N=35	N=137	N=52	N=623	N=141

Crime Rates Per 100,000

	1994	1933	1994	1933	1994	1933
Murder	22.5	8.8	13.6	7.1	4.7	5.
Robbery	731.7	155.5	370.6	70.8	154.	55.7
Aggravated Assault	841.7	52.9	615.7	62.2	370.8	41.6
Burglary: (Breaking in or Entering)	1546.2	428.1	1552.	449.8	1001.	318.6
Larceny Theft	4169.2	796.4	4356.	899.1	3434.9	730.1
Auto Theft	1413.6	423.7	917.	363.7	475.	201.3

Source: Data from United States Department of Justice: J. Edgar Hoover, Uniform Crime Reports, Volume 4, No. 4, January 1934, page 4; Crime in the United States, 1994 Uniform Crime Reports, November 19, 1995, pages 196-197.

Another illustration of behavior during the Depression Era is provided by the customer-payment procedure that was used in a fast-food Toddle House in New Orleans, where customers paid by an "honor system." A counterman punched the amount owed on a ticket. Then, upon leaving, the customer was expected to drop this amount, along with the ticket, in a bus-like, money chute by the door. Business was often so brisk that there was no way the counterman could check on whether or not a given individual paid. But the business prospered - it was protected by strongly held customer values about honesty.

Contrast this period with the one represented by New York City in the 1980's, when well-fed and adequately clothed looters gleefully smashed their way into furniture and appliance stores during a power blackout. Upon being questioned about their behavior by an on-camera reporter, one well-laden looter said: "Hey, man, we got this coming to us." Upon hearing of a criminologist's claim that such riotous looting is a "cry for help," columnist George Will characterizes it more as "a cry for a free color TV set."[6] Examples like this raise an interesting question. Does poverty cause most crime, as many people seem to believe, or is it just the other way around? Do characteristics such as poor education, need for immediate gratification, and anti-social attitudes tend to cause poverty and crime?

Certainly, the lower crime rates for the Depression years - when unemployment stood at 25 percent of the labor force and there was minimum government assistance - support the view that poverty is not the major cause. William Buckley, Jr. attributes the following to David Rubinstein of the University of Illinois: "How can one use 'the-poverty-causes-crime' argument to account for a black teenager conviction rate that is three times the rate of blacks aged 25 and 30, when the latter are typically more dependent upon work and money?" [7]

In addition, we find that, as early as the 1980's, our crime rates were significantly higher than those of Europe and many other countries - such as Egypt, the Philippines, and Thailand - despite the fact that we had fewer people in extremely depressed conditions of poverty and provided greater opportunity for upward mobility.[8] The table below shows the same thing when we compare our homicide rates with those of other developed countries that were not as well off, materially.

1988 Homicide Rates In Eleven Developed Countries
(per 100,000 people)

	Men	Women
United States	13.9	4.1
Czechoslovakia	3.4	1.3
Hungary	3.1	1.9
Canada	2.7	1.4
Australia	2.4	1.5
Italy	2.4	.6
Spain	2.	.4
France	1.5	.9
West Germany	1.1	1.1
Japan	.9	.6
United Kingdom	.8	.6

Source: World Health Organization Statistics, The New York Times, June 27, 1990.

Father William J. Byron, president of the Catholic University of America, cautions us: "Do not believe that to have is to be, that to have more is to be more fully human, and, worst lie of all, that to live easily is to live happily."[9] Presumably, he means that the pursuit of material well-being is less important to happiness than is emphasis upon meaningful work, personal growth, and behavior that enhances the lives of others. The high preference given to "true love" by our wealthiest Americans (in the box below) seems to support Father Byron's observation.

The Average Bid From 500 Of The Top-One-Percent-In-Income People In The U.S. For Each of The Following:

A Place in Heaven	$ 640,000
True Love	487,000
Great Intellect	407,000
Talent	285,000
Eternal Youth	407,000
To Be Reunited With A Lost Love	206,000
Great Beauty	83,000
To Be President of The U.S.	55,000
Fame	15,000
Relationship With Movie Star/Celebrity	4,000

Source: Survey by Roper Starch Worldwide for Worth, September, 1997, page 78.

More support for Father Byron's position is provided by public-opinion surveys conducted during the 1974-1983 period. They show that the people in Northern Ireland had the same level of contentment as those in the Netherlands, despite the fact that the per capita income of the Irish was only half as high; that the French were much less content than the Irish, despite the fact that they were twice as rich; and that even Americans scored below the Irish, despite having the highest per capita income of all![10]

In addition, we find support in research findings about the impact of inherited wealth. On the basis of his interviews with wealthy parents, their children, and the psychotherapists of wealthy patients, John Levy concludes that parental money should help to ease the way, but it should not be used to eliminate the need for their children to earn a living. And his conclusion is supported by interview data collected by the Inheritance Project in Blacksburg, Virginia. The following theme is clearly implied: "Abundant wealth has a way of separating heirs from the grist of life."[11]

Who Is Happiest?

"My impression is that those living in the materially developed countries, for all their industry, are in some ways less satisfied, are less happy, and to some extent suffer more than those living in the least developed countries."

Source: The Dalai Lama, Ethics For The New Millennium. New York: Riverhead Books, 1999, page 5.

We should consider, too, the power of values in the Nazi death camps. Did most of the captives - subjected to one of the most threatening environments ever created - abandon all ideas of decency and integrity and automatically regress to animal-like attempts to survive at any cost? According to authoritative reports from the survivors, the answer is "no."[12]

Of course, in addition to the positive power of values, there is strong negative power. Consider the absence of upward mobility for immigrants from Mexico and Central America, in contrast to the impressive achievements of those from China, Japan, and Korea. The latter cultures, along with many others, attach high value to education, work, achievement, and saving. While those cultures that are resistant to material progress tend toward passivity and fatalism, and are less committed to entrepreneurship and education.[13]

In his book, Does Africa Need A Cultural Adjustment Program?, Daniel Manguelle, a Cameronian, asserts that Africa's poverty, authoritarianism, and social injustice are due largely to such values as fatalism, a belief in sorcery, a distaste for work, and indifference to initiative, achievement, and saving. Similarly, many American reservation Indians are discouraged from displaying initiative and upward mobility by traditional values that stress fatalism and a high degree of egalitarianism. And David Fisher traces the roots of Appalachian poverty to a heritage from a poverty-ridden Scottish-Irish-English region characterized by distaste for work and disdain of education.[14]

Consider the number of innocent people who turn themselves in each year to get the punishment they feel they deserve - and will be even more miserable without. They have been programmed with such all-pervasive feelings of unworthiness and guilt that they have no idea of why they feel as they do and must manufacture fictitious crimes to maintain any semblance of self-acceptance.

Recall how pioneer Americans removed peaceful Indians from their land as Christian soldiers slaughtered their defenseless women and children, due to the belief that they were dealing with unworthy savages. Recall how the Nazis murdered millions of Jews, how the Communist Party deliberately starved millions of Russian kulaks, and how Mao promoted a famine that killed millions in China. Many of the perpetrators "did their duty" with the belief that they were creating new, superior societies. And, today, due to strongly held convictions, we have the continuing, brutal slaughter of innocent "outsiders" in Africa, Bosnia, and elsewhere under the banner of "ethnic cleansing." As an example, Pierre Rigoulot estimates that the North Korean Communists have eliminated some 3 million people over the last 50 years.[15]

Due to dysfunctional values, little girls are being sexually mutilated in some 25 African and Middle Eastern countries. In some places, only a piece of the clitoris is cut off; in others, the labia minora are removed; and elsewhere, all outer genitalia are removed and the two sides of the vulva are stitched together, leaving only a slight opening, until marriage.[16] In addition, girls in the United States face the possibility of such mutilation, if they happen to be daughters of immigrants from those areas.[17] And it is estimated that some 70 percent of Egyptian women have undergone some form of it. Yet, amazingly, an Egyptian court overturned a government ban on such mutilation as recently as 1997![18]

Salman Rushdie tells us about the increasing practice in India of setting brides on fire due to outrage over inadequate dowries, and adds that ritual child sacrifice is still being performed by some followers of the goddess Kali.[19] Lisa Beyer reports that male family members in Jordan and other parts of the Arab world may be permitted to murder female members who have threatened the "family's honor"; for example, for marrying or divorcing against the family's wishes, and even for having been raped against their will! [20]

A 1989 National Research Council report claims that boys aged 7-10 in the Sambia society of Papua, New Guinea, are routinely introduced to homosexual practices.[21] And Amnesty International's 1975 <u>Survey On Torture</u> identified more than 60 countries - both democracies and police states - that had systematically used torture, believing that the ends justify such inhumane practices.[22]

A spokesman for the Australian Anti-Slavery Society, Paul Bravender-Coyle, reports that some 104-146 million children in Pakistan, India, and Nepal - but mostly India - are making consumer goods for export as forced-laborers, due to the cruelty and insensitivity of their masters. Their living conditions are deplorable and "The punishments meted out to these children... defy description. They have been burned, branded with red-hot irons, starved, whipped, chained up, raped and kept locked in cupboards for days on end."[23]

When we look at the theological aspects of various religions - such as the identity of the one true god, the existence of heaven or hell or the devil, the reality of miracles or reincarnation, the specific requirements for baptism or for being "saved" - we find many conflicting beliefs. And far too often throughout history, fanaticism about the differences has created awesome, negative-value power. It has caused total disregard for the unifying core values of these same religions (discussed in Chapter 2) about how we should live together in harmony.

The Common Denominator of All Religions?

"The important point to keep in mind is that ultimately the whole purpose of religion is to facilitate love and compassion, patience, tolerance, humility, forgiveness, and so on."

Source: The Dalai Lama, Ethics For The New Millennium. New York: Riverhead Books, 1999, page 230.

When denominationalism is taken too seriously, it becomes a form of tribalism that has divisive effects upon those who profess a commitment to the brotherhood of man. For example:

Consider the tortures and executions of the Spanish Inquisition, the excesses of the Salem witch burnings, the bombings and murders in Ireland, the massacres in India, and the butchering of Arab women and children during the Crusades by Christian knights.

Lisa Beyer reports that in Jerusalem, in 1998, ultra-Orthodox Jews pelted men and women with excrement for praying together at the Western Wall, and that 47 percent of the Israelis at that time believed that a religious civil war was likely![24]

In certain places, the rise of Islamic fundamentalism has effectively criminalized the practice of Christianity. Michael Horowitz reports that one evening in 1994, most of the members of the largest evangelical Christian church in the Muslim-controlled Oromo region of southern Ethiopia were arrested. They died in jail and were denied proper burial. Their minister was permitted to live, but only after being tortured and having his eyes plucked out.

He indicates that the Armed Islamic Group in Algeria recently called for the "annihilation and physical liquidation of Christian crusaders," that Christian converts in Egypt have been imprisoned and tortured, and that there have been periodic beatings of Christian students for being "devils."

He tells us that Christians in Pakistan are permitted to vote, but only for token representatives to the National Assembly. He reports that, under apostasy doctrines in Iran, converts to Christianity are effectively barred from attending religious services, and that many have been arrested and tortured in attempts to make them renounce their faith, while others have lost their jobs, homes, or businesses.

Horowitz tells us that conversion to Christianity in Sudan is considered a criminal act punishable by flogging; that the Sudanese government denies food to famine-area Christians; and that it permitted thousands of Christian children to be taken from their families and sold as slaves there, as well as in Libya and other Islamic countries.[25] Nina Shea indicates that such persecution has caused more than 1.5 million deaths, as well as the relocation of whole villages to concentration camps where food is given only to those who convert to Islam.[26]

Macram Gassis, the Catholic bishop of Southern Sudan, testified at an anti-slavery conference at Columbia University in May of 1995 that Southern Sudanese are bought and sold for as little as $15; that Ushari Ahmad Mahmoud, author of a book on human rights violations, has described how Arab militias raid Sudanese villages, kill the men, then round-up their women and children and brand their ears to discourage escape.[27]

Divisive effects are also created by overly zealous Christian fundamentalists. They need to heed cautions given by such authorities as Origen, the great 3rd century church father; St. Thomas Aquinas; St. Augustine of Hippo; and Raymond

Brown, a leading Catholic scriptural scholar in the U.S., about overly literal interpretations of the Bible that can push one into the arena of dogmatic intolerance. Brown illustrates this pitfall by referring to the raising of Lazarus in the Book of John. The event is given as a prime reason for the arrest and execution of Jesus; yet, none of the other three Gospels even mentions the incident, though all are presumed to have been written before John wrote his.[28]

Lastly, Toler reports a powerful association between addictive behavior and value orientation. He found that alcoholics and heroin addicts - in comparison with those who are non-addicted - tend to rank personal values as being significantly more important and social values as being significantly less important.[29] And Rokeach has shown that the rankings of only two values, freedom and equality, effectively distinguish fascist, capitalist, socialist, and communist ideologies from each other.[30]

Ethical Reality Can Be Complex: There is debate today over whether or not rules and goals of desirable conduct can be agreed upon, let alone, prescribed for all. Some argue that there are no legitimate behavioral absolutes. "Realistically," they say, "moral judgments cannot ignore an individual's background relative to the situation at hand; therefore, to understand these factors is to forgive, and it would be unfair to hold the individual accountable for what happened." This is underscored by a 1997 survey conducted by the Lutheran Brotherhood, an insurance company, which found that 79 percent of Americans in the 18-34 age group believe that there are no absolute ethical standards.[31] On the other hand, some argue that the Bible or the Koran - or some other sacred source - provides absolute guidelines for everyone, everywhere, and under all circumstances.

Both approaches contain grains of truth. However, they represent simplistic attempts to deal with complex reality. Though we are attracted by the certainty and straight-forwardness they seem to provide, history and simple observation demonstrate their inadequacies. Life is full of challenging ethical dilemmas. For example, we had good reason to believe that we could save a million lives and shorten the war with Japan by dropping the atomic bomb, but some physicists argued that we shouldn't, due to the possibility of launching a new age of incredible horror. Who was right? Is it reasonable to abort a fetus before it becomes a viable human being when the expectant mother has neither the capacity or wherewithal to support an unwanted child? And when, realistically, does a fetus become a viable human being?*

*Cornell researcher Carl Sagan and Ann Druyan observe that:

"Every human sperm and egg is, beyond the shadow of a doubt, alive. They are not human beings, of course. However, it could be argued that neither is a fertilized egg...

"The Jewish Talmud teaches that the fetus is not a person and has no rights. The Old and New Testaments—rich in detailed prohibitions on dress, diet and permissible words——contain not a word specifically prohibiting abortion...The Catholic Church's first and longstanding collection of canon law (according to the leading historian of the Church's teachings on abortion, John Connery, S.J.) held that abortion was homicide only after the fetus was already `formed'——roughly, the end of the first trimester. Surprisingly, it was not until 1869 that abortion at any time for any reason became grounds for excommunication...

"When do distinct and characteristic human qualities emerge?...By the sixth week, the embryo is 13 millimeters (about $1/2$ inch) long. The eyes are still on the side of the head, as in most animals, and the reptilian face has connected slits where the mouth and nose eventually will be...Recognizably human brain activity begins intermittently around the middle of the seventh month."[32]

Biologist F. M. Sturtevant reports that a panel of the National Institute of Health on Research On Human Conception asserts that studies should be conducted on concepti less than 14 days old; that before day 14, the embryoblast can develop into an embryo proper, a tumor, a hydatidiform mole, a choriocarcinoma (cancer), twins or triplets, or (in at least two-thirds of the cases) nothing at all (due to genetic defects).[33]

In subsequent chapters we will consider other special ethical problems, such as those associated with business, political leadership, welfare programs, the criminal-justice system, and cross-cultural relations.

<u>A Preview</u>: A basic theme of this book is: *The key to resolving the "dilemma of the extremes" (absolutism vs. excessive permissiveness) lies in clearly distinguishing and nurturing basic core values - those which have proven their usefulness and general acceptance - from less-essential ones.* We will identify these core values, document why there is increased need today to nurture them, and discuss how this can be done.

In addition, we will examine such matters as:

Our often-overlooked, rich inheritance of core values from the founding fathers.

How a conscience develops, or fails to develop.

Why some people are predisposed at birth toward inappropriate behavior.

The role that values play in determining behavior.

The compatibility of core values from various religions and other cross-cultural sources.

What we can do to enhance ethical behavior in business, politics, the welfare system, the criminal-justice system, our schools, and our everyday lives.

Chapter 1

WHY CERTAIN CORE VALUES ARE
ESSENTIAL TO OUR WELL-BEING

George Washington

"...There is no truth more thoroughly established, than that there exists in the economy and course of nature an indissoluble union between virtue and happiness, between duty and advantage, between the genuine maxims of an honest and magnanimous policy, and the solid rewards of public prosperity and felicity."

Source: First Inaugural Address, 1789, reported by Constance Bridges in Great Thoughts Of Great Americans. New York: Thomas Y. Crowell Company, 1951, page 27.

Trust may be defined as "a psychological state comprising the intention to accept vulnerability based upon positive expectations of the intentions or behavior of another."[1] It is essential, if interpersonal relationships are to be meaningful and productive. Trust is nurtured by everyday commitment to shared values and goals and the capacity to honor this commitment through the practice of self-restraint. And these observations apply to all situations - whether we are dealing with relationships in a primitive tribe, family life, business, professional services, military operations, religious or charitable activities, sports, or everyday social encounters.

These realities were apparent to Charles Darwin many years ago. He observed that:

"The virtues which must be practised, at least generally, by rude men, so that they may associate in a

1

body, are those which are still recognised as the most important...No tribe could hold together if murder, robbery, treachery, &c., were common; consequently, such crimes within the limits of the same tribe are branded with everlasting infamy.

"There cannot be fidelity without truth; and this fundamental virtue is not rare between the members of the same tribe: thus Mungo Park heard the negro women teaching their young children to love truth...

"We have now seen that actions are regarded by savages, and were probably so regarded by primeval man, as good or bad, solely as they obviously affect the welfare of the tribe."[2]

A larger society or nation is really a "confederation" of smaller societies or cultures. It can be viable and productive to the extent that its members share certain over-arching values and goals - in the absence of seriously conflicting ones - that relate to personal behavior that affects other people.

Francis Fukuyama, a Rand Corporation scholar, stresses the need for this kind of intergroup sharing. He asserts that such trust is a key to markets, and ultimately, a nation's wealth; that kinship groups in low-trust societies may be tightly bound, but their members have difficulty in trusting "outsiders." He points out that it is only in more trusting societies that businesses can succeed more fully by reaching beyond kinship boundaries to thrive nationally and globally.[3] Consequently, he is particularly concerned about our preoccupation with group rights and with irresponsible experiments with multi-cultural reforms in education, because such efforts are diluting the common culture that pulls us together. He feels that the viability of a liberal state is grounded in old-fashioned virtues.[4]

In this regard, Joseph Plaud and Nancy Vogeltanz provide Bronowski's list of universal values that are required to create a social climate that will be supportive of intelligent inquiry and planning for the future: <u>honesty</u>; <u>freedom of inquiry, thought, and speech</u>; <u>justice</u>; and <u>respect for human dignity</u>.[5]

Generally, those who succeed in life - both psychologically and materially - do so as the result of positive attitudes, the pursuit of an adequate education through deferred gratification and self-discipline, and sustained hard work thereafter. True, a man can starve through no fault of his own and, understandably, steal a loaf of bread to feed his family. But this type of need hardly applies to many commonplace crimes today - such as rape, gratuitous assault, stealing to satisfy addictions, or auto theft - that reflect the absence of sound personal values.

The Need To Distinguish Peripheral Values: We need to distinguish a society's core values from less-socially- essential ones. That is, ones that have to do with personal indulgences and preferences that do little harm to others and are largely peripheral to the values required for mutual trust and harmony. Unfortunately, the need for this distinction is frequently overlooked by the ruling elders of a society. In their zeal to prescribe for others, they often forget their own youthful need for "breathing room" to further define and defend a fragile identity and to accommodate relatively harmless growing pains. As a consequence, many small communities have seen their young people alienated and lost to big cities because the local culture failed to adequately distinguish fads from basic values; individual style from substantial issues.

Undue Emphasis Upon Peripheral Values

(Essence of a Statute Passed in 1660 in the Massachusetts Colony)

Publick Notice

The obfervation of Christmas having been deemed a sacrilege, the exchanging of gifts, greetings, dreffing in fine clothing, feafting and similar satanical practices are hereby forbidden with the offender liable to a fine of five shillings.

Source: Atlantic Monthly, December 1979, page 91.

Choosing Core Values:
Ideally, a society should choose its core values by considering the *type of harm* that certain behaviors can cause - physical, economic, or psychological, or a combination of these - in relation to *the intensity of such harm*; for example, individual versus group harm, and the extent of monetary loss. However, more often than not, a society's values are created and retained by belief and tradition, rather than by objective investigation or analysis, as they are handed from one generation to another through instruction, stories, personal example, and the absence of proposed alternative beliefs and ways of doing things.

Our Inherited Core Values: We are fortunate that our inherited core values satisfy the positive criteria presented above. They are values that have made it possible for us to be free from the tyranny of an individual or a majority. In fact, they have made it possible for our democratic form of government to survive until now. Let's consider two important aspects of our heritage:

A *Common Philosophy:* We owe much to a commonly held political philosophy on the part of our founding fathers. Unlike the fathers of other revolutions, they not only wrote a constitution designed to facilitate and safeguard equitable democracy, they personally tried to uphold it in their everyday lives. For example, in Federalist Paper No. 2, founder John Jay, observes that:

> "Providence has been pleased to give this one connected country to one united people - a people descended from the same ancestors, speaking the same language, professing the same religion, attached to the same principles of government, very similar in their manners and customs, and who, by their joint counsels, arms, and efforts, fighting side by side throughout a long and bloody war, have nobly established general liberty and independence.
>
> "This country and this people seem to have been made for each other, and it appears as if it were the design of

4

Providence, that an inheritance so proper and convenient for a band of brethren, united to each other by the strongest ties, should never be split into a number of unsocial, jealous, and alien sovereignties."[6]

To stress the special requirements of our system, James Madison (or Alexander Hamilton) wrote the following in Federalist Paper No. 55:

"As there is a degree of depravity in mankind which requires a certain degree of circumspection and distrust, so there are other qualities in human nature which justify a certain portion of esteem and confidence. Republican government presupposes the existence of these qualities in a higher degree than any other form. Were the pictures which have been drawn by the political jealousy among some of us faithful likenesses of the human character, the inference would be that there is not sufficient virtue among men for self-government; and that nothing less than the chains of despotism can restrain them from destroying and devouring one another."[7]

John Stuart Mill - eminent English philosopher, economist, and ethical theorist - in his essay, "On Liberty," adds:

"Despotism is a legitimate mode of government in dealing with barbarians, provided the end be their improvement, and the means justified by actually effecting that end. Liberty, as a principle, has no application to any state of things anterior to the time when mankind have become capable of being improved by free and equal discussion..."[8]

"All that makes existence valuable to anyone, depends on the enforcement of restraints upon the actions of other people. Some rules of conduct, therefore, must be imposed, by law in the first place, and by opinion on many things which are not fit subjects for the operation of the law."[9]

And George Washington cautions us:

"Do we know that the first form of self-government is governing ourselves - not through indifference or rigidity, but through respecting our fellows and wanting to play an honorable part in the world...Do we understand that liberty isn't a vacation from restraint, but a duty to govern?[10]

Lord Moulton, Noted English Judge, On The Virtues Of Commitment And Self-Restraint

"The real greatness of a nation, its true civilization, is measured by the extent of...Obedience to the Unenforceable."

Source: Talk presented to the Authors' Club in London, prior to his death in 1921, (printed in The Atlantic, July, 1924, page 2).

Based upon his stay in France in the early 1790's and his experience as our ambassador there starting in 1792, Governor Morris was convinced that our system of government, to succeed, places special requirements upon its citizens. In fact, he predicted the failure of the French Revolution due to the absence of these special requirements:

"I wish much, very much, the happiness of this inconstant people. I love them. I feel grateful for their efforts in our cause...But I do not greatly indulge the flattering illusions of hope, because I do not yet perceive that reformation of morals without which liberty is but an empty sound...

"When a man of high rank and importance laughs today at what he seriously asserted yesterday, it is considered as in the natural order of things...The great mass of the common people have no religion but their priests, no law but their superiors, no moral but their interest."[11]

Louis D. Brandeis, Former Associate Supreme Court Justice

"Democracy in any sphere is a serious undertaking. It substitutes self-restraint for external restraint. It is more difficult to maintain than to achieve. It demands continuous sacrifice by the individual and more exigent obedience to the moral law than any other form of government."

Source: A 1922 letter reported by Constance Bridges in Great Thoughts Of Great Americans. New York: Thomas Y. Crowell Company, 1951, page 206.

In addition to stressing the need for liberty to be coupled with self-restraint, our founding fathers supported the idea that certain basic, non-conflicting individual and minority rights must be protected, while giving priority to the shared values and goals of the majority. Thus, we see stated or implied in the material presented above the core values of duty, accountability, honesty and truthfulness, education, self-discipline, respect for others, and liberty - with abstinence from treachery, theft, and murder.

The Issue Of Slavery: As a matter of record, most of the founding fathers opposed slavery. President Lincoln observed: "If those who wrote and adopted the Constitution believed slavery to be a good thing, why did they insert a provision prohibiting the slave trade after the year 1808?" He also pointed out that free Negroes were voters in five of the original 13 states.[12] Here is a sampler of founding-father views:

George Washington: "There is not a man living who wishes more sincerely than I do, to see a plan adopted for the abolition of it."[13]

John Adams: "Every measure of prudence, therefore, ought to be assumed for the eventual extirpation of slavery from the United States...I have through my whole life, held the practice of slavery in...abhorrence."[14]

Benjamin Franklin: "Slavery is...an atrocious debasement of human nature."[15]

James Madison: "We have seen the mere distinction of color made in the most enlightened period of time, a ground of the most oppressive dominion ever exercised by man over man."[16]

Thomas Jefferson: "The whole commerce between master and slave is a perpetual exercise of...the most unremitting despotism on the one part, and degrading submissions on the other."[17]

John Jay: "Those who know the value of liberty, and are blessed with the enjoyment of it, ought not to subject others to slavery..."[18]

As evidence that this was not meaningless rhetoric, some 5000 slaves from every part of America who fought in the Revolutionary War were freed (except those from South Carolina and Georgia) - though Alexander Hamilton had proposed this type of emancipation for South Carolina as well, while he served on Washington's military staff.[19] The House of Representatives of New York, a slave state, formally resolved in 1776 that slavery is "utterly inconsistent with the avowed principles in which this and other states have carried on their struggle for liberty."[20] Subsequently, it, and seven other states, abolished slavery, either gradually or immediately: Vermont in 1777, New York in 1799, Pennsylvania in 1780, Rhode Island

8

and Connecticut in 1783, Massachusetts and New Hampshire in the 1780's, and New Jersey in 1804.[21]

According to Thomas West, Jefferson proposed a law in 1779 that provided for the gradual emancipation of slaves in Virginia. It was not passed. Then, he proposed a law in Congress in 1784 to ban slavery from the entire Western territory, and this came within one vote of passage.[22] But these failures were short-lived. In 1787 Congress passed the Northwest Ordinance which outlawed slavery in the future states of Ohio, Indiana, Michigan, Illinois, and Wisconsin.

Slavery remained legal in the South; however, surprisingly, the first census in 1790 reported 32,000 free blacks there. And by 1810, this number had grown to 108,000, due largely to the action of certain slave owners who willingly relinquished the investment involved.[23] To appreciate the magnitude of their financial sacrifice, consider that a young, healthy, male slave sold for as much as $1000 in the 1850's - the equivalent of some $50,000 today![24] Another interesting fact is that the owning of slaves was not, uniquely, a white phenomenon. According to Sandburg, as least one in every 100 free Negroes owned one or two slaves - and a few owned as many as 50 or more! [25]

Abraham Lincoln

"I never knew a man who wished himself a slave. Consider if you know any *good* thing, that no man desires for himself."

Source: Carl Sandburg, Abraham Lincoln: The Prairie Years And The War Years. New York: Galahad Books, 1993, page 495.

If the ideals expressed by the founders and the language of the Constitution were sincerely meant, why was emancipation such a drawn-out and painful process? West points out that the founding fathers were confronted with two conflicting principles: the concept of equal rights and the right of consent to be governed, with the latter right (via voting) belonging just as much to the prejudiced as to the more enlightened.

Given the strongly held feelings of those slave owners who were bent upon protecting their investment and their way of life, it seems clear that insistence upon immediate freeing of all slaves would have precluded the continuation of the union. But even had the owners been willing, compensating them would have been quite an undertaking. There were some 3,204,000 slaves in the South valued at more than 1.5 billion dollars![26]

In addition, desire for immediate emancipation was tempered by another concern. As was pointed out earlier, many of the founders felt that our new system of government - more than any other system - requires commitment to certain values on the part of its citizens; that it would take a period of time for former slaves (or others who were alien to our system) to become sufficiently educated and well-versed in these values before they could properly function as citizens. Consequently, many anti-slavery advocates favored the concept of gradual emancipation and honestly believed that abolition was inevitable despite the concessions they were making to the Southern states to preserve the union.

In this vein, Jefferson, Madison, Henry Clay, Daniel Webster, and (later) Lincoln believed that slaves had a right to *liberty*, but not to *immediate citizenship*. Therefore, they felt that the best way to give full and immediate freedom would be to assist the former slaves - via compensation to their owners, money, educational opportunities, and protection - in going to other places where they could establish communities according to their own values and stage of development, just as the English colonists had left Europe to found a new form of government in the new world.[27] But there was little enthusiasm on the part of free Negroes for doing this.[28]

That these concerns were warranted is suggested by the undemocratic and destructive exercise of self-government by free blacks and ex-slaves and their descendants in Liberia (see the end of Chapter 6) and by the behavior of many blacks in the post-Civil War Reconstruction Governments of the South. With regard to the latter, historians Morison and Commager point out:

"The vast majority of the freedmen were quite unprepared for the exercise of any political responsibility...their innocence exposed them to temptation and their ignorance betrayed them into the hands of astute and mischievous spoilsmen who exploited them for selfish and sordid ends...

"The resulting state administrations were characterized by extravagance, corruption, and vulgarity."[29]

And Frederick Douglas, the noted black abolitionist, stated in 1848:

"What we, the colored people, want is *character*...[O]ur general ignorance makes [intelligent and educated blacks] exceptions to our race...Character is the important thing, and without it we must continue to be marked for degradation and stamped with the brand of inferiority...."[30]

A Little-Known Instance Of Emancipation

In 1827, the slave ship Guerrero was wrecked on Carysfort reef in Key West, Florida, and all but 41 of the 561 chained-together slaves were saved by the local residents. Since maritime slaving had been illegal since 1808, the survivors were declared free and were returned to Africa at federal expense.

Source: Bureau of Archaeological Research, Florida Department of State.

Unfortunately - though it occurred in the North - the expected gradual withering away of slavery did not occur in the South. To the contrary, as the South became increasingly dependent upon slave labor to produce its cotton, there was a resurgence of pro-slavery sentiment. This led to a total rejection of the Constitutional concept of liberty for all - in the future as well as the present - and the inevitability of the Civil War. The Southern position was clearly stated by Alexander Stephens, the Confederate vice president:

> "The prevailing ideas entertained by [Jefferson] and most of the leading statesmen at the time of the formation of the old constitution, were that enslavement of the African was in violation of the laws of nature; that it was wrong in *principle*, socially, morally, and politically... the general opinion of the men of that day was that, somehow or other in the order of Providence, the institution would be evanescent and pass away...

> "Our new [Confederate] government is founded upon exactly the opposite idea...that slavery - subordination to the superior race - is [the Negro's] natural and normal condition."[31]

<u>Support For Core And Related Values Today</u>: Survey data show that most Americans still support the core values presented in this book, and - as we will see - anecdotal and research data provide impressive evidence as to why they should.

Duty, Honesty, Integrity, And Being Responsible: The importance of integrity is underscored by the testimony of Vice Admiral James Stockdale who honorably survived eight years of deprivation, humiliation, and torture as a prisoner of the North Vietnamese and wears the Congressional Medal of Honor:

> "Are our students getting the message that without integrity intellectual skills are worthless?...The linkage of men's ethics, reputations, and fates can be studied in...vivid detail in prison camp. In that brutally controlled environment a perceptive enemy can get his hooks into the slightest chink in a man's ethical armor and accelerate his downfall. Given the right opening, the right moral weakness, a certain susceptibility on the part of the prisoner, a clever extortionist can drive his victim into a downhill

slide that will ruin his image, self-respect, and life in a very short time."

Admiral Stockdale goes on to quote from an ancient source - the Enchiridion, the Roman philosopher Epictetus's "manual" for the Roman field soldier:

"It's better to die in hunger, exempt from guilt and fear, than to live in affluence and with perturbation. ...Lameness is an impediment to the body but not the will....If I can get the things I need with the preservation of my honor and fidelity and self-respect, show me the way and I will get them. But, if you require me to lose my own proper good, that you may gain what is no good, consider how unreasonable and foolish you are."[32]

It is instructive that these values of honesty and integrity, as well as other core values, have been selected by thousands of parents to be taught and emphasized in our schools. These programs are discussed in Chapter 7. In addition, core values were stressed by a Council of the Parliament of the World's Religions in Chicago in 1993. In their "Declaration Toward a Global Ethic," they state:

"We take individual responsibility for all we do. All our decisions, actions, and failures have consequences... We must speak and act truthfully and with compassion, dealing fairly with all."[33]

Four national surveys conducted between the years 1968 and 1981 revealed that a representative sample of American adults still gave high priority to being honest and responsible and to providing family security.[34] More light on what this means was provided by a Wall Street Journal/NBC poll conducted in 1998 - based upon a representative sample of adults 18 or over via telephone interviews. Seventy-four percent said that adultery is always wrong, with an additional 14 percent saying it is wrong almost always. Sixty percent said divorce should be harder to obtain, and less-stable marriages were identified as the single most important factor associated with negative change in the American character since the 1950's.[35]

Such emphasis upon the importance of intact families has been validated by extensive research findings. For example, Henry Biller and Richard Solomon surveyed over 1000 studies of single-parenting outcomes and found that children so raised do significantly poorer on any criterion of social health, including delinquency.[36] Single-parent homes supply 70 percent of our juvenile offenders,[37] and even when we control for income and race, boys from single-parent homes are significantly more likely to become criminals than those from two-parent homes.[38] A child raised by a single parent is six times more likely to take drugs, drop out of school, and participate in the birth of an illegitimate child![39]

Furthermore:

> Since 1976, as the divorce rate soared, the rate of child abuse increased 331 percent.

> Children from fatherless homes comprise 60 percent of our rapists and 72 percent of our adolescent murderers.[40]

Why is single parenting usually inadequate? Here are some important reasons:

> When single-parent births are the result of promiscuity, a frequent result is the absence of adequate nurturing of the babies. The diagnostic label for this is "reactive attachment disorder."[41] It occurs, as several psychiatrists have pointed out, because continuing sex without commitment tends to erode one's feelings of self-worth, and this undermines one's ability to nurture others.[42]

Urie Bronfenbrenner, founder of the Head Start program, thinks that the greatest disadvantage of single parenting is the inability of the single parent to provide sufficient periods of personal interaction that are needed to supply enough intellectual and emotional stimulation for the child. Though

14

extended family members and others may try to fill this need, it is difficult for them to do so and, typically, they are not as effective as mutually supporting parents.[43]

Hart and Risley support this view. They describe extensive observational studies of children that were conducted over a period of 2 $\frac{1}{2}$ years or more. They found that less interaction with significant adults was associated with diminished cortical and psychological development, and they point out that early deficits are hard to remedy because cortical development is largely finished by the age of four.[44]

Adding to these problems, Bryce Christensen reports that single parenthood resulting from divorce is one of the most common causes of childhood depression, as well as other mental and physiological afflictions. He notes that over one-third of these children are still troubled and depressed five years after a divorce.[45] Also, divorce tends to make boys more hostile and withdrawn than peers from intact families.[46]

In addition to the need for adequate economic and emotional support and interactive stimulation, there is a need for the firm and consistent administration of discipline. Andrew Thomas, an assistant attorney general for the state of Arizona, observes that:

"While many of America's single mothers have shown inspiring courage in the face of indifferent former lovers and ex-husbands, it is now undeniable that many of these mothers are simply unable to control their children...Teenage boys today are often ungovernable because they lack one of the basic and crucial deterrents to juvenile misconduct - fear of answering to an angry father...Anyone who questions parental awe's unique capacity to deter naughtiness in young males should enter an inner-city school and compare the behavior of boys in classrooms headed by male and female teachers."[47]

A member of a black gang in Los Angeles describes the difference:

> "Most of the time your momma knows what's going on, but Momma's not going to be the one to tell the kid to stop it...Moms are too gentle. When I started gangbanging, my mother tried to get me to stop. I wouldn't; she saw that's what I wanted."[48]

To whom do fatherless teenagers turn for male role models, emotional support, peer acceptance, a sense of common cause, and protection from a hostile environment? They turn to anti-social gangs and their irresponsible and immature leaders. Andrew Thomas reports that by 1990, some 90,000 young people had joined gangs in Los Angeles County, alone.[49]

In reviewing 1976 U.S. crime data, Dady and Wilson found that a child who had lived with one or more substitute parents was some 100 times more likely to be fatally abused than a child living with biological parents; that a child who lived in a Canadian city in the 1980's was 70 times more likely to be killed by a parent when living with a parent and stepparent than when living with two natural parents. And children under ten were 3-4 times as likely to suffer non-fatal abuse (depending upon their age and the particular study) when living with a parent and stepparent than when living with two natural parents.[50] Furthermore, studies in both England and the U.S. estimate that 60-80 percent of felons came from the foster-care system.[51]

The report of the Council on Families in America makes a point that is often overlooked:

> "The parental relationship is unique in human affairs. In most social relationships, the reciprocity of benefits is carefully monitored, since any imbalance is regarded as exploitative. But in the parental relationship, as has often been pointed out, 'the flow of benefits is prolongedly, cumulatively, and ungrudgingly unbalanced'...No amount of public investment in children can possibly offset the private disinvestment that has accompanied the decline of marriage."[52]

16

This view is strongly supported by the experience of kibbutzim (agricultural communes) that raised thousands of children over many decades in Israel. By design, the "family" became a voluntary association of adults and children, with the children being raised by qualified personnel in on-site nurseries.

However, after only one generation, this "ideal arrangement" was questioned. Both children and parents preferred spending their evenings and nights "at home" together. Though the placement of all children in Kibbutz day-care centers has survived - since both parents work - there has been a significant increase in parental authority and involvement in running them. Irving Kristol observes that: "Amid continual soul-searching and self-criticism, family relations came more and more to resemble those in the bourgeois world that the founders had rebelled against."[53]

Even well-run, day-care centers here in America may not turn out to be a happy panacea for absentee parents. Ron Haskins found that early-care children who had spent more time in day care suffered greater ill effects regardless of the quality of the care. He found that they were "more likely to ...hit, kick, and push than children in the control group...[also] to threaten, swear, and argue." And their teachers were more likely to rate them as being seriously over-aggressive.[54] And Rutter, Bagley, and Bronfenbrenner report similar findings from other studies.[55]

More recently, a joint U.S.-Israeli study found that kibbutzim children who had received 24-hour day care were at greater risk of developing mental disorders. And a long-term National Institute of Child Health and Human Development study of 1364 diverse-background children in 10 states found that day-care placement provides a significant prediction of poorer mother-child interaction and reduced linguistic and cognitive development.[56]

Interestingly, a recent Roper Poll shows that 75 percent of Americans believe that mothers who have children under the age of three are threatening family values when they work outside of the home. And the Pew Center found that only 41 percent of women who work full time feel confident that the arrangement is good for their children.[57]

Being Ambitious, Hardworking, And Aspiring: Four national surveys conducted between the years 1968 and 1981 revealed that a representative sample of American adults still gave high priority to being ambitious, hardworking, and aspiring.[58] In addition, a Wall Street Journal/NBC poll conducted in 1998 - based upon a representative sample of adults 18 or over via telephone interviews - revealed that 83 percent ranked "hard work" as very important.[59] And the value of "performing to the best of one's ability" was selected by a majority of 1200 adult members of the Parkway School District in the St. Louis area after due deliberation.[60]

There is little question that ambition and hard work - coupled with integrity, a sense of responsibility, and the practice of self-restraint - underlie personal achievement, productivity, economic well-being, and the blessings of personal freedom. America did not become a leading world power - offering unparalleled levels of individual freedom and economic opportunity - due to manna from heaven, government welfare, or merely the presence of abundant natural resources. Productivity has been the key to our well-being, and this productivity has been the result of imaginative enterprise and innovations that are grounded in individual freedom, ambition, hard work, and interpersonal trust.

J. Hector St. John De Crevecoeur On America (1782)

"The American ought therefore to love his country much better that that in which he or his forefathers were born. Here the rewards of his industry follow with equal steps the progress of his labor...without any part being claimed either by a despotic prince, a rich abbot, or a mighty lord. Here religion demands but little of him - a small voluntary salary to the minister, and gratitude to God..."

Source: Constance Bridges in Great Thoughts Of Great Americans. New York: Thomas Y. Crowell Company, 1951, page 24.

In 1776, the average farm family, working from sunup to sunset, produced enough food to support itself and one other person. Today, due to imaginative enterprise and innovative technology, a typical American farm family can feed itself and 35 others! During this same period, however, farm output in many other parts of the world remained the same or even declined. Why so? Typically, we find that factors such as corruption and/or the lack of personal ambition, interpersonal trust, and foresight are the causes of poor-performing economies to a greater extent than the absence of natural resources. As cases in point, consider the high productivity of Hong Kong and Taiwan. Their output cannot be attributed to an abundance of natural resources.

Millions of immigrants who embrace American core values have come here and prospered. Koreans have developed a thriving community of some 400,000 in Southern California. In fact, through mutual financial support and personal assistance, one in ten Korean adults now owns a business.[61] And Thomas Sowell reports that, as of 1980, a larger percentage of West Indians, Japanese, Filipinos, and Chinese were lawyers, doctors, and teachers in America than were Anglo-Saxons! He also points out that certain ethnic groups - such as the Japanese, Jews, Poles, Chinese, and Italians - made more money.[62]

Workable individual freedom presupposes individual accountability for responsible behavior toward others and the long-term ability to support one's self. When freedom is provided without these constraints, predatory and self-destructive behaviors are encouraged, and burdens of dependency and lawlessness are created that society cannot tolerate or afford. Unfortunately, many today appear to have lost sight of this basic reality, though our founding fathers were well aware of it. The largely unregulated economic system they created worked as well as it did at times because leading citizens were constrained by personal commitment to certain values (influenced greatly by involvement in their religions) and knowledge that the community would strongly censure individuals who tried to seek personal gain without contribution.

For example - even during the Great Depression - most respectable citizens could not imagine an honorable individual who, by filing for bankruptcy, would claim exemption from personal responsibility to pay his or her creditors, however long it might take. Yet, today, many people consider this attitude almost laughable. The present trend toward unlicensed individual freedom without responsibility to others is an invitation to disaster. As Andrew Thomas observes:

> "Indeed, one of history's iron lessons is that the speed of a nation's descent ultimately depends on its citizens' degree of willingness to forgo private pleasures for public duty. The choice...is both manifest and simple: freedom practiced responsibly or no freedom at all."[63]

Emphasis On Learning: Four national surveys conducted between the years 1968 and 1981 revealed that a representative sample of American adults still gave high priority to "seeking wisdom or a mature understanding of life." [64] In addition to other areas of accomplishment, this includes a need for passing scores on special examinations in math, science, and English as a precollege requirement, and teacher accountability for student progress on standardized national tests. It also implies parental/ community moral and economic support for educational achievement.[65]

Thomas Jefferson

If a nation expects to be ignorant and free, in a state of civilization, it expects what never was and never will be.

Source: Letter in 1816 to Charles Yancey, reported by Constance Bridges in Great Thoughts Of Great Americans. New York: Thomas Y. Crowell Company, 1951, page 42.

It should be apparent why competence in reading, writing, and speaking English are basic requirements for responsible citizenship in our present-day, complex democracy. It may be less obvious, however, why *even greater academic achievement* is necessary for personal opportunity and success in today's economic world: technological advances have caused an accelerating increase in the proportion of higher-skilled jobs in relation to lower-skilled ones.

Timothy Parks, president of the Pittsburgh Alliance, observes that the proportion of U.S. unskilled jobs shrank from some 60 percent in 1950 to only 25 percent in 1997; that it will decline even further to 15 percent by the year 2000![66] Detroit lost 51 percent of its manufacturing jobs between 1967 and 1987. And, by the late 1980's, inner-city black men who had not completed high school experienced a 44 percent jobless rate in the Northeast, 58 percent in the Midwest, 49 percent in the South, and 66 percent in the West.[67]

The needs of Lincoln Electric and Scott Paper illustrate this trend. Lincoln manufactures motors and welding equipment. To qualify for recent, entry-level openings an applicant must be able to do high-school trigonometry, read technical drawings, and have the aptitude and motivation for learning how to operate computer-controlled machines.[68] Workers at Scott's new tissue products plant must develop production schedules, enter data for computer spreadsheets, buy supplies, take attendance, interview applicants, vote on merit pay raises for each other, and deal with customers and production staff. Then, to become regular employees, they must pass standardized English and high-school algebra tests and complete some 740 hours of training their first year in such matters as using Microsoft Windows software, performing lab tests for fiber strength, operating fork-lifts, and handling confrontations with fellow employees.[69]

Obviously, training for all of the specific skills mentioned above cannot be presented in high school. However, adequate academic preparedness greatly facilitates on-the-job learning. This is pointed out by Barbara Rogoff and Pablo Chavajay who report a clear-cut relationship between logical thinking and formal schooling.[70] And further evidence is provided by a growing high-school-graduate/dropout earnings gap. Graduates, on average, earned $6,415. more per year in 1999, according to the U.S. Census Bureau, and each year's dropouts will cost America more than $200 billion in lost earnings and unrealized tax revenue during their lifetimes.[71]

Furthermore, staying in school is important for reasons other than the knowledge gained. Eighty-two percent of U.S. prisoners are high-school dropouts,[72] and staying in school increases a student's IQ score to a higher level than it would have been had the student dropped out. For example, it was found that children of Indian ancestry whose schooling was delayed (due to the unavailability of teachers) experienced a drop of five IQ points for every year without schooling. More precisely, studies show that students lose ground from both their end-of-the-year IQ and end-of-year academic scores in each passing month![73] Why is this important? General intelligence (as measured by IQ score) is an important predictor of the level of job complexity one can handle.

Providing Equality Of Opportunity: Four national surveys, conducted between the years 1968 and 1981, revealed that a representative sample of American adults still gave high priority to this value.[74] And the value of "providing equal rights to all" was selected by a majority of 1200 adult members of the Parkway School District in the St. Louis area for presentation in their schools.[75] In addition, representatives of all of the religions of the world met as a Council of the Parliament of the World's Religions in Chicago in 1993, and produced the following "Declaration Toward a Global Ethic":

> "We must strive for a just social and economic order, in which everyone has an equal chance to reach full potential as a human being."[76]

The giving of equal opportunity implies that we should judge people more on the basis of their personal qualities and achievements than by their ethnic or economic backgrounds or by the status of their parents. In addition, equality of opportunity creates significantly different quantity and quality levels of individual productivity. Therefore, one should be rewarded on the basis of her or his contribution. It follows then, that the concept of equal opportunity is not compatible with the idea of equality of income.

Though the problem of racial discrimination is still very much with us, David Horowitz reminds us that "it is America's white racial majority that ended slavery, outlawed discrimination, funded massive welfare programs for inner-city blacks, and created the very affirmative action policies that are allegedly necessary to force them to be fair."[77] There are few if any other nations - including those in Africa - wherein the leaders, black or white, have made similar efforts of this magnitude.

Though certain aptitudes - like those for artistic expression, sports, singing, and instrumental performance - are inherited from one's parents, high levels of developed skill and achievement in these activities are not. They are the product of aptitude coupled with persistent hard work. Respect for this fact has helped to make America the leading land of opportunity. We have intuitively understood that an approach based upon it motivates individuals to excel; whereas, one based upon parental status and connections breeds mediocrity and a rigid class system, and discourages promising young "outsiders." However, we cannot afford to forget that equality of opportunity requires respect for others, respect for property, and a justice system that assures the rights and personal liberty of every citizen. To realize these values, we must discourage and suppress theft, treachery, mob rule, physical violence, and murder.

Conclusion: When diverse people are not able to govern themselves, they invite some form of absolutism; usually, a brutal and insensitive tribalism that ignores the humanity of non-members. Then, "outsiders" are viewed as "non-humans" who - regardless of their behavior - do not deserve the protection and support of strongly held "insider" values and goals about justice and interpersonal relations. They are subjected to unprovoked

23

murder, robbery, torture, rape, and other abhorrent behaviors which are not only condoned - but are often encouraged - by other insiders.

In the short run, a society of such extremists can be quite cohesive and effective in pursuing its goals; however, in the longer run, it cannot sustain desirable change and creativity, and properly accommodate the legitimate individual needs of its own members, as well as those of people from other cultures. Our founding fathers realized this as they launched a truly unique experiment in self- government.

Our allegiance to their creation is based more upon an ideology of shared values than upon race or ethnic identification. We have no "old country" as many Europeans and others have. Rather, we share certain core values that distinguish us and make us viable as a nation, despite our diverse backgrounds and customs and our physical dispersion over half a continent. Above all, we value our freedom, but it cannot survive for long without self-restraint that is guided by shared values.

Chapter 2

THE COMPATIBILITY OF OUR CORE VALUES WITH THOSE OF VARIOUS RELIGIONS AND OTHER SOURCES

As the evidence presented below will show, when we focus upon appropriate rules for living, rather than theology, we find little evidence of disagreement among the religions of the world - with each other, with our core values, with notables from the past, or with the Universal Declaration of Human Rights of the United Nations.

Buddhism: Among the teachings of Buddhism in the Dhammapada (Path of Virtue) we find emphasis upon:

resisting the domination of our desires and senses,

earning a living in a manner that is not harmful to others,

doing any job well,

accepting responsibility for our actions,

being tolerant of the intolerant,

while abstaining from:

greed,

hatred,

lying,

killing,

stealing, and

coveting another's wife.

Thich Nhat Hanh's revision of the Five Precepts provides these additions:

do not let others kill,

prevent others from enriching themselves from human suffering,

practice sexual expression only with love and commitment,

do not spread rumors or criticize things you are not sure of; avoid words that cause division and hatred and try to resolve or reconcile conflicts,

do not destroy your body with alcohol and other intoxicants.[1]

E.F. Schumacher observes that the Buddhist view of work is at least threefold: "to give a man the chance to utilise and develop his faculties; to enable him to overcome his ego-centeredness by joining with other people in a common task; and to bring forth the goods and services needed for a becoming existence."[2] Thus, Buddhism would look disapprovingly upon certain occupations that are prevalent in the West - processing tobacco, selling arms to questionable regimes, or misrepresenting goods and services. This viewpoint is characterized by Denise and John Carmody in the following way: "Neither profit nor pleasure should rule over peace, self-possession, purity of intention, and compassionate help for others."[3]

<u>Confucianism</u>: Among the values stressed by Confucianism since the 11th century are:

courage,

integrity,

faithfulness, loyalty,

filial piety (loving, respecting, serving, supporting, and obeying one's parents)

loving kindness of parents toward their children, (the family being the most important social institution, partly because it is the natural ground for moral training)

harmony in social relations,

love for all mankind,

propriety (proper attitude and expression),

rule by moral example rather than force,

righteousness in preference to profit,

sincerity and truthfulness, and

the seeking and application of knowledge through objective study.[4]

Hinduism: Though there is no single source of ethical guidance for traditional Hinduism, there are many exemplars in Indian theology and mythology for the following:

kindness,

helpfulness,

honesty,

love,

wisdom,

integrity,

self-sacrifice.[5]

    <u>Islamism</u>: Among the values encouraged by the Koran, the sacred book of Islam written in the 7th century, are:

a sense of modesty on the part of women,

egalitarianism for all members of the faith,

kindness to orphans,

honesty and truthfulness,

monogamy - when a man cannot do justice among more wives (and some Koranic modernists argue that justice for more than one is not possible)

support for the poor via obligatory taxes, and

the seeking of knowledge.

Among the Koranic prohibitions are:

adultery,

alcohol,

gambling,

slavery, and

usury and other forms of economic exploitation.[6]

<u>Judaism</u>:   Judaism established courts of justice and
proscribed:

    murder,

    adultery,

    lying,

    bearing false witness,

    stealing or defrauding others, and

    coveting what belongs to another.

These rules also appear among the Ten Commandments in the <u>Bible</u> (in the Book of Exodus, the second book of the Old Testament). In addition, they reflect what was common morality throughout the ancient Near East hundreds of years before Christ.[7] They stress the avoidance of any deed that is potentially harmful to fellow human beings.

The <u>Torah</u> (comprising the first five books of the Old Testament) emphasizes service to others as a key obligation, and for its injunction - "Love your neighbor as yourself" - it expressly includes strangers (thus expanding the concept of "others" to include people outside of one's tribe or community). Additionally, it discusses one's right to life, leisure, liberty, possession, work, clothing, shelter, and restitution for damages done by others.[8]

The Sermon on the Mount (in Chapter Five of St. Matthew in the New Testament) stresses the ideas of peacemaking, generosity toward the needy and one's enemies, avoidance of unwarranted anger and judging others, striving to be a good example for others in one's everyday life, and trusting one's security and well-being to faith in the Lord rather than to one's possessions.

Lest the last point be interpreted as sanctioning a disregard for supporting one's self, we find several New- Testament references that indicate otherwise. For example, Chapter 3, Verse 10 of Thessalonians (Book 2) provides the admonition that able-bodied persons who are unwilling to work should not eat. Chapter 6, Verse 5 of Ephesians indicates that one should respect the legitimate directives of one's employer. And the parable presented in Verses 14-30 of Chapter 25 of Matthew emphasizes that one should make productive use of one's material resources.

We see, then, strong cross-cultural and cross-denominational compatibility among the major religions of the world about appropriate rules for living. We note the themes of self-restraint and not hurting or exploiting others. We see a clear emphasis upon true fellowship - at least in dealing with the members of one's own faith or tribe. Though a number of the values stressed by one or two religions are not stressed by the others; they tend to be complementary rather than contradictory.

"[All religions] are similar in that they all emphasize the indispensability of love and compassion in the context of ethical discipline."

Source: The Dalai Lama, Ethics For The New Millennium. New York: Riverhead Books, 1999, page 227.

Declaration Of The World Conference Of Religions For Peace: This theme of unity is expanded upon in a declaration adopted by the World Conference of Religions for Peace in 1970 in Kyoto, Japan:

"We have found that we have in common:

"a conviction of the fundamental unity of the human family, of the equality and dignity of all men and women;

"a sense of the sacrosanctity of the individual and his or her conscience; a sense of the value of the human community;

"a recognition that might is not the same thing as right, that human might is not self-sufficient and is not absolute;

"the belief that love, compassion, selflessness and the power of the mind and inner truthfulness have, in the end, more power than hatred, enmity and self-interest;

"a sense of obligation to stand on the side of the poor and oppressed against the rich and the oppressors;

"deep hope that good will, in the end, will triumph."[9]

Declaration Toward A Global Ethic: More recently, in 1993, representatives from all of the religions of the world met in Chicago, as a Council of the Parliament of the World's Religions. Their purpose was to discuss and endorse a "Declaration Toward a Global Ethic." The Declaration was composed in Tubingen, Germany, with the hope that it would prompt a continuing process of discussion and acceptance throughout the world. Here are some excerpts from a summary and from the Declaration itself:

"We affirm that a common set of core values is found in the teachings of the religions, and that these form the basis of a global ethic.

"We affirm that this truth is already known, but yet to be lived in heart and action.

"We take individual responsibility for all we do: All our decisions, actions, and failures have consequences.

"We must treat others as we wish others to treat us...

"We must strive to be kind and generous. We must not live for ourselves alone, but should also serve others, never forgetting the children, the aged, the poor, the suffering, the disabled, the refugees, and the lonely.

"We commit ourselves to a culture of non-violence, respect, justice and peace. We shall not oppress, injure, torture, or kill other human beings, forsaking violence as a means of settling differences.

"We must strive for a just social and economic order, in which everyone has an equal chance to reach full potential as a human being. We must speak and act truthfully and with compassion, dealing fairly with all, and avoiding prejudice and hatred. We must not steal. We must move beyond the dominance of greed for power, prestige, money, and consumption to make a just and peaceful world. Earth cannot be changed for the better unless the consciousness of individuals is changed first. We pledge to increase our awareness by disciplining our minds, by meditation, by prayer, or by positive thinking.

"We condemn sexual exploitation and sexual discrimination as one of the worst forms of human degradation. We have the duty to resist wherever the domination of one sex over the other is preached - even in the name of religious conviction; wherever prostitution is fostered or children are misused. Let no one be deceived: There is no authentic humaneness without a living together in partnership!"

The Declaration was endorsed by representatives of Bahai; Brahma Kumaris; various Buddhist sects (Mahyana, Theravada, Vajrayana, Zen); the Roman Catholic Church; Orthodox, Anglican, and various other Protestant churches; Native religions (Akuapi, Native American); Hinduism (including Vedanta); Jainism (Digambar, Shwetambar); Judaism (Conservative, Reform, Orthodox); Islam (Shiite, Sunni); Neo-pagans; Sikhs; Taoists; Theosophists; Zoroastrians; and various inter-religious organizations.[10]

Declaration Of The United Nations: The Universal Declaration of Human Rights of the United Nations (adopted by the General Assembly December 10, 1948) follows some notable milestones: the English Magna Charta of 1215, the English Bill of Rights of 1689, our Declaration of Independence of 1776, the French Declaration of the Rights of Man of 1789, our Bill of Rights of 1791, and the Declaration of International Human Rights of the Institute of International Law in 1929. Here are some universal values we may reasonably infer from the 30 articles of the UN declaration:

We should regard all human beings as being free and equal in dignity and rights under our laws, and we should act toward one another in a spirit of brotherhood.

We, as well as the state, should respect the right of private property, and we should refrain from stealing or harming such property.

We should not deprive another person of life, liberty, or property, freedom of peaceful assembly and association, or the free expression of differing opinions or religious beliefs outside of non-discriminating laws or the demands of self-defense.

We should not subject anyone at anytime to cruel, degrading, or inhuman treatment.

We should assume that a person is innocent of a criminal offense until that person is found to be guilty according to law.

33

We should not arbitrarily interfere with a person's family, home, correspondence, freedom of movement, or freedom of thought, or arbitrarily attack that person's honor or reputation.

We should not deprive a person of a job who is morally and functionally qualified, and we should establish reasonable limitations to working hours and give equal pay for equal work.

We should respect the needs of motherhood and childhood for special care and assistance.

We should respect and encourage objective inquiry and learning on the part of all.

It is the duty of all able-bodied persons to support themselves and to contribute to the common good.

We are individually responsible for constraining our own behavior in order to accommodate the obligations listed above, and for protecting each other against third-party violations of these obligations, and for providing assistance to those who have been injured by such violations.

Lastly, we have the results of cross-cultural interviews that Rushworth Kidder, president of the Institute of Global Ethics, conducted with 24 men and women around the world - from a Maori wisewoman to a Vietnamese activist. He asked each: "If you could create a global code of ethics, what would be on it? What moral values, in other words, would you bring to the table from your own culture and background?"

Here are the common elements from the interview data:
Love - regard for others, compassion, mutual assistance,

Truthfulness - being honest and trustworthy,

Fairness - justice, The Golden Rule,

Freedom - equal opportunity and freedom of expression, with personal restraint and accountability,

Tolerance - of differences that do not injure others,

Responsibility - individual interests must not damage community interests, and

Respect For Life - thou shalt not kill.

Kidder reports that this enumeration is strikingly similar to lists of values developed by participants in many ethics seminars conducted around the U.S. by the Institute staff.[11]

<u>Value Orientations of Some Notables From The Past</u>: It is interesting, also, to consider values that were important to some of the most notable leaders from different cultures of the past:

Marcus Aurelius, a distinguished Roman emperor, honored the virtues of justice, truth, temperance, fortitude, and keeping one's promises.[12]

Immanuel Kant, the noted German philosopher, stressed the need to "Act according to a maxim which can at the same time make itself a universal law..."[13]

George Washington demonstrated the virtues of devotion to duty, absolute integrity, and personal opposition to slavery. Also, he was notable for his steadfast refusal to seek or use power for personal gain, despite the fact that he was the most powerful man in America. For example, when the State of Pennsylvania proposed a Congressional entertainment allowance for him before he became President, he declined. When the Virginia legislature presented him with 150 shares of stock in two newly chartered canal companies, he accepted on condition that any dividends be given to charity.

Furthermore, Washington ably administered the office of President without fear or favor. He sought to relinquish it after his first term and insisted upon relinquishing it after his second, despite the fact that he had been unanimously elected to both terms and undoubtedly would have been elected to a third.[14]

Robert E. Lee, the esteemed general of the Confederate States of America, emancipated the slaves which his family inherited when his wife's mother died in 1862. As a person of authority, he exercised power in the same manner as Washington. He wrote that:

> "The power which the strong have over the weak, the employer over the employed, the educated over the unlettered, the experienced over the confiding, even the clever over the silly - the forbearing or inoffensive use of all this power or authority, or a total abstinence from it when the case admits it, will show the gentleman in a plain light...
>
> "He can not only forgive, he can forget; and he strives for that nobleness of self and mildness of character which impart sufficient strength to let the past be but the past. A true man of honor feels humbled himself when he cannot help but humbling others."

When the widow of one of his officers sought his advice about how to rear her son, he advised: "Teach him he must deny himself."[15]

Abraham Lincoln declined some shares of stock in a new bank that had been organized in Illinois by an old acquaintance under the then-new National Bank Act. He declined with thanks, indicating that he did not feel that he should profit from a law that had been passed during his administration. The banker later observed that "He seemed to wish to avoid even the appearance of evil."[16]

In addition, Lincoln repeatedly denounced slavery and observed that "As I would not be a *slave*, so I would not be a *master*. This expresses my idea of democracy. Whatever differs from this, to the extent of the difference, is no democracy."[17]

He was compassionate about the people in the South. He wanted to welcome back as active citizens all Southerners who were willing to take an oath of allegiance to the U.S. Tragically, he was assassinated before he could attempt to implement his non-vindictive plans for reconstruction.[18]

Conclusion: When we consider the core values of various religions and cultures for living together - not the theological or peripheral ones - we find surprising levels of agreement and compatibility. Furthermore, there is some evidence today - despite the deplorable exceptions presented in the Introduction - that the various cultures of the world are moving away from divisive differences toward even greater agreement.

Chapter 3

OUR CORE VALUES ARE BEING SUBVERTED

We Americans have good reason to be proud of our country. We have the finest medical facilities and the best higher-educational system in the world. We enjoy a high standard of living and the ultimate in individual freedom without chaos. In just four years, military drafts of civilians from all walks of life were developed into our armed forces, and they fought in World War II with great courage, endurance, and honor to defeat seasoned and determined enemies. (For detailed evidence, see Citizen Soldiers, by Stephen Ambrose, Simon and Schuster, 1997). And, despite having become the most powerful nation on earth, we have continued a tradition of being more altruistic than aggressive, as we have championed world peace and justice.

In addition, despite our current problems - and they are very real - we have come a long way from the earlier days of our country. We now have significantly improved women's rights, literacy levels, living and working conditions, health and sanitary conditions, protection of the environment, control of spousal and child abuse, consumer protection, and tolerance of minority groups.

In the recent past, there has also been greater respect for the office of the President than in the days when otherwise responsible newspaper editors described President Lincoln as an ape, buffoon, despot, fiend, fool, gorilla, ignoramus, land pirate, liar, monster, and tyrant,[1] and the Chicago Times reacted to his Gettysburg Address with the observation that "The cheek of every American must tingle with shame as he reads the silly, flat, and dish-watery utterances of the man who has to be pointed out to intelligent foreigners as the President of the United States."[2]

In those days, General George McClelland snubbed his Commander In Chief: As Lincoln and one of his cabinet members waited to see him at his home one evening, McClelland returned and went straight up to his room, ignoring the porter's message that the President was waiting. When another servant was dispatched a half hour later to get him, the return message was that the general had gone to bed.[3] Another subordinate, General Hooker, told a newspaperman that the President and Government at Washington were imbeciles and should be replaced by a dictator.[4]

In addition, there were serious challenges to our core values:

Draft dodging was rampant, with thousands of would-be federal draftees fleeing the country to Canada and Europe,[5] while 39,877 failed to report for their examinations in New York City, and others bought exemptions at $300 apiece. In addition, thousands of others rioted for three days through the city as they killed people and burned 13 buildings and numerous stores and factories.[6]

With regard to corruption, General James Wilson reported that: "In tents, a lighter cloth or a few inches off the size; in harness, split leather; in saddles, inferior materials and workmanship; in shoes, paper soles; in clothes, shoddy; in mixed horse feed, chaff and a larger portion of the cheapest grain...Every contractor had to be watched."[7]

Such practices were so widespread that General Sherman wrote in a personal letter that "Corruption so underlay the Government, that even in this time of trial cheating...is universal."[8]

Nor was cheating limited to war contractors. The mayor of New York City sold nominations for Supreme Court judgeships and city contracts to super-high bidders who knew how to show their appreciation.[9]

Samuel Morrison and Henry Commanger, two eminent historians, detail the extravagance, corruption, and vulgarity of the post-Civil War Reconstruction governments in the South, and how another notorious politician, Boss Tweed, with the help of his henchmen, robbed New York City of over seventy-five million dollars.[10]

Fortunately, since those days - and until recent times - we have not had much cause for alarm. Certain values have been clearly dominant, accepted, and relatively unchanging in our society. We have tended to take them for granted with little questioning about their validity or origin.

Traditionally, we have made room for healthy foreigners who are willing to work and wish to jump into the melting pot and "become Americans;" that is, adopt - or at least respect and conform to - our dominant values. Given this purpose and the reasonable control of immigration volume and quality in the past, we have felt little threat to our dominant culture. Nor have we felt threatened by other less-assimilated groups such as the traditional Chinese, ultra-religious Jews, and the Amish - as long as their existing or projected sizes remained proportionately small, they continued to be economically self-sufficient and law-abiding, and they honored dominant values and goals when they engaged in social or commercial interaction with "outsiders."

However, we have felt threatened by immigrants whose values clash with our dominant values, such as those who have attempted to transplant the Mafia culture from Sicily and the padrone political culture from Mexico and elsewhere. And a major challenge to certain core values was presented by the "hippies" of the 1960's. A popular slogan of the time was "tune in [to the new values], turn on [to drugs], and drop out [of mainstream society]."

Today, as evidence in this chapter will show, our culture is being attacked and undercut by people who are indifferent to - or actively hostile to - our laws and majority values. Among them are immigrants who need not meet any criteria in terms of their personal aspirations or their ability to support themselves; those who see dependency upon the state as a way of life; drug addicts from all strata of society; angry young people from broken or dysfunctional families who resent all persons in positions of authority; and growing numbers of amoral opportunists who strive to profit from the exploitation of others - especially our young - regardless of the social costs involved.

In addition, demographic trends are adding fuel to this potential for subversion, because growing numbers - due to birth or immigration - of the members of diverse groups are not seeking to adopt mainstream values and/or be law-abiding and self-supporting to the extent that traditional Americans do. Henry Grunwald warns us not to become complacent about the need to take stock to determine when corrective action is needed:

> "We have a hard time accepting the notion that history is not a steady ascent, that it can move us from democracy to dictatorship, from licentiousness to prudery - and back. During the past hundred years, let alone the past thousand, we have made almost unbelievable material and social progress; what has not changed is the nature of humanity and our never ending challenge: to keep working, to keep mending, to keep building."[11]

Evidence Of Negative Change In Levels Of Honesty And Trust: To begin with, we have the discouraging case of the American Seed Company of Lancaster Pennsylvania having to drop its long-standing program for young people in 1981:

> For more than 60 years, American Seed had profitably distributed garden seeds to enterprising youngsters to sell in their neighborhoods. Then, between 1975 and 1981, some 400,000 young business people sent for the seeds - but pocketed all of the proceeds - rather than deduct their commission and remit the rest, claiming to have been "mugged."[12]

Additional discouragement is provided by Patricia Hersch. She reports a 1989 survey of 5000 Girl Scouts which found that 65 percent would cheat on tests, and a 1992 survey of high-school students which revealed that 75 percent had already done so.[13] And Rushworth Kidder reports a 1991 survey of some 16,000 students that found that 76 percent of those pursuing graduate degrees in business admitted to having cheated at least once on a test as undergraduates.[14]

Percent Who Seriously Lie* (By Age Groups)

Age Group	18-24	50 percent
	25-44	34
	45-64	29
	65+	19

* Engage in lying that hurts people, violates a trust, has legal consequences, or is totally self-serving

Source: An anonymous survey of a random sample of 2000 adult Americans reported in James Patterson and Peter Kim, The Day America Told The Truth. New York: Prentice-Hall Press, 1991, page 46.

In 1996, Tony Bouza, a top-level administrative police officer, described how some 30 percent of 4H farm youngsters were discovered to have been feeding a steroid-like drug, Clenbuterol, to the livestock they exhibited. The practice had not only resulted in the rescinding of ribbons and cash prizes, it had produced tainted meat that had been fatal for a number of people.[15]

A recent survey of voters found that seventy-five percent believe that we are in a state of moral decay and that government policies should be guided more by moral values.[16] In fact, Harris Polls show that public confidence in all branches of government, organized religion, business leadership, and the press has declined dramatically since 1966.[17] There are about eight times as many bankruptcies today as there were during the Great Depression![18] And many states are excessively lenient. For example, Paul Bilzerian sank some $6 million into his Florida home just before filing for bankruptcy, and his creditors can't touch a penny of it.[19]

Finally, we see increasing, behind-the-scenes influence on the part of special-interest groups, an increase in greed-driven litigation, and the growth of self-serving behavior and irresponsible spending on the part of our elected representatives.

Evidence Of Negative Change About Regard For Others: Martin Seligman reports that increasing numbers of people are becoming depressed today due to a change in values toward "an exalted sense of commitment to the self and a concurrent decline in commitment to religion, family, the nation and community." He found that those born after 1950 have experienced a twenty-fold increase in depression compared with those born before 1910, and that depression now occurs much earlier in life than before. He points out that our parents were more likely to ask what they owed the world; whereas, our children are more inclined to emphasize what the world owes them.[20]

Several other developments support this idea of an increasing lack of concern for others. Consider, for example, the current abuses of Medicare - one of our most important social-support programs. Eugene Methvin reports that Medicare fraud is costing us some $30 billion a year! And, even more alarming, are *the types of people* who are engaged in these abuses. Methvin tells us that most of them are social workers, school counselors, probation officers, doctors, ministers, and pharmacists who repackage and sell out-of-date drugs. In fact, one of these pharmacists, when told of the complaints of elderly nursing-home users as to the ineffectiveness of the drugs, replied: "What difference does it make, they're going to die soon anyway."[21]

HMO Executive On The Industry's Approach

"We see people as numbers, not patients...We're a mass-production medical assembly line, and there is no room for the human equation in our bottom line."

Source: Robert Goldberg, "What's Happened To The Healing Process?," The Wall Street Journal, June 18, 1997

To assess the growing disdain for the property of others, we only have to look at the unwelcome and offensive graffiti on abandoned buildings and other property, and read about the widespread and carnival-atmosphere looting of innocent establishment owners in many of our recent riots and electrical brown-outs.

In addition, we are seeing a marked increase in incivility - the lack of mutual consideration and respect in casual face-to-face relationships. For example, we are being victimized by "road rage." The number of incidents in which angry drivers attempt to injure or kill other drivers has increased 51 percent since 1990 - and 65 percent of the offenders used guns or other weapons, while 35 percent used their cars![22]

Also, we have growing numbers of "air rage" cases. For example, United Airlines experienced 527 disruptive-passenger incidents in 1997 - more than double the number for 1995. The incidents include sexual offenses and the physical or verbal assault of fellow passengers or crew members.[23] Even school buses are becoming unsafe. The 20/20 Television Program of January 6, 1999 showed tapes made by school-bus video cameras. Viewers saw fights, sexual harassment of girls (via groping), and several boys kicking a girl in the head as she lay on the floor. Also, the commentator told of frequent spitting and hitting attacks on the drivers (who were not permitted to touch the students).

In view of these developments, the results of a recent survey are not surprising: Some 89 percent of the respondents think that ill-manneredness is a serious problem that contributes to violence, and 78 percent feel that the problem has worsened in the past ten years.[24] One may wonder, "How can incivility produce violence?" Everyday life is full of unplanned events: having to miss or be late for a business or social appointment, accidentally bumping into someone on the sidewalk, dialing the wrong phone number, getting into the wrong traffic lane, and so on. Increasingly, such events are being responded to with rudeness or negative gestures before the "offender" has a chance to explain or apologize, and this often triggers a negative spiral of escalating insults and recriminations that ends with physical violence.

In effect, we are witnessing a trend toward unlicensed individual freedom without responsibility to others - a breakdown in the kind of self-control that is essential to the functioning of a healthy society. We are seeing that lack of positive influences in American life has caused many people to gravitate toward two new Golden Rules: "Do unto others as you wish - only do it before they can do it to you"; and "Whoever has the gold, makes the rules."

Evidence Of Negative Change In Rates Of Crime And Violence: William Bennett reports that violent crime rose 560 percent between 1960 and 1993,[25] and we had a 90 percent increase in the juvenile arrest rate for homicide between 1987 and 1991.[26] In fact, there was a 172 percent increase in the number of violent crimes committed by juveniles during the last decade! Weapons violations were up 482 percent, drug charges up 523 percent, and the total number of arrests for under-16 offenders had increased 105 percent. As early as the 1980's, the chances of a 15-19 year-old being arrested had increased to 16 times that of a 50-54 year-old being arrested.[27] And a survey of 165 mothers of children aged 6-10 in a moderate-violence, low-income area of Washington, D.C. revealed that 32 percent had been victims of violence, and that 72 percent had witnessed it.[28] Needless to say, there were reports of distress symptoms and concerns about personal safety for children in both surveys.

Given such examples - and the high levels of employee theft and admitted cheating by school students - we may get the impression that it is inherent for most people to cheat if given a low-risk opportunity. Yet, during the Depression years this was *not* the case, as the discussion of the power of values in the Introduction illustrates. There were certainly more opportunities for dishonest and violent behavior then: stores did not have video monitoring systems, libraries and other organizations did not have electronic detection equipment, law-enforcement agencies did not have the sophisticated technology they now have, and many people did not lock their doors. Nevertheless,

46

crime rates were much lower, as the table in the Introduction shows.

<u>Evidence Of Negative Change In The Social Environment</u>: There has been a dramatic change in the character of popular music in recent years. Andrew Thomas observes that:

> "Rap and heavy metal music are the preferred music of the biggest bloc of crime citizens, young black and white males respectively. This music is often filled with lyrics that, prior to recent court rulings, could have been banned as leading to imminent violence."[29]

For examples, look over songs such as "Fight the Power," "Cop Killer," "Black Korea," "F_k the Police," "We Had To Tear This Motherf__r Up," and "Eat Me Alive."

Although violence on television is not the only factor that encourages inappropriate aggression, it is an important one. A 22-year study, involving 875 boys and girls and most of their parents in semi-rural New York State - conducted by psychologist Leonard Eron and his team - found that the influence of viewing violence or aggressive behavior "is relatively independent of other likely influences and is of a magnitude great enough to account for socially important differences."[30]

Brandon Centerwall, an epidemiologist, took advantage of the fact that from 1945-1974, English-speaking South Africans had no television. He found that during this period, the white homicide rate in America increased 93 percent and the rate in Canada increased 92 percent, while the rate in South Africa *declined* 7 percent! And other factors - such as economic growth, civil unrest, age distribution, urbanization, alcohol consumption, capital punishment, or the availability of firearms - could not account for these findings. However, Brandon found that homicide rates for whites rose as they began to acquire TV sets in large numbers, just as homicide rates for minorities rose approximately five years later when they began to acquire sets in large numbers.[31]

Another study focused upon inappropriate physical aggression among 45 first and second-graders in a remote Canadian community. Within two years of acquiring television, the rate of inappropriate physical aggression for both boys and girls increased 160 percent for those who previously had been aggressive, as well as for those who had not; whereas, the rate remained the same for two similar communities that had had television for years.[32]

Some time ago, David Phillips documented the phenomenon of "copycat acts" that come after well-publicized suicides and notorious crime sprees.[33] And more recently, the Arts and Entertainment channel presented a program on the role of violent movies in triggering violent acts on the part of unstable individuals. Dr. Robert Butterworth, a child-trauma psychologist, pointed out that young people will have been exposed to some 40,000 murders and some 200,000 other violent acts in movie theaters and on television by the time they reach adulthood.[34]

But violence, alone, is only part of the problem. Many of these programs imply that violence provides a useful way to solve differences, as they glamorize criminals and depict them "getting away with it." This observation is supported by a 1996 study conducted by psychologists at several universities. They found that - over the preceding two-year period - 58 percent of TV's violent acts portrayed no painful consequences and that perpetrators went unpunished in 73 percent of the violent scenes.[35] Also, we see the same trend toward violence without negative consequences in the movies.

Many who oppose the idea of censorship overlook the successful administration of it by Hollywood's Hays Office from the early days of motion pictures until 1967. Its existence reflected the sound conviction that it was in the public interest to stress that crime produces negative consequences and ultimately doesn't pay. The Hays Office code discouraged:

> on-screen violence,
> revealing the details of criminal methodology,
> glamorizing criminals; creating sympathy for
> them,

48

showing criminals winning out in the end.

In addition to abandoning such censorship, we have another negative development in the so-called docudrama - in both television and films - that blurs fact with fiction. Randy Fitzgerald illustrates this with Hollywood's distortion of the relationship between Lewis and Clark during their historic 1804-1806 expedition to explore and map the American West. Rather than showing the documented close friendship and mutual support that were essential to their success, the script has them bickering and under-cutting each other's efforts at every turn. Among other examples Fitzgerald notes how ex-teamster boss, Jimmy Hoffa, is largely absolved of a working relationship with organized crime in the film Hoffa, despite considerable evidence to the contrary; and how the film Panther unjustifiably demonizes law enforcement.[36]

Physical abuse is another factor that contributes to aggression and violence. Dodge, Bates, and Petit found that young children who are physically abused are substantially more likely to develop chronic aggressive behavior later on.[37]

Another problem is posed by dysfunctional gambling. Durand Jacobs, an authority on problem gamblers, observes that: "After a decade of increased availability, promotion and glamorization of commercial gambling, it may well be time for American society to re-examine the long-range consequences of its love affair with [it]." He found that 75 percent of the children of problem gamblers report that their first experience with gambling occurred before age 11 and, as of 1995, he estimated that 4-6 percent of 12-17 year olds were pathological gamblers.[38]

Evidence of Negative Change In The Maintenance Of Healthy Family Life: A decline in the number of two-parent homes and a decline in the quality of family life are creating problems.

Decreasing Number Of Two-Parent Homes: The probability that white children would live with both parents fell, from 81 percent in the early 1950's to 30 percent for those born in 1980.[39]

And the National Parenting Association's Task Force reports that the proportion of married adults declined, from 72 percent to 62 percent between 1970 and 1990, and the divorce rate exceeded 40 percent in 1995.[40] By 1990, only some 33 percent of divorced fathers saw their children as much as once a week.[41]

As of 1990, in comparison with 1960: the number of children with single mothers had trebled, the teen suicide rate had more than doubled, and the violent crime rate had increased 560 percent.[42] Furthermore, as of 1992, some 50 percent of all unwed teen mothers were on welfare within a year after assuming motherhood, and 77 percent were on welfare within five years.[43]

More direct evidence of the impact of family structure is provided by a longitudinal study that tracked 6403 boys (aged 14-22 in 1979) up through their early 30's. The researchers, Cynthia Harper at the University of California and Princeton's Sara McLanahan, controlled for various variables such as family background, income, race, neighborhood, and cognitive ability. Among their findings:

> Boys raised outside of intact marriages were more than twice as likely to end up in jail. Each year without a father in the home increased the odds of future incarceration by about 5 percent.

> The boy of an unwed mother was about 2 $^1/_2$ times as likely to wind up in prison, while one whose parents split during his teenage years was about 1 $^1/_2$ times as likely.

> Boys in stepparent families were almost three times as likely to face imprisonment as those from intact families.

> However, teenage boys who lived with their single fathers were no more likely to commit crimes than boys in intact families. But boys living with remarried fathers

faced incarceration rates as high as boys living with remarried mothers.

Finally, poverty did make it more likely that a boy would be imprisoned as an adult, but family structure was a more important factor.[44]

Decline In The Quality Of Family Life: Not only do problems result from the physical disintegration of the family unit - they result also from the declining quality of the units that remain intact: the decrease in meaningful family-member interactions due to the advent of dual-wage earners, increased television viewing, a more-permissive, "anything goes" attitude on the part of parents and, possibly, cohabitation.

There has been a dramatic increase in the number of unmarried couples who live together. According to a report from the National Marriage Project, based at Rutgers University, cohabitating couples experience:

> more than three times the rates of depression of married couples,

> more episodes of domestic violence to women,

> more physical and sexual abuse of children, and

> greater tolerance for divorce when they marry - their divorce rates were 46 percent higher than for those couples who had not lived together.

These findings are quite provocative; however, they leave a key question unanswered: Do those who choose to live together before marriage differ significantly (from those who do not) in ways that would produce these negative outcomes?[45]

Eighty-three percent of the respondents in a 1999 nationwide survey of 2011 adults said that lack of parental involvement in children's lives is a "very serious problem" confronting the nation.[46] And William Bennett reports that American teenagers

51

average about five minutes per day alone with their fathers and about 20 minutes per day alone with their mothers, and that the majority of this time is devoted to jointly eating or watching television.[47]

This trend is documented by Patricia Hersch who became a confidant of eight representative teen-agers over a period of three years. On the basis of regular, in-depth discussions with each of them privately and a considerable amount of time devoted to observing their in-school behavior with each other and their friends, she reports that:

> "The adolescents of the nineties are more isolated and more unsupervised than other generations...Mom is at work. Neighbors are often strangers. Relatives live in distant places. This changes everything. It changes access to a bed, a liquor cabinet, a car. The kids have all the responsibilities for making decisions, often in a void, or they create an ersatz family with their buddies and let them decide."[48]

Kathleen Bergeron, a high school English teacher in Gainesville, Florida, instructed each of her students to talk to a parent for 10 minutes and then write a brief summary of the conversation. This evoked the following kinds of protest: "What would I talk to a parent about?" "When will I be able to do it, I won't see a parent for that long before the deadline?," or "Can I break it into shorter periods, like talking to my dad during the TV commercials?" When Ms. Bergeron suggested the family dinner table, she found that only two or three of the entire class regularly ate dinner as a family - either someone was too busy at work, had this or that practice, or was away from home for some other reason.[49]

For the sake of comparison, psychologist James Garbarino reports that current studies show a 10-12 hour reduction per week of the time in which adults are available to children compared with 30 years ago.[50] And Richard Zoglin observes that young people "are growing up, too frequently, in abusive or broken homes, with little adult supervision and few positive role models"; that the rate at which youths in the 14-17 age group committed homicides jumped 16 percent between 1990 and 1994.[51]

Number Of Hours Per Week Spent In Nonparental Care By
Children Under Five Of Working Mothers

35 or more hours	41 percent
15-34 hours	25
1-14 hours	16
None	18

Source: Urban Institute calculations from the 1997 National Survey of American Families's sampling of 44,000 households with working mothers, in Indicators Section of Time, April 17, 2000.

Kay Hyonowitz tells us that the proportion of girls who say they had sexual intercourse before the age of 15 rose from 11 to 19 percent between 1988 and 1995, and that a middle school counselor told her, "We're beginning to see a few pregnant sixth-graders." She adds that "eight to 12 year old 'tweens' are the vanguard of a new decultured generation, isolated from family and neighborhood, shrugged at by parents, dominated by peers, and delivered into the hands of a sexualized and status- and fad-crazed market place."[52] And Patricia Hersch documents how these trends are leading us down the wrong paths. She reports that the Search Institute based in Minnesota - which had surveyed 250,000 students by 1996 - found that only ten percent of them satisfied standards for optimal healthy development![53]

Percent Who Feel They Received A Large Portion Of Their
Current Values From The Influence Of Their Parents

Age Group 18-24	50 Percent
25-6	61
65+	78

Source: An anonymous survey of a random sample of 2000 adult Americans reported in James Patterson and Peter Kim, The Day America Told The Truth. New York: Prentice-Hall Press, 1991, page 62.

Increased Use Of Drugs: There is little doubt that the breakup of families, and the declining quality of relationships within them, have encouraged the use of drugs by young people. In addition, a recent national poll found that 76 percent of 12 to 17 year-olds believe that current popular culture - in the form of TV, movies, magazines, and music - contributes to the problem.[54] Such factors caused the use of "pot" by teenagers to nearly doubled between 1992 and 1995.[55]

"True," some will say, "But, surely marijuana is not as harmful as many would have you believe." Unfortunately, this is not true, due to the more subtle - but quite disabling - *delayed* effects of pot.   Though physically less harmful than heavy drinking, marijuana inhibits one's social and emotional development. As Lance Morrow points out:

"The age of development through which a child passes from ages 12 to 18 is critical. Adolescence is the labor that gives birth to the adult. It is a painful, indispensable process.   Adolescence quite precisely requires the pain and difficulty of learning in order to come out well. Among the lessons, of course, are how to love and support others and how to be responsible."[56]

54

In addition, the earlier one starts to use marijuana, the likelier he or she will move on to other drugs. Morrow indicates that Dr. Joycelyn Elders, former U.S. Surgeon General, reported that "Children who smoke pot before age 12 are 42 times likelier to use drugs like cocaine and heroin than those who first smoked after age 16."[57]

The latest fad in the drug culture is methamphetamine (called meth, crank, or speed), which is sometimes referred to as "the poor man's cocaine." It not only destroys the user, but also threatens the neighbors, because it can make causal indulgers clinically psychotic. Even when one stops using it, the drug carries almost a two-week residue of paranoia that often produces violent behavior. David Morales, a truant officer, often has to deal with the problem in the form of 10- and 11-year-olds who are either users or are suffering abuse at the hands of spun-out relatives.[58]

Joseph Califano of Columbia's Center of Addiction and Substance Abuse reports that "Our children are crying out for help. They're telling us that drugs are by far the most important problem they face growing up."[59] And most of them do not understand that the majority of people cannot experiment with drugs and, then, readily walk away from them. This fact is illustrated by a professional friend of mine - a recovering addict who has been a successful member of Narcotics Anonymous for many years. She reports that only 1-2 percent of NA's crack addicts - and only 5-6 percent of their other addicts - stay clean indefinitely. And despite her outstanding success in staying off of drugs, she feels that she will need to attend weekly NA meetings for the rest of her life! Equally discouraging is the report that only one percent of the 80,000 low-income drug addicts and alcoholics on Social Security disability benefits ever recover or obtain jobs.[60]

Evidence Of Negative Change In Part Of The Black Culture: Many of the negative changes discussed above have developed more fully in a part of the black culture. As a task force chaired by former U.N. Ambassador Andrew Young put it, African-American men and boys are "the nation's most troubled

55

population."[61]   And in his recent book, <u>Code Of The Streets</u>, black sociologist Elijah Anderson describes the predatory behavior that poisons life in the inner city. He targets those for whom the chief guiding principle is "ruthless might makes right" and norms of decency are totally lacking - young men who must "prove themselves"   by violating someone weaker.[62]   Let's consider other evidence:

Delinquency, Violence, and Crime:

A survey of 53 African-American mothers of fifth-graders in a high-violence, low-income area of New Orleans revealed that 51 percent had been victims of violence, and that 91 percent had witnessed some type of violence.[63]

Carmichael found that black-American delinquents in custody indicated their highest respect for assailants, drug dealers, and murderers.[64]

During the Los Angeles riots thousands of blacks went on a rampage and indiscriminately damaged or destroyed some 2000 businesses of Korean-Americans, though these people had absolutely no association with the Rodney King affair![65]

As of 1998, half of the murderers and victims in the U.S. were black - a victimization rate seven times that of whites.[66]

The Washington-based Sentencing Project reported that one of every three black men aged 20-29 was either in jail, paroled, or on probation as of the end of 1995. And Paul Butler, a George Washington University law professor, reports that, increasingly, inner-city juries are acquitting black men they know to be guilty.[67]

Illegitimacy And Broken Families:

Whereas the rate of illegitimate teenage births soared from 15 percent of all teenage births in 1960 to 75 percent in 1995, it had reached 95 percent for blacks.[68]

The National Parenting Association's Task Force reported that two-thirds of all black births - in comparison with one-third of all white births - occurred in single-parent households in 1995.[69]

Yet, we have reason to believe that the disintegration of the black family in part of the black culture was not preordained by historical precedent. Jared Taylor reports that - even prior to the emancipation of American slaves - most black children were born to two-parent families.[70] And Bill McAllister tells us that from 1890-1950 more black than white women were likely to be married![71] In addition to the many problems associated with single parenting that were discussed earlier, the 1992 poverty rate for black, single-parent families was 55 percent, compared to 15 percent for black two-parent families.[72]

Disregard For Academic Attainment: Negative value orientation - rather than racism - appears to be the greater cause of poor, black, male, educational achievement. Department of Education data indicate that college attendance by black women soared during the last 20 years in comparison with that of black males, creating a current ratio of 62 percent to 38 percent.[73] And George Gilder reports that the average black, full-time worker earns one percent more than the average white full-timer - *when we control for age, IQ, and gender! In addition, he indicates that mostly white employers have given larger average earnings to black women in comparison with comparable white women.*[74]

Bill Maxwell, a black columnist and faculty member of a community college, stresses the current disregard - even disdain- of many black males for academic attainment and their preoccupation with immediate gratification over investing in their futures.[75]   And his observations are supported by Sophfronia Gregory.   She describes crumbling, black communities that do not see academic achievement as essential to survival and prosperity, and reports that young blacks who study hard face isolation, scorn, and rejection. For example, she tells about a gang of black girls in Oakland, California who terrorize bright black students with anonymously phoned threats that they will be killed. And she describes how achievers are ridiculed for speaking standard English, having white friends, joining non-sport activities, and even for arriving in class on time.

In effect, the phrase "acting white" is the insult of choice by black underachievers for their peer achievers.   Thus, for a conscientious black student in many settings, social success and personal safety depend upon academic failure and rejection of traditional paths to self-improvement.[76]   This conclusion was supported by interviews with black students and counselors on ABC's 20/20 program of June 7, 1999. All of the participants indicated the very negative behavioral effects of being accused of "acting white."

What Will Rescue The Youngster Imprisoned In Social and Cultural Isolation That Has Doomed Whole Peoples For Centuries?

"When we promote cultural provincialism under glittering labels, we must confront the hard question whether we are throwing... a lifeline or an anchor."

Source: Thomas Sowell, distinguished social theorist, "Race Culture and Equality," Forbes, October 5, 1998, page 149. Reprinted by Permission of Forbes Magazine © 2000 Forbes 1998).

Equally disturbing is the fact that an association called Concerned Black Educators In Higher Education in Florida opposed raising the passing requirement for a teacher licensing test in math, writing, reading, and professional education above an eighth-grade level. Walter Mercer, a spokesman for the group, said that such action would be like fashioning "an academic electric chair" that could make black teachers an "endangered species"![77]

Rejection Of Positive, Black Role Models: Disregard for these basic values by part of the black community stand in sharp contrast to the views of black achievers like Booker T. Washington, a former slave who became an outstanding educator and leader. Washington stressed that African-Americans should contribute positively to society by gaining the respect and confidence of their neighbors; that they could do this by practicing personal discipline, mutual aid, racial solidarity, and by developing habits of thrift, intelligence, and high moral character.[78] However, the very success of many eminent blacks who could serve as positive role models has apparently alienated them from the ones they could help the most.

For example, Bill Maxwell, the columnist, describes how he became an exile among his relatives and peers during his first summer home from college:

> A former boyhood friend greeted him contemptuously at the bus station with "What's wrong, Billy Max? Don't tell me you done become one of them book-toting, proper-talking college niggers too good for his friends."

> One morning when he said he was going to the library his father confronted him with: "Who in hell do you think you are? You keep your head stuck in a book like some honky. Them books done gone to your head. Next you'll be thinking you better than everybody."

> And when he traveled to another city to see his mother, he found her to be somewhat distant, as his siblings and childhood playmates shunned him.

Maxwell concludes that:

"Today, little has changed for me and hundreds of thousands of other educated, middle-class African Americans. The rejection continues. When we're not in our cozy circle, we feel the profound resentment of blacks unlike us...

"they resent us because of the way we earn our money, the way we talk and think, the way we spend our leisure, the way we raise our children."[79]

Another illustration of this type of alienation is provided by Joe Klein of Newsweek. He writes about the arrival of some 16,000 jobs in the Brooklyn neighborhood of Fort Greene with the development of a $1.25 billion tax-subsidized enterprise zone called Metroplex. Despite the appearance of many entry-level jobs and a stable and active black middle class, there appears to have been little economic impact upon the local underclass. He quotes Eric Blackwell, publisher of the Fort Greene News, with regard to the black middle class:

"There's a lot of resentment...They have their own [public] schools, their own churches. They're like foreigners."[80]

Lack Of Mutual Economic Support: The lack of "economic solidarity" among blacks prompted TV journalist Tony Brown to observe that "The Chinese help the Chinese, the Koreans help the Koreans, the Cubans help the Cubans, but blacks help everyone else. We have conducted the most successful business boycott in history - against ourselves."[81]

This is illustrated by William Hunter, research director of the Federal Reserve Bank of Chicago. He reports that African-American banks on the average are not as helpful to needy blacks as other banks; that they have a greater tendency to favor wealthy local borrowers over lower-income applicants, and some even discriminate against equally qualified black applicants.

However, a large part of this problem is the poor repayment rate by black borrowers. The more that black banks lend in black communities, the higher their risk of failure.[82]

John Kasarda observes that:

"In Washington, D.C., a predominantly black city, only 3% of blacks are self-employed, compared to nearly 20% of Asians and 16% of non-Hispanic whites.

"In St. Louis, Asian self-employment is 25% and black self-employment only 2%... Between 1977 and 1982, the most recent years for which figures are available, the number of Asian-owned companies with paid employees expanded by 160%, while the number of such black-owned companies declined by 3%."[83]

Unwarranted Black-Against-Black Discrimination: Among blacks - a group that has benefited the most from affirmative-action programs and other efforts to compensate for historical discrimination against opportunity and advancement - we find a surprising carryover of historical racism and resistance to the ideas of meritocracy.

Being a New Orleanian, I remember reading and hearing of the rigid social discrimination that was practiced many years ago in the black community by those of differing shades of color: seven-eighths-white octoroons shunned three-quarters-white quadroons; who, in turn, shunned half-white mulattoes; and so on, down the line of color-shading.

I am surprised and disappointed to learn that such practices are still alive and well. For example, Jane Mayer and Jill Abramson report that Justice Clarence Thomas was acutely sensitive to color differences and talked bitterly of the "light-skinned elite" while at Yale; that his mother, Leola Williams, recalls him saying "What would I want with a woman as black as Anita Hill."[84] And Bill Maxwell, the columnist, indicates that, even today, many black fraternities and sororities reject those of darker skin, out of hand - that after graduation, many friends, business partners, churches, and even spouses are selected on this superficial basis.

He laments the lack of change, and observes that "Civil rights activists, including me, had hoped that the 'black is beautiful' movement of the 1960's and early 1970's would sound 'taps' on black America's obsession with degree of skin color. Sadly, though, that didn't happen." He quotes the editors of Essence magazine:

> "Quiet as it's kept, it is still...among us. Color still affects our thoughts, attitudes and perceptions about beauty and intelligence, about worth and self-esteem."[85]

It is truly ironic that many black Americans do not hold each other and themselves to the same high standards against arbitrary discrimination that they demand and expect from all whites.

Conclusion: We have reviewed the evidence about negative changes in our levels of trust and regard for others, in the incidence of crime and violence, in environmental factors that influence us, in the maintenance of healthy family life, and in a part of the black culture. The evidence is compelling. These changes affect many aspects of our daily lives and call upon us to turn things around. Chapters 6-10 are devoted to means for doing this. But first, it will be useful to discuss how values are acquired (Chapter 4) and their role in causing behavior (Chapter 5).

Chapter 4

HOW WE ACQUIRE VALUES

Values may be created by the evaluation of experience. This was the approach used by our founding fathers. Based upon their review of history, they concluded that individual freedom requires a certain form of republican government. However, for the most part, values are created and retained more by belief and tradition than by objective investigation or analysis. They are handed from one generation to another through instruction, stories, personal example, and the absence of proposed alternative beliefs and ways of doing things.

We give the label *ethics* to those values which relate to the "rightness" and "wrongness" of human behavior. And the most potent vehicle of ethics is the human conscience, because it facilitates compliance with ethical values (or right behavior) through the influence of personal feelings of guilt or virtue. Consequently, it is important for us to answer the following questions: What factors influence the initial development of a conscience? Why may there be inadequate development? When, and why, will a conscience inhibit rationality? And how can "growing up" modify the values in one's conscience?

How A Healthy Conscience Develops: We are not "born good" with a clear-cut sense of what is right and wrong. If we were, this would require the rebellion of children born into tribes that practice cannibalism, or those that subject all "outsiders" to theft, torture, or dishonesty. We know, however, that there are non-rebellious and virtuous children in such cultures. No, a conscience is not possessed, full-blown, at birth. It appears to be created - or not created - by the following processes:

When we enter this world, we are predisposed by our genetic makeup to explore the audio and visual stimuli around us - to seek food, protection, and love - and to avoid pain and perceived danger. We do not have other strongly held values and goals. We acquire these as a result of interacting with the people and things around us.

Since we are wholly dependent upon primary caretakers for our well being, we learn to associate their strong approval or disapproval with certain attitudes, behaviors, and objects, and we adopt their orientations as a means for retaining their support and avoiding their rejection.

The strength and speed of this learning depend upon the *amount* of interaction with significant others, as well as the *perceived agreement* among them as to what is being taught. And the first few years of life are the most crucial period during which this learning occurs. Hart and Risley explain why:

"We know that by age 2 the growth and mylenization of nerve cells is almost complete and that by age 4 cortical development is largely finished...Given the nature of babies and their interactions, the very first years of life establish an entire general approach to experience...Children learn through words and actions what the world means, who they are, and what is valued."[1]

If we are biologically normal and have supportive caregivers, we feel warm, secure, and loved when we comply with their wishes; and we feel lonely, upset, and threatened when we do not. These feelings are the result of cause/consequence conditioning that gives either positive or negative "emotional charging" to various attitudes, behaviors, and objects. Then, in time, we begin to internalize these emotionally charged ideas of right and wrong as part of a developing "conscience" - that helps to define what we should and shouldn't do, what we stand for, and who we are.

On the other hand, if we had aloof, hostile - or otherwise maladjusted - caregivers, we tend to acquire dysfunctional programming. And there is evidence to suggest that some people grow up with a weak, or even non-existent, conscience - despite the presence of appropriate caregivers - because they are *biologically incapable* of feeling empathy or love for others.

When we violate the "do's" and "don'ts" of our conscience, we feel the same kind of uneasiness or guilt we felt when we rebelled against the sentiments of the significant others in our early environment. This is why we can be very irrational about defending highly charged values and uncritically accepting of any positive support for them. In other words, much of the subsequent influence of the "do" and "don't" commands of a conscience stems from the way significant others trained us - *not* necessarily from any logical appeal these values may offer, nor from our own analysis as to their appropriateness at the time we acquired them. We may not recall or understand the reasons for many of these prescriptions and proscriptions, *but we have an emotional stake in complying with them.*

If we were fortunate, our caregivers were well-adjusted, as well as being supportive, and served as positive role models as they practiced and taught us sound values. The moderately charged (and appropriate) behaviors and values they imparted encourage us to act in socially useful ways, and they help us to know "who we are" and "what we stand for." Without these moderately charged values, we would be more readily confounded by the many choices that life presents, and we would be more likely to give in to short-term self-indulgences that are socially dysfunctional and, in time, self-destructive.

On the other hand, early exposure to the wrong kind of caregivers can program us with *excessive* (rather than moderate) emotional charging - that is, unquestioning commitment to certain imperatives. This can make us think of good and bad in simplistic "all" or "nothing" terms. For example:

> It can create religious fanatics who believe that some sacred source provides absolute guidelines for everyone, everywhere, under all circumstances, and *only on the basis of their interpretations.*

It can create commitment to an absolute "nothing but the truth" doctrine which, at times, can be needlessly brutal when there should be room for compassionate and socially constructive evasions.

It can make it difficult for us to visualize situations where blind adherence to a proscription against some activity in a different culture may do more harm than good to individual or organizational long-term interests.

In summary, the ideal is to have enough emotional charging of appropriate values to provide us with needed constraints and a sense of direction in life, but not so much that we cannot assess our programming in the light of mature experience and intelligent analysis, and modify it when appropriate.*

---

* This approach is based upon the insightful ideas of Seymour Epstein, "Integration of the Cognitive and the Psychodynamic Unconscious," <u>American Psychologist</u>, August 1994, pages 709-724, and Camilla Anderson's two books: <u>Beyond Freud</u> (Harper and Brothers, 1957) and <u>Saints, Sinners, and Psychiatry</u> (The Durham Press, 1962).

<u>Further Development Through Conscious Analysis</u>: A normal conscience leaves ample room for rational decision making with which to solve problems and develop and select non-emotionally-charged values. And such rationality increases as our brains mature, we gain more experience, and the decisions involved do not challenge excessively charged values, behaviors, or objects. For example:

Consider the complex rational analyses behind the development of the atomic bomb, the evolution of computers, space exploration, and modern medical science.

Consider the millions of people everyday who logically solve their problems, plan their activities, carefully budget their funds, and live harmoniously with their families and others.

Consider how well we operate automobiles and other machines in complex and dangerous environments with relatively few accidents.

However, many logical adults fail to make adequate allowances for the stages of intellectual development that young people must go through before they are capable of adult logic. They make unreasonable demands, behaviorally, and often succeed in making children feel inadequate. Jean Piaget provides one formulation of these stages of development. On the basis of his careful observation and experimentation - assuming the same exposure to Western-style formal schooling - he identified four:

1) From birth until about four years of age there is trial and error learning.

2) From approximately 2-7 years, children tend to perceive things in terms of their own activities - for example, the sun follows them around, and they don't see the relationship between mother's headache and her unwillingness to answer questions.

3) From approximately 7-11, they learn to make certain transformations - for example, that water poured from a squat glass into a same-capacity, tall glass remains the same quantity; that the left side of the street going in one direction becomes the right side going the other way.

4) From approximately 11-15, they learn to deal with abstractions - for example, to establish presumed relationships between things, such as is done to formulate scientific hypotheses.[2]

The Genetic Factor: The genes we get from our parents influence our capacity for complex learning (our level of intelligence) and the ease with which we acquire certain values and skills. Studies of twins suggest the following approximate percentages for the heritability of the following attributes:[3]

Body mass	70 percent inherited
Anxiety	40-50 percent
Assertiveness	60 percent
Ability to be enthralled by an aesthetic experience	55 percent
Thrill seeking	59 percent

In addition to these personal differences, we have genetic characteristics as a species that guide the manner in which we develop. Melvin Konner notes that: [4]

The human species is only moderately pair-bonding, with a significant polygynous tendency: Of 849 human societies, 83 percent practiced polygyny, and 16 percent practiced monogamy. Furthermore, there is a tendency for most of the single mates in a majority of the monogamous societies to have a succession of mates.[5]

Men have as many days per month of physical discomfort as women, but these are not as predictable as some female bad days due to the menstrual cycle.[6]

There is good evidence that early indulgence of an infant's instinctual, attachment behaviors will produce reduced dependency behavior in later years.[7] Tendencies toward anger, aggression, and grief are near-universal characteristics of bereavement.[8]

In comparing males and females in any given culture: females tend to be more nurturing toward infants and children and more altruistic; males tend to be more egotistical and aggressive, and only men commit rape.[9]

Konner provides a dramatic illustration of the role of biology in behavior with the case of 19 baby "girls" in three intermarrying rural villages in the Dominican Republic in his discussion of research led by Dr. Julianne Imperato-McGinley. All of the babies were born genetically male, but lacked a single enzyme of male sex-hormone synthesis due to a genetic defect. Consequently, their physical appearance and behavior were female. Eventually, the effects of delayed testosterone release in their systems over-rode the effects of having been reared as girls to produce the transformation described in the box below:

Female to Male Without Special Assistance

"...[They] were viewed and reared as completely normal females by their parents and other relatives...After twelve or more years of rearing as girls, with all the psychological influences encouraging that gender role in a rather sexist society, they are able to completely transform themselves into almost typical examples of the masculine gender - with family, sexual, vocational, and avocational roles...Imperato-McGinley reports that it cost some of them years of confusion and psychological anguish. But they made it, without special training or therapeutic intervention."

Source: Melvin Konner, The Tangled Wing. New York: Holt, Rinehart, and Winston, 1982, pages 124-125.

James Satterfield of The National Center for Hyperactive Children reports that there is clear evidence for a significant genetic factor in childhood hyperactivity.[10] If left untreated, such children are 10-20 times more likely to become delinquent than normal children.[11]

A Danish study and a Swedish study provide additional evidence to suggest a significant genetic component in delinquent behavior. The Danish study involved 14,427 adoptions registered in Denmark between the years 1927 and 1947. In those families where neither a biological nor adoptive parent had been convicted of a crime, 13.57 percent of the sons had criminal records. In families where an adoptive, but not a biological parent had been convicted, the rate was 15.7 percent. However, in families where a biological parent had been convicted, but not an adoptive parent, the rate was 20 percent![12]

The Swedish study involved 1775 adopted men and women who were born between 1930 and 1949. Of the men who had been born to law-abiding parents and reared in good adoptive homes, only 3 percent had been convicted of a crime. Of those born to law-abiding parents and reared in unfavorable adoptive homes, 7 percent had been convicted. However, of those who had been born to a convicted parent and reared in good adoptive homes, 12 percent had been convicted, and of those born to a convicted parent and reared in unfavorable adoptive homes, the rate soared to 40 percent![13]

As was mentioned earlier in our discussion of the development of a conscience, it appears that certain individuals are inherently deficient from birth in their ability to empathize with others. They have sporadic or weak feelings of genuine love, compassion, or contrition - if, indeed, they have them at all. And they are unable to restrain the immediate gratification of their desires.

Perhaps, this latter characteristic is an aspect of what we call "poor willpower": an inability to consciously and deliberately resist the temptation to betray one's values and goals; an inability to use conscious determination and focused attention to persist in a course of action despite pain, danger, or fatigue.

Many such genetically deficient individuals possess what Yochelson and Samenow call a "criminal personality." Their profile of it is based upon years of in-depth research and rehabilitation activity:

Defining Elements of the Criminal Personality

The restraints of responsible living are unacceptable and even contemptible. In such a person's reality, society's values and rules are absurd or unimportant.

Crime does not come to the criminal-to-be, he goes to it in search of excitement.

In whatever he does, he has to be a unique Number One; to be like anyone else is to be a failure. Instead of friendship, he seeks avenues of triumph.

He may work hard to be the best at something he likes, but then will quit when he tires of it. More often, he expects to be an overnight success, not through hard work, but by taking shortcuts. Throughout life, he is a sprinter, never a long-distance runner.

Lying is a way of life; lies of omission are more frequent than lies of commission.

He disregards the right of others to live safely or to expect promises to be kept, but demands from them the utmost trust, respect, and consideration. He claims he can live without depending on others, but demands that others provide whatever he wants.

He rarely sees anything from another's point of view, and it doesn't bother him to injure people.

He never develops a realistic concept of family life, an education, a vocation, or a sense of community.

He blames forces outside of himself for what he does. Others are always to blame, not he.

Kindness is weakness and people are expendable. They are valuable only to the extent that they can be controlled and exploited.

He does not know how to get along with responsible people on a day-to-day basis; he practices the extremes of total withdrawal or inappropriate intimacy.

He is fragmented in his thinking, largely ignoring the past and the long-term future. He may be sincere one day and completely insincere the next. Whatever he wants to do at a given moment is "right." He fails to listen to or take stock of himself. For him, just thinking something largely makes it so.

Source: Samuel Yochelson and Stanton Samenow, The Criminal Personality Volume II: The Change Process. New York: Jason Aronson, 1977, chapter 1.

George Horvat, former chief of psychological services at California's U.S. Terminal Island prison, attested to the validity of this profile: "Most psychologists working here find this one of the most accurate descriptions of the criminal personality they have ever seen."[14] And further support was provided by a special-education-teacher friend of mine. She translated the profile into children's language and administered it to her chronically troubled wards in the form of a self-description questionnaire. They were astounded. Several wanted to know how she had learned so many of their "secrets" without their help!

But, back to the origin of the profile. Having worked for 15 years with hard-core criminals at Saint Elizabeth's Hospital for the Criminally Insane, Dr. Yochelson, a psychiatrist, and psychologist Stanton Samenow undertook research to better understand the prisoners. They conducted 15 to 30 hours of interviews with each of them; conducted extensive interviews with their family members, teachers, playmates, and any others who could contribute useful information; and collected inclusive material about parental conflict, neglect, educational level, and economic circumstances.

In addition to producing the profile, their work also supports the idea that the formation of the criminal personality is largely due to inheritance:

> They found that only one or two of several children in a given family of quite normal siblings and parents had acquired it (and these were families of widely varying socio-economic circumstances), and they had very limited success with one of the most ambitious and rigorous individual/group rehabilitation programs ever undertaken - an intensive, long-term effort that was conducted for some 255 volunteer, criminal-personality individuals who professed to wanting to turn their lives around.

Group meetings lasted four hours per day, five days per week, for a year. And these were not self-justifying or "therapist-snowing" bull sessions. Each participant had to keep a daily record of his thought processes, report these to the group, and relate them to various dysfunctional thinking patterns, as well as to what he had learned that day. But only 30 of the prisoners completed the rigorous program. And then, only ten of them could be counted as successes several years later! Furthermore, for those few to achieve this level of success, they had to behave almost like saints: they could not deal with everyday moral gray areas or fine circumstantial discriminations. One slip off the carefully prescribed straight and narrow path was like a "cured" alcoholic attempting one drink.[15]

Fortunately, however, when heritable tendencies toward antisocial behavior are less extreme, there is good evidence that appropriate and early intervention can effectively curb - and even eliminate - them. The nature of such intervention will be discussed in Chapter 6.

Conclusion: A conscience is an essential blessing, but it does interfere with our ability to be objective in situations that involve emotionally charged factors. However, our ability to be more objective in such situations increases with brain growth, experience, and use of the techniques discussed in Chapter 6.

Genetic inheritance influences the types of values acquired and, at the extreme, largely precludes one's ability to experience genuine love, compassion, or contrition - thereby undermining the socialization process. This inherited defect predisposes the development of a criminal personality.

Chapter 5

THE ROLE OF VALUES IN CAUSING BEHAVIOR

If the only barrier to a happy and productive life were knowledge about how to attain it, most of us would have little trouble, because (as was discussed in Chapter 2) generally-agreed-to (and proven) rules for effective living have been available for a long time. The underlying problem is that we had little to do with much of our early "do's" and "don'ts" programming. Though this programming can be altered later, by our growing capacity for logical analysis and conscious effort, we always remain captive to it to some degree. In this chapter we will look at the roles which our values play in triggering and guiding our actual behavior.

It has been said that one of the ways that humans differ from animals is that they can cry...and one of the reasons they can cry is that they are able to perceive the difference between what they are and what they could be!

Source: Quoted by psychologist Joyce Brothers on her radio program.

Values Influence Our Energy To Act: Our energy to act is generated - largely at an unconscious level - by such factors as hunger; thirst; sexual arousal; fear; mood changes; response expectancies; discrepant feedback; the need for affiliation, optimal arousal, achievement mastery, and the need to know; and by conditioned anticipation of punishment or a desired reward.

In addition, energy to act is created consciously when we value winning and overcoming adversity. For example, we "psych ourselves up" for an athletic event or we exercise will power by focusing upon energizing thoughts such as "I can't give up." Lastly, "do's" and "don'ts" and other emotionally charged program values generate energy to act.

Values Influence Conscious Analysis: Strongly charged program values undermine rational analysis;   however, as we gain experience and mental maturity, we improve our ability to identify these strongly charged values (by discerning that we are behaving inappropriately or over-reactively) and, when appropriate, to discount their influence upon our thinking and behavior.

Values Interact With Situational Factors:

* The force of our values is weakened when we feel pressured to conform to the expectations of others by the threat of disapproval, rejection, or even physical harm.

* Our values are strengthened, weakened, or altered by the thinking and behavior of peers, relatives, teachers, religious leaders, law-enforcement officials, and those others whom we admire.

* Our values are strengthened, weakened, or altered by the positive or negative consequences of our own behavior and the behavior we read about and see in the movies or on television.

When there is consistency in the values represented by these various influences, we are made more clearly aware of the "social imperatives" of a given society. And when these values are compatible with our own values, we are strengthened in our sense of individual identity and belonging to that particular society. For example, consider the feelings and behavior of people at a funeral or church service. They are almost wholly determined by the demands of the situation, because few, if any, people there have values that require otherwise. Consequently, those in attendance experience minimal conflict with those around them, and observe little variation in their behavior. On the other hand, when there is inconsistency in the values represented by these various influences - or there is conflict between our conscience and the subculture we live in - we may become "loners" and/or experience a weakening of our moral imperatives.

Other situational factors that can affect our values are: the presence or absence of the material wherewithal required for action; physical deprivation or abuse; uncertainty about continuing employment; reward without performance; opportunities to cheat; and deteriorating economic conditions.

Dramatic illustration of the importance of situational pressure is provided by the experimental research of Stanley Milgram of Yale University. In 1965, he reported his findings about human tendencies toward questionable submission to authority:[1]

> Non-student adults, aged 20 to 50, were recruited as subjects for the experiment. They were told that their job would be to administer electric shocks to "learners" to determine the effect of punishment upon memory; that they would increase the level of shock for each error made as the "learner" tried to recall paired comparisons.

> Unknown to the experimental subjects, the "learners" were confederates of the researcher, and the errors made, the indicated shocks, (from a "slight shock" of 15 volts to a "severe shock" of 450 volts), and the audible responses (from complaints of discomfort to agonized appeals to stop) of the "learners" (who were strapped in an "electric chair") were not real.

> These deceptions were quite successful, as was indicated by the stressed reactions of the subjects to giving higher-level "shocks" as well as post-experiment, interview data obtained from them.

Milgram describes what happened:

> "With numbing regularity good people were seen to knuckle under the demands of authority (orders from the

researcher) and perform actions that were callous and severe. Men who are in everyday life responsible and decent were seduced by the trappings of authority, by the control of their perceptions, and by the uncritical acceptance of the experimenter's definition of the situation.

"Cries from the victim were inserted; not good enough. The victim claimed heart trouble; subjects still shocked him on demand. The victim pleaded that he be let free, and his answers no longer registered on the signal box; subjects continued to shock him! At the outset we had not conceived that such drastic procedures would be needed to generate disobedience, and each step was added only as the ineffectiveness of the earlier techniques became clear."[2]

However, in follow-up studies an increasing number of subjects did defy Milgram's instructions to administer larger shocks when they were placed close to the victim and could both see his convincingly acted agony and hear his feigned cries.

Next, we have the dramatic experience of Ron Jones, a teacher at Cubberley High School in Palo Alto, California. In his 1967 world-history class, he created a highly authoritarian, military-like organization, called The Third Wave, to illustrate how ordinary Germans could have gone along with the excesses of Nazism under Adolph Hitler. He reports that:

"The experiment that was initiated as a one-day exercise in the 'power of discipline' became a five-day nightmare. Over 300 students eventually took part in The Wave. The desire to be 'a part of the group,' to be 'successful,' and 'actively involved' in the experiment, replaced student curiosity and expression. Uniform behavior, salutes, tattling, fear and violence became expected conduct. The experiment climaxed in a rally in which students gave up their freedom for the promise of being superior to their classmates."

As "the leader," Ron Jones became more personally involved during the experiment than he had anticipated. He derived the following observations from this experience:

"It doesn't take money or power to be kind to a stranger, stand by a loved one, or fight injustice. It's not the big things in life that make up our history, but the small events - the everyday decisions that give meaning to our future."[3]

According to Leslie Weinfield,[4] Jones' Third Wave experiment caught the attention of Philip Zimbardo, a psychologist at Stanford University, who simulated prison environments several years later by randomly assigning college students as "guards" and "prisoners" (with all attendant powers to the "guards"). The subjects were selected after screening, with none having any history of emotional, physical, social, or intellectual disability. Yet, the simulation had a dramatically negative impact upon them.

The student "guards" became increasingly impersonal and abusive toward their fellow-student "prisoners" - verbally so, because they were not permitted to be physical - as they converted, on their own initiative, all of the "prisoner's" prescribed rights (even time of eating, sleeping, or going to the toilet) into privileges to be awarded at their discretion. As a result, the "prisoners" became increasingly passive and dependent, with flattened emotions - after initial bouts of rebellion and hostility toward each other. Within the first three days, five "prisoners" had to be released from the experiment due to extreme depression, crying, rage, and acute anxiety. In fact, when the study was prematurely stopped after only six days, most of the "guards" appeared to be distressed. They had come to enjoy the extreme levels of control and power they had exercised.[5]

In the real world - according to the May 22, 1996 Dateline television program - a unique, criminal subculture thrives in Murphy Village, South Carolina. The town serves as home base for scam artists (called "travelers") who exploit various people throughout the U.S. - especially the elderly - with reasonable-sounding propositions for repairing or painting their houses. Then, when the scam artists demand exorbitant fees for their shoddy or non-existent work, they enforce compliance through the use of threats and other forms of intimidation. In addition, Murphy Village has a unique culture that nurtures bizarre behavior on the part of its "traveler-related" young people. Child marriages, child mothers, and the intermarriage of first cousins are commonplace.

The survey data in the box below suggest that the longer we stay in a given work environment the more likely we are to be influenced by that environment - even when its values are contrary to the ones we started with. We see ambitious young business executives who compromise their values to get ahead and use suppression and denial to minimize unpleasant feelings of guilt and lost self-esteem. Most of them do not understand the emotional price that these psychological defense mechanisms may exact; that, in time, this "solution" to their uneasiness can generalize to other relationships and activities. They may lose their general capacity to feel and experience listlessness in their everyday lives.

1443 Various-Level Managers Rank Reasons For Unethical Behavior

(1 = most important)

1 Behavior of Superiors	4 Society's Moral Climate
2 Behavior of Peers	5 Formal Policy (or Lack
3 Ethical Practices of	Thereof)
of Industry	6 Personal Financial Need

To the question "Would you resign if your boss insisted on you doing something you strongly feel is unethical?," 33 percent of the first-line managers and some 25 percent of the middle managers said "not sure" or "probably would not."

Source: Based upon Barry Posner and Warren Schmidt, "Values and the American Manager: An Update," California Management Review, Spring 1984, pages 206-216.

A dramatic illustration of the power of institutional custom - coupled with peer influence - is provided by the "tailhook scandal" of the Tailhook Association: a private organization of active and retired Naval and Marine aviators and defense contractors whose members received financial support from the Navy to help them with annual-meeting- attendance expenses. A Pentagon investigation concluded that at least 83 women and 7 men, both naval officers and civilians, had been assaulted in an indecent manner while being forced to involuntarily walk a hotel-corridor "gauntlet" at the 1991 meeting.

An admiral's aide and helicopter pilot, described how she was assaulted when she stepped off of the elevator. Someone grabbed her buttocks so hard that he lifted her off of the floor. As she physically and verbally protested, another grabbed her buttocks, and someone else reached under her skirt and grabbed the crotch of her panties. She was terrified.[6]

Apparently, a milder version of such "hazing" had started years earlier, and then had escalated as it became a "custom" of annual Tailhook conventions. New, younger members assumed that such behavior was "expected" and permissible, given the lack of "interference" by more senior-officer "graduates" of the process. Even after the adverse publicity given to the event, many attendees said that such conduct should be overlooked for an elite group of "returning heroes" from the Desert Storm operation who, by facing such dangers there, were somehow immune to normal conduct requirements.[7]

Clearly, this behavior was dominated by situational factors. These college-trained men had to be highly recommended - and then survive rigorous training and high standards of personal conduct - to enter and complete the aviation-training program. Consequently, it seems reasonable to assume that few, if any, of the perpetrators or apologists would have behaved as they did under everyday circumstances.

81

Still, such situational factors should not be over-emphasized. A majority of the pilots did not participate in the offenses, just as a significant proportion of those subjected to the Nazi death camps did not abandon respect and caring for others, even though they were confronted with extreme forms of situational pressure .[8]

Values Influence Our "Can Do" Feelings: The *ability* required to intervene successfully in a situation is the product of aptitude, training, and experience. However, *the capacity to use such ability* is influenced by one's value with regard to "self-efficacy" – one's "can do" feelings.

Bandura explains that, at any point in time, the belief in one's self-efficacy is not primarily determined by the ability one has - it is determined more by one's judgment as to what she or he can do with that ability. This observation is based upon studies that show that one's self-efficacy score is a better single predictor of future performance than is an objective record of past performance.[9]

How These Factors Interact To Cause Behavior: Research findings suggest that ethical behavior is caused by four interacting factors (Energy to Act, Conscious Values or Goals, Situational Factors, and Feelings of Self-Efficacy) as presented in the box below:

Ethical   Energy   Conscious Values or Goals
Behavior = To Act X   (to channel energy)

X Situational Factors X Feelings of Self-Efficacy*

*The formulation of this model was influenced most by David McClelland. In one study, through the use of just three of the terms - Energy to Act, Conscious Values, and Feelings of Self-Efficacy - he was able to account for some 70 percent of the variation in the actual affiliation behavior of 48 subjects. See his article "How Motives, Skills, and Values Determine What People Do," <u>American Psychologist</u>, 1985, <u>40</u>, 812-825.

For example, I may agree that helping a neighbor is a good idea, and I may be quite able (physically, financially, and time-wise) to do so, but - in the absence of energy to act (see first page of this chapter) - I will do nothing! Another example is provided by Chris Argyris, a behavioral consultant who has counseled many executives. He observes that managers will often commit to intended changes in their behavior and then utterly fail to execute the changes. They will create, "by their own choice, a world that is contrary to what they say they prefer and contrary to the managerial stewardship they espouse."[10]

<u>Conclusion</u>: It is simplistic to assume that doing what is right is merely the result of knowing what is right - various factors *interact* to cause ethical behavior. Among these are situational factors. They are potent, but not all-controlling. Mature logic and the strongly held values that comprise a healthy conscience and feelings of self-efficacy can negate or facilitate compliance with negative external pressures: All of the subjects did not succumb to Milgram's experimental commands, all of the guards did not become brutal in Zimbardo's study, most prisoners of war do not sell-out to the enemy, and only a minority of officers engaged in Tailhook misbehavior. The better we understand the model, the more we are enabled to constructively influence our own behavior and that of others.

Chapter 6

HOW TO NURTURE CORE VALUES IN OURSELVES AND OTHERS

Herman Melville

And freedom is only good as a means; is no end in itself...it is easier to govern others, than oneself.

(In <u>Mardi</u>. Reported by Constance Bridges in <u>Great Thoughts Of Great Americans</u>. New York: Thomas Y. Crowell Company, 1951, page 93)

As we discussed in Chapter 5, consistent ethical behavior is not simply the result of being aware of good and bad consequences: it requires an understanding of the limits to rationality - caused by our biological makeup and our early programming - and the ability to overcome these limits when they interfere with our effective functioning in everyday life. There are proven tools of Behavior Management that can aid us in doing this. They are presented below.

<u>Dealing With Emotionally Charged Values</u>: We are fortunate when those who rear us endow us with moderate emotional charging for constructive values. This provides us with a conscience that prods us toward practicing self-discipline and doing what is right, and it greatly facilitates mutual trust and compatibility with other constructively programmed members of the culture. On the other hand, we are unfortunate when our culture incorporates dysfunctional values or when early programming prods us in the direction of inappropriate behavior. As an example of the latter situation, a typical "spoiled child" is one who has been emotionally rewarded for being demanding

85

and self-indulgent and for disruptively seeking attention, while escaping censure for ignoring the needs of others.

If certain inappropriate beliefs are *excessively* charged, we tend to be compulsively captive to them in adulthood. We find ourselves in the unpleasant position of feeling compelled to act inappropriately on certain occasions, *even though we know that the related behavior is illogical and contrary to our best interest or the best interests of others.* Here are some examples of inappropriate beliefs which prompt behavior that interferes with good interpersonal relations, the full use of our abilities, and our willingness to accept responsibility for our actions:

Typical "Entitlements"

If I feel bored or distressed, it is the duty of those around me to make me happy.

An apology entitles me to full forgiveness.

If I feel helpless, I am entitled to help from others.

If I am non-assertive, I'm entitled to get my share.

Typical "Musts"

People must recognize my opinions as final.

I must feel virtuous and blameless at all times.

I must feel that everyone who knows me likes me.

I must always be in control of a situation and never at a disadvantage.

I must outshine and show up others to feel comfortable.

Typical "Don'ts"

Don't be thoughtful of others for this is a sign of weakness and they will take advantage of you.

Don't work hard or others will think you are a sucker.

Don't be honest or others will take advantage of you.

A husband shouldn't do housework, real men don't do this.

A husband shouldn't tolerate disobedience by his wife.

Never ask for help or admit an error, because others will think less of you.[1]

Albert Ellis has developed an approach called Rational Emotive Therapy that can help to free us from the influence of such dysfunctional beliefs:

First, we must identify the inappropriate behaviors we tend to repeat and remind ourselves *why* these behaviors are undesirable. Then, we must consciously reaffirm our resolve to discard them.

We must identify the circumstances in which these behaviors occur; that is, we must look for and note the cues that seem to trigger them. Then, we must look out for these cues and consciously challenge ourselves to act in more constructive ways when they appear.

Finally, as with the development of any skill, we must engage in repeated practice to obtain significant change.[2]

Qualified therapists can assist us in this work. They can help us to understand when and why we are behaving dysfunctionally, and they can encourage and support us in our efforts to break out of such habits. As we learn to accept and practice more desirable behaviors, we may long for greater feelings of brotherhood and tolerance. Religious conversion has provided one means for enhancing such feelings. Another means is provided by participation in a properly led encounter group. In this regard, I recall the comment of a minister with whom I participated in a successful, week-long encounter experience: "The most important thing I have learned here is that there is another way (other than religious conversion)!"

<u>Dealing With The Urge For Immediate Gratification</u>: Excessively charged values are not our only problem. Our natural susceptibility to immediate rather than delayed consequences - regardless of their relative importance - is another. For example, many smokers, drug addicts, excessive drinkers, and compulsive gamblers refuse to quit despite overwhelming evidence about the destructive effects that will eventually overtake them. Clearly, their behavior is driven more by the immediate physiological highs they gain, than by consideration of the deadly, but delayed, consequences they will reap. There are two useful means by which we can discourage this urge for immediate gratification and nurture the core value of self-restraint:

Cue Control: Temptations are cues that encourage immediate gratification: the sight or aroma of inviting food, a pack of cigarettes or an ashtray, a bottle of alcohol or a bar, people enjoying a cocktail, an attractive and willing member of the opposite sex, and so on. "Cue control" involves removing such cues or focusing our attention on "counter cues" that will discourage the undesired activity. For example:

We can remove cue stimuli from view and easy access. This includes avoiding TV shows, movies, or places in which the undesired activity is likely to occur and avoiding - at least initially - people who engage in the activity.

88

We can reflect upon all of the harmful effects of the activity when we feel the urge to engage in it.

We can assure consideration of often-overlooked factors by completing a "Decisional Balance Sheet": by listing all of the objective "pros" and "cons" that go with a choice, as well as how we think all "relevant others" will react to it (spouse, family members, business associates, clients, close friends, etc., and even children yet to come!).

In situations that tempt fraud or theft, we can help ourselves and others to be honest by removing any doubt as to what constitutes dishonest behavior through adequate discussion and explanation; we can put up signs that warn of surveillance, prosecution, or harmful consequences; and we can insist that more than one person be involved in accounting for cash or other assets.

We can help to assure desired action by establishing individual or group goals that are specific and understood, and then committing them to writing, with target times or dates specified. When a goal is long-range, we can commit to a series of more-immediate sub-goals.

An effective use of "counter cues" is being made by Project Northland, which involves some 1200 Minnesota teenager participants, and was launched in 1990. The participants view videotaped interviews with imprisoned drunken drivers, participate in mock DUI accidents and trials, accompany police officers to investigate store owners who are selling liquor to minors, and stage all-night "lock-in" parties which are kept free of alcohol. After being in the program for three years, eighth graders were 20 percent less likely to drink on a monthly basis. Currently, a nine-year, $9 million program is being launched that will increase the involvement of peers, parents, teachers, prisoners, prosecutors, town-council members, and the police.[3]

Consequence Control: Another way to discourage the urge for immediate gratification is to use "consequence control." This involves formalizing what many of us did informally in school to prod the completion of our homework: agree with ourselves that we would see a particular movie, have a favorite dessert, or view a preferred TV program only after successfully completing an assignment.

Bandura on Immediate Gratification

"People are more likely to resist tyrannical authority than the immediate gratification of self-interest."

[however]

"It is because people are able to do whatever they wish with the rewards they control that they can be agents of their own motivation."

Source: Albert Bandura, Social Foundations Of Thought And Action. Prentice-Hall, 1986, pages 45, 367.

As Bandura points out in the box above, because we are able to do as we wish with the rewards we control, we can manage them to prod ourselves in the right direction:

First, we can make a list of the realizable consequences (rewards) we value the most. Then, we can consider which are most practical to administer on an on-going basis. For example, it helps if the reward can be administered as soon as possible after completion of the target behavior. (To illustrate the value of this, consider why most people do not drive foolishly in heavy, fast-moving traffic - potentially bad consequences are immediate and usually quite serious).

Next, we draw up a written contract with ourselves that specifies exactly what will be done, exactly when, and what consequence-reward we will receive. At the same time, we need to specify that we *cannot* enjoy a substitute reward if we fail to comply (no "gamesmanship-with-self" permitted)!

If possible, we should show the contract to someone who will be able to monitor our compliance or non-compliance, and whose approval we value. In addition, we might have this person exact an agreed-to penalty for failure.

Initially, we should receive the reward after every occurrence of the desired behavior. Then, we should shift to a "variable-ratio schedule," whereby we are rewarded for every second or third occasion of the behavior *on the average*. (We can have it be truly "on the average" by drawing one of two or three numbers from a hat each time - one of which permits the reward).

When it is feasible to do so, we should add cue control to enhance the effects of consequence control.

You may think: "I'd give anything to change, but there just isn't a legal or civilized consequence that is powerful enough to do the trick." Don't believe it! Most of the time, we can assure success by arranging for a large enough amount of money or a treasured asset to be held by a third party for forfeit due to failure. Usually, after a sustained period of success, there is no need to continue with conscious rewarding - the effects upon us of achievement, and/or the positive effects upon others, will sufficiently maintain the behavior.

In addition to, or in place of a reward, overt punishment may be used as a consequence. However, punishment does not weaken behavior as effectively as an appropriate reward will strengthen it. Here are some of the disadvantages associated with punishment as a first-choice consequence:

It may cause high levels of resentment and tension.

It may undermine performance, endurance, and creativity.

It may make the person punished want to avoid the punisher. This can interfere with good interpersonal relations, effective two-way communication, commitment to the cause, and the effective use of a reward approach in the future.

It may work only when the punisher is perceived to be present. As the old saying goes: "When the cat's away, the mice will play."

On the other hand, these disadvantages can be eliminated or minimized when punishment is used as *a last resort and in conjunction with the rewarding of desired behavior*.[4] In practice, this "last resort" standard may apply most frequently to young, active children between the ages of $1\frac{1}{2}$ and 6 who, typically, have poor understanding of the consequences of their behavior. For example, when a child is out of control - especially if the behavior poses a danger to the child or others - one or two mild slaps on the bottom may provide the *only* means for effective constraint. According to Michael Lemonick, more than two thirds of recently polled pediatricians agree with this assessment.[5] And Daniel Costello reports that a decade-long study by Diana Baumrind of the University of California at Berkeley found that the combination of positive encouragement and reasonable discipline - including spanking - produced the best outcomes in terms of personal achievement and feelings of self-worth.[6]

With regard to dealing with heritable tendencies toward antisocial behavior in children, the results of one of the most comprehensive studies yet conducted by David Reiss and his associates imply the following:

Antisocial behavior in children is reduced significantly by close parental behavior monitoring and the administration of firm discipline when needed. It is essential, however, that the parental response be constructive and effective, and not punitive. True, it is difficult to be loving toward an initially unlovable child; but, except in extreme cases of negative heritability, the child's behavior will change for the better.

Ineffective parental monitoring and disciplinary attempts - as well as retaliatory discipline - encourage antisocial behavior, as does a parental shift toward permissiveness - thus leaving the young person as the "victor." Parents should seek professional help rather than "quit the field."

Effective parental monitoring is also needed to influence the choice of peer associates, because heritable tendencies toward antisocial behavior influence the choice of peer groups, and these groups have a significant influence upon subsequent behavior.[7]

What About Objections To Behavior Management?: Some people oppose the use of rewards to influence behavior because: "You shouldn't have to bribe a person for doing what he or she is supposed to do anyway." This objection is aimed most often at gaining compliance from children or employees in a company. In the case of children, genuine approval and praise - as well as spending money and TV privileges - are potent rewards. Before labeling them as demeaning "bribes," remember that punishment for failure to conform is a form of "negative bribe." In addition, appropriate rewards are preferable to punishment as a first-choice response.

As for employers demanding that employees "do their duty," there is an interesting inconsistency - many U.S. managers overlook the absence of a similar imperative for themselves. They regard high salaries, big bonuses, stock options, and all sorts of special "perks" as being absolutely essential to their motivational well-being!

Some people fear that material rewards will undermine the motivating potential of self-esteem, a sense of achievement, and satisfaction for a job well done. To the contrary, research by Eisenberger and Cameron shows that rewards increase motivation and creativity as long as they are tied to specific standards of success rather than the mere fact of performing without regard to the quality of the performance.[8]

In 1996, more than 22 million children participated in the Pizza Hut "Book It" program which provided a personal pan-pizza to each student who met a teacher's reading goals. Stephen Flora surveyed 171 college students who had participated as children to determine the program's long-term effects. He also surveyed students who had been given money rewards for reading. In both cases, the respondents told him that rewards had not only boosted their interest in reading, but had also enhanced their skill. They indicated that subsequent reading activity had been sustained by the pleasure it gave and the opportunity it afforded to acquire new knowledge.[9]

In addition to the evidence given above, it appears that most outstanding authors, corporate leaders, doctors, lawyers, and other professionals are not demotivated by money. To the contrary, they appear to study and work harder, and to defer their retirement, despite rising material success.

What Is Wrong With Life In The West

B.F. Skinner, one of history's most eminent psychologists, made the following observation:

"What is wrong with life in the West is not that it has an abundance of reinforcers, but that they are not contingent upon the kind of behavior that sustains the individual or promotes the survival of the culture or species."

Source: From an address at the 1985 American Psychological Association Convention, reported by Dawn Bennett, "Pleasing Reinforcers Sap Strength of West: Skinner," APA Monitor [of the American Psychological Association], October, 1985, page 9.

<u>Enhancing Feelings of Self-Efficacy</u>: As we discussed in Chapter 5, self-efficacy - confidence that we can accomplish something - is not determined solely by the skills we have, but primarily reflects our judgment about what we can do with these skills. To enhance our feelings of self-efficacy, we can:

Focus upon visual cues that are associated with our achievements - pictures, trophies, scrapbooks, letters of appreciation, certificates - to counteract our thoughts of failure.

Try to "mentally relive" some of our greatest successes.

Formulate and achieve meaningful personal goals through the use of consequence contracts as discussed above.

Counteract feelings of unworthiness by devoting at least one-half an hour each day to recalling instances in which others unselfishly gave us love, encouragement, genuine forgiveness, or material help without questioning whether or not we deserved it. We should try to "mentally relive" these instances.

<u>Encouraging Truthfulness And Full Disclosure In Group Problem Solving</u>: In a typical group setting, we hesitate to give candid opinions that might offend those who control the things we need and want, and we tend to limit how much we contribute so as not to impose upon the contribution opportunities of others. Consequently, many decisions are made without the benefit of deliberation based upon truthful, full disclosure. These observations are supported by research findings. For example, I conducted a study in which groups were led to unanimous public votes on the same issues by both autocratic and participative leadership. Yet, many of the autocratically led participants - in comparison with the participatively led ones - maintained private opinions that differed significantly with the way they voted.[10]

Here are proven guidelines for assuring candid inputs and an unbiased participative, problem-solving process:

1) Whenever possible, pursue just *one* of the following purposes in a given meeting:

    Identify, discuss, and rank problems, positions, or options.

    Solve a particular problem.

    Debug and/or refine a written proposed solution, program, or other document.

2) Collect, number, reproduce, and distribute anonymous inputs from all participants prior to the meeting, sufficiently in advance to permit any desired participant reflection or brief research about them.

3) Solicit additional, anonymous inputs on 3X5 cards at the beginning of the meeting and transcribe these to flipchart pages to display on the wall (with the pre-meeting handout serving to display the pre-meeting inputs). Maintain the display throughout the meeting, noting any permitted changes on the items.

4) Assure opportunity for discussion of all the items before any voting, limiting the discussion to desired clarification of, and presentation of any pros or cons for, an item.

5) Allow a single, unexplained objection to block any proposed change to the wording of any item, or for the combination of two or more items (though the purpose here is *not* to classify items into categories). However, no one's approval is required to add an item to those on display.

6) Use anonymous voting to rank 15 percent of the finalist problems, positions, or options; to rank solutions; or to approve final changes to a document by majority vote.

7) When the first vote to prioritize problems, positions, or options produces inconsistent rankings that suggest that adequate discussion or clarification had not been given to certain items, provide for a second vote (if a majority of group members wants it). When a second vote is desired, discussion is reopened for a subset of the items on display, and the second vote determines which "winners" from this will be added to the list of clear-cut "winners" from the first vote. In addition to clarifying results, the presence of this option discourages collusion or "gamesmanship" in the initial voting.

Note: For fuller discussion of these procedures, and the research findings that underlie them, see my book: Effective Group Problem Solving, Jossey-Bass, 1987.

How The Factors Influence Ethical Behavior: Recall our formula for the causes of ethical behavior:

Ethical   Energy   Conscious Values or Goals
Behavior   =   To Act X   (to channel energy)

X Situational Factors X Feelings of Self-Efficacy

We have discussed ways in which we can enhance each of the causal factors to strengthen our ethical behavior and help others to do the same. To summarize:

Setting goals helps to generate energy as well as to channel it.

Identifying and challenging dysfunctional values helps to "defuse" negative energy-to-act, as it facilitates rational decision making.

97

Making desired rewards contingent upon performance (consequence control) further strengthens motivation.

Seeking out and attending to positive cues - and removing or avoiding negative ones (cue control) - help to make the immediate situation encourage - rather than discourage - desired behavior. And using cue control in conjunction with consequence control is even more effective.

Enhancing feelings of self-efficacy strengthens both energy to act and persistence.

Assuring anonymity of inputs, distributing the inputs before the meeting, displaying them throughout the meeting, and providing full discussion opportunity for all inputs before voting, anonymously, are means for encouraging truthfulness and full disclosure in group problem solving.

<u>Increasing The Likelihood For Creating Healthy And Stable Families</u>: The creation of a healthy family begins with desired conception on the part of self-supporting and responsible parents. Then, it is sustained by maintenance of caring and conflict-free relationships. Let's examine some means for accomplishing these goals:

By Encouraging Couples To Seek Pre-marriage Counseling: Given the disabilities that broken or conflicted homes impose upon our children - and subsequently upon society - we should pay more attention to improving the odds for success in marriage. One good approach is pre-marital counseling. Mark Merrill, president of Florida Family Council, reports that the divorce rate in Peoria, Illinois dropped 20 percent in five years after churches there began to require such a program.[11]

By Discouraging Inappropriate Conception: It seems strange that we require licenses to drive a car, practice medicine, build bridges, sell real estate, and do other things that can adversely affect society; yet, make no comparable effort to discourage the production of children on the part of those who neither want them nor are ready or able to support them. Can anyone think of another unregulated activity that is more potentially destructive to society? And to further dramatize our inconsistency, think of those who oppose the establishment of any restrictions upon childbearing, but offer no objection to our rigorous adoption criteria. In fact, they often criticize the inadequacies of these criteria! Why should we insist upon responsible parenting *only* for adopted children?

It would be nice if would-be parents had to satisfy the following criteria before conception could occur:

> Both would state in writing that they desire a child, or an additional child, and provide evidence at the time of application to show that, jointly, they could provide at least minimum financial support for themselves as well as the child, or children.

> Both would agree that, jointly, in terms of both personal time and financial contribution, they would continue to be legally liable - within the limits of their resources - for the support and nurture of the child, or children, until each child came of age, whether or not they were married at the time of application, or remain married.

"Fine," you might say, "But how could we enforce such requirements short of establishing a police state?" Perhaps in the future, practical means for accomplishing fully reversible or temporary sterilization will be devised, and it will be feasible to require all boys or girls to submit to it. In the meantime, we have a promising new procedure. It is a form of reversible, non-surgical sterilization for women that may avoid the downside effects of implants. It is called Selective Tubal Occlusion or S/TOP. Five years or more (from 1997) may be required for adequate testing of its safety and contraceptive effectiveness, according to its developer, Dr. Amy Thurmond. She reports that a trained gynecologist can complete the procedure in about 10 minutes without the need of anesthesia.[12]

Meanwhile, we can encourage a decrease in unwarranted pregnancies through the use of such contraceptives as the pill, the newer injectable Depo-Provera (effective for three months), and doctor-administered abortion drugs such as RU-486, which was approved by the Food and Drug Administration for use in the U.S. in late October of 2000. In addition, we should consider implementing Noel Perrin's financial incentive system (or some variation of it):

> "Every girl when she reached puberty would notify her local population center...If the girl went the next year without having a baby, she would get a government check for $500, placed in the bank account at the center now opened for her. She could take it all out [or leave it in as part of a growing fund]...The next year, if she still hadn't had a baby...her second check would be for $600. The year after $700. A young woman reaching the age of 20, and still not having had a child, would receive a check for around $1,200.

> "If at 21 she proceeded to have a baby...payment...would abruptly drop to zero...if she did not have another baby the next year, back would come a check for $500...and so on up the modest pay ladder.
> "The cost wouldn't level off for about 40 years - and when it did, it would still be under what we now pay as welfare...The current figure [1990] is 770 billion a year."[13]

Among other programs for discouraging inappropriate conception, two school-linked ones for teenagers have been successful:

The Johns Hopkins Pregnancy Prevention Program incorporates comprehensive medical care and contraceptive services. It has succeeded in reducing the early onset and frequency of sexual activity, increased the use of contraceptives, and reduced teenage pregnancy rates by 30 percent (while comparison school rates rose 58 percent)[14]

The Teen Outreach Program, has produced lower rates of sexual intercourse, school suspension, and course failure for participants, as compared with controls, according to a national evaluation. The program combines volunteer community service with classroom discussion about one's choices as to one's future.[15]

Another interesting effort is a weekend program called "Baby Think It Over" sponsored by Alachua County, Florida. Participants (aged 12-21) are responsible for life-like baby dolls that cry at random during sessions that last 5-35 minutes. A participant can appease her crying doll only by inserting a "care key" (attached to her wrist) in the doll's back. Failure to insert the key within one minute is counted as "neglect." In addition, participants must prepare an expense budget for one year of baby supplies, and are asked to maintain a diary of their training experience. Follow-up visits revealed that most of the participants had decided that they were not yet ready to undertake the responsibilities of motherhood. For more information, contact Jenna Prusakowski at (352) 395 0680, extension 88218.[16]

Finally, we might consider the requirement that any pre-menopause mother on welfare who has an unsanctioned additional child (and has not reported for regular Depo-Provera injections) will have to submit to sterilization as a condition for retaining her present child (or children) and continuing to receive support payments.

By Dealing Effectively With Irresponsible Young Fathers:
In 1982, Charles Ballard decided to do something for angry young fathers who were suffering from low self-esteem and the absence of positive role models. Armed with some grant money, he created the Teen Father Program in Cleveland, Ohio. As word spread, the number of young men seeking his assistance increased dramatically. However, before he agrees to help them, he insists upon three things:

> Legitimize your child,
>
> enroll in school or a GED class, and
>
> get a job, no matter how menial, to learn financial responsibility.

Ballard - who had grown up poor and fatherless in rural Alabama and had quit school in the 10th grade - reflects that:

> "The young men who come into our program are just like I was. Angry, with minimal self-esteem and without positive role models. When they decide to walk through our door, that is an important first step. We encourage them to develop potential that is already there.
>
> "If you want to change how a man acts, you must change how he thinks about himself, about taking responsibility for his child and respecting the child's mother. When we achieve that, then the rest of the community can be saved."[17]

Later, his program expanded into the National Institute for Responsible Fatherhood and Family Development. By 1994, it had helped more than 2000 high-school-dropout fathers to become more responsible. Seventy percent of them now have diplomas and 97 percent are providing support for their children. New offices have been opened in Washington, Baltimore, Nashville, Kansas City, and Detroit.

<u>Improving The Quality Of Family Life</u>: After meeting the requirements for having a child responsibly, it is not enough that parents simply stay together and provide adequate child support. They need to devote enough quality time to their children, for young people learn to value themselves and become productive adults by imitating and interacting with caring and responsible grown-ups.   Harry Triandis of the American Psychological Association cites research findings that confirm that parental supportiveness is very important across all cultures:

> Children whose parents reject them - by withdrawing affection, disliking them, being disapproving of them, resenting them, being indifferent to them, or neglecting them - are more hostile toward peers, more dependent on others, and show low self-esteem in comparison with other children. In addition, they have a negative world view, are emotionally unresponsive and unstable, and are low in generosity and nurturance as adults.

> Children whose parents are warm and affectionate - who hold them, praise them, console them, hug them, and play with them - show less hostility to peers, are less dependent, and have higher self-esteem. In addition, they have a positive world view, are emotionally stable, and are generous and nurturing as adults.[18]

In 1995, <u>The Wall Street Journal</u> reported that students who had indicated spending the most time with their parents had had significantly lower rates of alcohol and tobacco abuse,[19] and it has been found that parental guidance is among the significant factors associated with resistance to drug pushers.[20] In addition, Dr. Joy Osofsky of the LSU Medical Center in New Orleans reports that a positive family environment can play an important role in countering the negative effects upon children of witnessing violence.[21]

A crucial period for quality time is from birth to age 4, because one's cortical development and general approach to experience are largely finished by then. Researchers Betty Hart and Todd Risley specify what constitutes good quality time during this period of development:

> Talking and listening well beyond what is necessary to provide adequate care; for example, naming and describing what the child is watching, reading to the child, describing what to expect and how to cope with new situations,
>
> providing children with wholesome new experiences like visiting the zoo and watching TV programs such as Sesame Street,
>
> describing or offering choices, such as suggesting alternative behaviors in response to an unacceptable behavior, rather than just saying "no," or "stop that," or "you are bad (or stupid)," and
>
> providing enough, but not too much, help.[22]

These guidelines are also supported by the research findings of the Fullerton Longitudinal Study led by Allen Gottfried of California State University-Fullerton.[23]

While providing wholesome new experiences, parents should be equally concerned about discouraging unwholesome ones. According to a 1999 Kaiser Family Foundation study of 3000 young people, aged 2-18, two-thirds of those who were eight and older had television sets in their bedrooms. And, typically, they spent five and one-half hours per day consuming media material (computers and music, but mainly television). Yet, half the parents had no rules about the use of these media. Amy Dickinson suggests the following guidelines:

> Television should not be on during mealtime or during homework or study time.
>
> It is useful for parents to review program listings with their children to agree about what they will watch, and their sets should be turned off during other times.[24]

Needless to say, the majority of present day-care centers do not provide the kind or amount of quality care that is needed. Yet, working mothers have to be at work during all or most of these critical baby years. Changing the quality of day care should be one of our top priorities. Another approach, according to Harriet Presser, an authority on shift work, is for working parents to commit to back-to-back work shifts. She reports that 30 percent of all dual-earner couples with children under the age of five are now doing this.[25] In addition, it would help for lawmakers to give tax credits to businesses that accommodate mothers or fathers who leave the work force during the first critical years of child development.

Hetherington, Bridges, and Insabella cite research findings that show that the level of conflict between parents is a more important source of psychological problems for children than whether or not the parents are divorced. They report that the most destructive type of conflict is that in which parents denigrate each other and demand that the children give their allegiance to one or the other.[26]

Mark Merrill points out that post-marital intervention can save troubled marriages. For example, the success rate for the international Retrouvaille Program for troubled marriages has been better than 80 percent.[27] The program was started in Canada in 1977 and was then shared with other communities, worldwide, starting in 1982. It involves a weekend experience in which couples are helped to re-establish communication and to gain new insights about themselves as individuals, and as couples. They are led by team couples who offer knowledge and hope, because they have successfully resolved their own deeply troubled marriages. This weekend experience is then followed by 12 presentations during the ensuing three-months. For further information, contact Retrouvaille International, 231 Ballantrae Lane, Houston, Texas 77015, or call 1-800-470-2230.

Reducing The Incidence Of Delinquency And Crime: In addition to measures that parents can take to discourage delinquency and crime, we now consider important measures that can be taken outside of the home.

By Dealing Effectively With Troubled Young People: The fifteen-year-old Monitor Program of the Oregon Social Learning Center (a nonprofit research organization in Eugene) has been able to attract top professionals on 24-hour call for half the pay they might command elsewhere. The approach used, known as "treatment foster care," has been successful in changing the behavior of violent juveniles (other than murderers or those who threaten the community).

A four-year study of 37 Monitor "graduates" found that they had spent 60 percent fewer days in jail during the year after their admission to the program, compared with similar young people in group homes. And though Monitor's foster parents are paid about twice as much as regular foster parents, it is estimated that the program saves taxpayers $9757. per youngster per year, in comparison to the costs of regular juvenile programs.[28]

In July, 1997, Boston - unlike any other American city with a population over one-half million - had been free for two years of anyone under 17 being killed by a firearm. This success was due to the following interventions that are supported by more than a dozen agencies (including a coalition of 43 churches):

Court ordered curfews (for example, being required to stay home from 7 p.m. until 7 a.m. seven days per week) for youths who have been apprehended for drug possession,

requiring probation officers to make regular surprise visits to curfew homes to check on probationers,

requiring school police to notify the city and federal officials of every gun charge, so that all data can be fed into the computers of the Youth Violence Task Force.

In addition, this program has prevented city gangs from hanging out with impunity on crack corners late at night.[29]

Another useful approach is to place more police on the streets. They help to deter crime by their physical presence, by gaining the confidence and cooperation of members of each neighborhood through interactions with them, and by serving as role models for young people. For example, Larry Tye reports that an increase in foot patrols in the 1980's reduced crime 12 percent in Baltimore County, Maryland, and reduced auto thefts, robberies, and burglaries 25-50 percent in Newport News, Virginia.[30] Unfortunately, lack of funds has prevented the greater use of foot patrols. Adam Wallinsky proposes an interesting solution: creation of an ROTC-style program to produce a Police Corps. Its members would commit to four years of service on their hometown forces in exchange for tuition assistance while in college.[31]

The importance of involving members of a neighborhood in a program is underscored by experience with New York City's Model Block Program - the second phase in an anti-drug initiative to maintain a drug-free street block that had been achieved by the first phase. During the beginning of this second phase, the police saw to it that the street was tidied up: better lighting was installed, potholes were fixed, graffiti was removed, and regular garbage pickups were assured. Three sergeants and 24 officers were posted on the street around the clock.

When asked by a resident how long the police would stay to keep the drug traffickers from returning, Commissioner Safir replied:

"As long as it takes. There are no overnight solutions. The community itself has to become a full partner with the police. Once the block is stabilized, you will have to form building and block associations to let us know of any new problems. We will supply you with radios. You call us, and we'll be back."

Associations were formed and residents of a building who hadn't known each other for twenty years became acquainted, got to know the block beat officer, and began to work together to maintain the gains made. In addition to the patrols, the police utilized the Trespass Affidavit Program, whereby landlords agreed that officers could challenge someone in a building who didn't live there. And they used the Nuisance Abatement Act,

107

which allowed them to obtain court orders to padlock and recycle to legitimate families any apartments that had experienced three incidents of drug trafficking or prostitution. The program has been so successful that law-enforcement representatives from 40 states and 24 countries have visited New York to study it.[32]

New York City's Mayor Giuliana About His "Quality of Life Agenda"

"Improving the quality of life is not a destination. You never get there. It's a work in progress. But along the way, you keep making things better."

Source: Parade Magazine, May 10, 1998, page 6.

Tae Kwon Do (martial arts) classes provide a means for troubled young people to enhance their self-discipline, self-respect, and respect for others. Typically, Tae-Kwon-Do instructors set strict rules for behavior, and they administer penalties for violations ranging from push-ups to padded paddling or demotion in rank. For example, Gregg Tubbs will not promote trainees until he reviews their report cards and teachers' comments, as well as parents' reports on the performance of home duties. Typically, the classes produce better school grades and greater respect for parents.[33]

Another "tough-love" approach is provided to juvenile offenders in Cumberland County, North Carolina. They are turned over to a retired Army drill instructor who administers a hard-knocks, military-style program that includes 5 a.m. reveille, push-ups, five-mile runs, and ethical orientation. So far, only 15 of the 775 graduates of the five-year old program have been charged with crimes.[34]

A 20-60 percent decline in drinking, smoking, and drug abuse among high school students has been produced by the Project STAR program in Indianapolis schools. It encourages the organization of neighborhood smoke-outs and drug-free sporting events and the setting of anti-drug policies in the home.[35]

Whatever the program, a key consideration is the *interaction* between nurture and discipline - one without the other can be quite damaging. The necessary constraining, prodding, and punishing of young people works well *only* when they are convinced that the administering person *really cares* about them and their welfare. Many of them feel: if she or he doesn't care, why should I care? *And it is hard to demonstrate that one really cares without investing personal time and effort in the relationship.* This truth was dramatized by the outstanding success of Vince Lombardi, one of the most demanding football coaches. I have heard former team members attest to what a tough disciplinarian he was, but immediately add that he had their highest regard - that they played their hearts out for him. Why? Because they were convinced that he cared about them. They enjoyed telling about how he had gone to bat for them - and for other players - long after they had left the team.

Two additional examples are provided by our experience with the Civilian Conservation Corps for young people during the Depression Era and the success of the Peace Corps in more recent years. It is apparent that the proper combination of challenge, responsibility, and nurture has been successful many times. In view of such evidence, we should seriously consider a national policy of requiring - under proper direction and nurturing leadership - some minimum amount of compulsory civilian service for our young people, or at least for those who have been in trouble.

By Dealing Effectively With The Homeless And The New And Long-Term Unemployed: We find that advocates for the homeless have been concealing a "dirty little secret." Gina Kolata of The New York Times discovered, from interviews with several authorities, that drug and alcohol abuse are major reasons for the homelessness of men, women, and families, and that many of these drug and alcohol abusers suffer from mental illness. For example, the Cuomo Commission found that 65-80

109

percent of those in New York shelters tested positive for drugs in 1992.[36]

James Willwerth reports that many of the mentally ill were released from hospitals - having been stabilized with drugs - to fend for themselves without assistance. They are left with no one to monitor their continuing medication, to assist them in finding work, or to turn to for counseling. Now, under various psychosocial rehabilitation programs, the more fortunate ones are assigned to treatment teams comprised of psychiatric and "life skills" specialists. One of these programs, Partners in Care, was launched in 1998, and now has been established throughout the country. Participants have only one-third the relapse rate of traditionally treated individuals.

In addition, there are support groups. For example, Schizophrenics Anonymous has 80 chapters. The New York area has Awakenings (with 12 chapters), Fast Track to Employment (with many cooperating firms), and INCube (which has helped the recovering mentally ill to start 300 new businesses over the last decade).[37]

A highly effective approach for other homeless people was started by Joe Carroll, a Catholic priest, who administers St. Vincent de Paul Village in San Diego. He gives high priority to the new-homeless who are able and willing to work, or upgrade their skills, and really want to get off the street rather than have someone support them. For them - and they must be referred by a church - there are clean, phone-equipped, semi-private bedrooms with round-the-clock access, a barbershop, a clinic whose staff members make room calls, free bus tokens, budgeting and resume-writing courses, and a school across the street for their children.

Other first-time residents are given a month to earn a place in a six or 18 month program of personal development. They are assigned responsibilities and are tracked for class attendance and performance on basic-skills tests. Only 20 percent make the cut for the longer programs; however, about 70-80 percent of the "graduates" do obtain jobs and housing. Those who fail and other applicants - the chronically homeless majority - sleep in bunk beds in a dormitory with modest food and fewer services.

In response to public interest aroused by Father Carroll's impressive record of success, St. Vincent de Paul Village conducts three public tours per week. His approach is now being used at a $4 million Travelers Aid Society shelter in Salt Lake City, a Catholic Charities shelter in Maui, Hawaii, and a $1 million shelter in Charlotte, North Carolina.[38]

Private industry is also playing an important role in rehabilitation. Richard Barclay, vice president of Barclay Enterprises of Riverside, California, makes the point that businesses need honest, dependable, and conscientious candidates for semiskilled or unskilled work more than they need graduates of government-sponsored training programs. Of course, qualification in both regards is best, but for lower-level jobs, it is easier for business to take care of the training than to develop the missing values. But present regulations pose a real obstacle. They deny an employer the freedom to give untried workers a chance, to thoroughly assess them, and then dump them - when necessary - without penalty.

To remedy this, Barclay proposes that each state create a special "untried worker category" that would suspend certain worker rights during a six-month probationary period. Here are some provisions that he thinks would help to motivate employers to give these candidates a chance:

Drug and alcohol abuse would not be legally protected illnesses that prohibit discharge,

any injuries by or to the worker would not penalize the employer's worker's compensation account unless it could be shown that the employer had been negligent,

drug tests could be administered at the employer's discretion,

upon termination, the employer's unemployment insurance account would not be charged, and the employer would be exempt from wrongful-termination suits.[39]

Barclay's concerns are already being dealt with by a company called America Works, of Hartford, Connecticut and New York City. It specializes in welfare recipients, but recruits only those who it judges are seriously committed to placement - those who are punctual in attending a week-long, uncompensated, pre-employment program that covers proper English, placement interviewing, the development of self-esteem, and appropriate attitudes that will help them to "fit-in" on the job.

Some 50-60 percent of those who complete the program are placed in jobs from which, for the first four months, they may be removed by the employer for any reason. During this period, the employer pays America Works $7 per hour and America Works pays wages plus benefits. In addition, America Works gets a one-time fee of approximately $5000 from the state welfare department after each applicant holds a job for seven months. This saves taxpayer money, since the typical mother-of-two client on welfare gets about $14,000 per year. An America Works staff member makes on-site visits to the employee several times per week, to provide support and guidance, prepare a weekly written evaluation and, if necessary, act as a mediator with his or her supervisor. Employers retain approximately 70 percent of these probationary workers, and about 90 percent are still on the job after a year.[40]

Another major company, The Marriott Corporation, has discovered that such continuing "hand-holding" and oversight is necessary for the success of its welfare-to-work program, called Pathways to Independence, through which it has put some 600 people in the last few years. Mariott employees drive welfare trainees to work, arrange for day care for their children, negotiate with their landlords and case workers, help them buy clothes and open bank accounts, and reassure them with regular home visits and personal coaching.[41]

The program costs about $5000 per trainee, but government funds pay for some $2700 of this. Since the company's overall employee turnover rate is about 37 percent - compared with about 25 percent for the welfare-program trainees - the company does better than break even, in addition to performing an important community service. However, Marriott's well-organized support efforts were not as effective with a special class of homeless participants in early 1997. Since half of them washed out, the company will no longer attempt to work with the homeless in separate groups.[42]

Needless to say, companies that fail to provide such support activity find that recruiting welfare people does not make much sense financially. Only a minority of their recruits remain after a year. A co-manager of the Marriott Pathways program explains that these people think differently; that someone else is always responsible for bad things that happen to them.[43] And these observations are supported by interview data from 179 Chicago-area firms. Only 12 percent of the respondents felt that lack of job skills is a major problem for inner-city applicants. The chief obstacles they identify are: lack of a work ethic, nondependability, and negative attitude.[44]

Marriott is also noteworthy for its leadership in establishing first-rate "early-learning centers" in Atlanta and Washington, D.C. for the children of hourly-paid employees and lower-wage families. By entering into joint-financial sponsorship with other businesses and the government, the non-profit centers are offering three meals a day, classes on an extended-hours basis, a sick bay for minor ailments, health fairs, dental screenings, and parent workshops. Tuition is adjusted for a family's income. Donna Klein, Director of Work/Life Programs for Marriott International, observes that "If you earn $20,000 a year, you can't afford child care in this country, and we as a nation haven't faced this. We are reliant on female labor, and as long as child-rearing is a female issue, there is no way we can avoid this problem."[45]

The privately funded Strive Program is active at 19 sites in New York, Boston, Chicago, and Pittsburgh. It takes all comers, but insists that they satisfy strict standards of maturity and responsibility. Consequently, some 35 percent of each class quit after a three-hour orientation, and another six percent leave during a required three-week workshop. However, Strive offers all departees the opportunity to start over as many times as they like. In five years, 14,000 people have been put to work at a cost of about $1500 per person, and 80 percent of Strive's graduates are still working after two years.[46] Other providers of successful mentoring-type programs are Wildcat Services in New York, the South Bronx Overall Development Corporation, and GAIN (Greater Avenue to Independence) in Chicago.[47]

Chief executive Craig Hoekenga of Microboard Processing in Seymour, Connecticut is willing to take on high-risk people (former welfare recipients, felons, and former drug addicts) who are recommended by trusted sources (such as churches). He provides a supportive environment and ample opportunity to prove themselves. He observes that several months are usually required for their attendance behavior to straighten out. He puts some high-risk hires in educational and training programs, starting with English-language instruction if needed, and he starts others as temporaries doing landscaping or odd jobs. Then, he considers them for factory jobs if they prove to have good work habits. He will wait as long as 6-9 months for some of these candidates to come through. And this turns out to be profitable, for he partly attributes the growth of his company to the hard work and loyalty of his high-risk hires, since some 70-80 percent of them become valued workers within six months.[48]

Another successful program for the unemployed was developed by four researchers - Robert Caplan, Amiram Vinokur, Richard Price, and Michelle van Ryn. It comprises eight, three-hour sessions over a two-week period, and it covers the following areas through the use of role-playing, positive reinforcement, and other techniques:

Strategies for identifying job-related skills,

use of social networks to obtain job leads,

techniques for contacting employers,

presenting application data,

practice in being interviewed,

114

getting past secretaries to potential employers,

emphasis upon the need to be persistent.

Trainees were compared with control-group members who received only a booklet on job-seeking tips. One-month, 4-month, and 30-month follow-up assessments indicated that significantly more trainees were reemployed, that they earned more, and found their jobs more satisfying. Even those who did not find reemployment right away, were less depressed and exhibited greater job-seeking confidence.[49] Significant success has also been experienced by the Chicago Manufacturing Institute and the California-based Center for Employment Training.[50]

Poor, but deserving, would-be entrepreneurs - half of which are on welfare - are accommodated by some 328 microenterprise programs in the U.S. The average "microloan" they get is about $4500 - enough to buy a used truck or professional tools or equipment. The money is drawn from a revolving fund provided by public and private sources. To qualify for a loan, applicants must complete two months of classes on finance and marketing, present an acceptable business plan, and commit something they value as collateral - even if it's only an old television set. Local bankers, or other experienced businessmen (such as SCORE retirees), voluntarily conduct the classes and offer business advice to the borrowers. In the meantime, the loan committee follows each borrower's business progress closely. Surprisingly, the default rate is very low. For example, in Pike County, Ohio, no outright defaults have occurred during the program's six years of existence (from 1991), though several loans have been restructured.[51]

In 1972, at the Delancey Street Foundation in San Francisco, criminologist Mimi Silbert founded a program for former convicts that is similar in spirit to the programs described above. Her work shows that many hardened ex-criminals who are both unskilled and functionally illiterate can succeed, given the right kind of environment and encouragement. However, a former convict must ask to be accepted and make a verbal commitment to stay for at least two years (although most believe they will remain only a few months). Actually, eighty percent stay at least two years, and many "graduates" become highly skilled workers and professionals.

Dr. Silbert says that she is well aware of the typical feelings of bitterness, despair, and defensiveness on the part of most newcomers. When one of them scowls at her with contempt, she responds with: "Hey, we know you're trying to manipulate us. Our job is to out-manipulate you! And we're better at it than you are." Among program specifics:

> Newcomers must cut their hair, look presentable, and even change the way they walk - "through external imitation, something gets internalized."

> They must perform maintenance chores at the bottom of the chain of command and are told that they are responsible for the next new arrivals - "based on the premise that people will change simply by 'doing' for somebody else."

> Each must learn at least three marketable skills and earn a high-school-equivalency diploma.

In addition, these former convicts have access to marathon, group therapy sessions and volunteer community and social projects. Dr. Silbert says that it is "like holding hands while climbing a mountain. Together we rise or together we fall. And that's what happens here every day." The program has been successful in nurturing sound values.

A new, 500-resident facility - assessed at $30 million and constructed almost entirely by the residents - was opened in 1990. For the most part, it is self-supporting. The residents net about $3 million per year by running businesses such as discount stores; printing, picture-framing, and catering shops; and an upscale restaurant. Similar programs are now operating in Brewster, New York; Greensboro, North Carolina; and San Juan Pueblo, New Mexico. In addition, Dr. Silbert has established a training institute for applicants from around the country who want to devote several months of internship to understanding the Delancey Street approach.[52]

In contrast to such approaches, we have seen an endless proliferation of rules, regulations, and generous spending programs at state and federal levels that are aimed at trying to compensate for the decline in commitment to core values on the part of recipients. Many such attempts are doomed to failure. We need to rediscover what our founding fathers stressed time and again - one cannot legislate morality, and there is no substitute for responsible personal behavior in a free society.

By Dealing Effectively With Hardened Criminals: It is estimated that some seven percent of New York City's population accounts for most of its crime, and that only one percent of these lawbreakers are criminal-personality types who do far more than their share, accounting for several felonies per day per person.

Prior to Mayor Rudolph Giuliani, New York's police commanders had been rewarded more for keeping their units from being corrupt and too aggressive, than for reducing crime rates. But starting around 1993, the Mayor mounted a concerted war on crime with the following action:

Installation of a computer-based program called "Compstat" to provide timely reports and analyses of crime data - and thus a more solid basis for precinct accountability - and

A change in promotion policy so that subsequent promotions for commanders would require double-digit crime reduction.

From 1993 to 1998, murders declined 70 percent and felonies dropped 46 percent![53]

Discouraging Fantasies About Life In Africa: Could it be that many blacks have illusions about what existed, and exists today, in Africa; that this is one reason that they acclaim being *African* Americans and fail to appreciate the unique strength of

117

mainstream American values? If so, they are sorely in need of accurate information.

For example, Hugh Thomas, the distinguished British historian, points out that most of the initial enslavement of Africans resulted from wars within Africa.[54]   And uninformed blacks need to consider what has happened in Liberia - a country that was founded in 1822 by former U.S. slaves with the backing of President Monroe, the U.S. Congress, and various charitable organizations, and was intended to symbolize "freedom."

After enjoying the financial support of the American Colonization Society for 26 years, Liberia was declared an independent republic in 1847 with a constitution based upon ours.   Yet, the descendants of the settlers formed a haughty aristocracy of Americo-Liberians who kept the indigenous natives "in their place."   In fact, an investigation by the League of Nations in 1931 confirmed the practice of forced labor and brutal slavery.   These findings prompted the resignations of the president and vice-president.   And by 1959, little had been done by the Liberian government to improve the lot of the people. There was a 93 percent illiteracy rate and only one-quarter of the school-age children were actually attending school.   Corruption was so endemic that President Tubman personally signed all vouchers for more than $100.   As one Liberian diplomat put it, sardonically, "Liberia had not had the benefits of colonialism."[55]

Matt Mofett observes that Ethiopia did not outlaw slavery until 1942.   And he reports that slave trading in women and children still thrives today in large parts of Asia and Africa; that adults are openly bought and sold in Sudan.[56]   Robert Block reports that the per capital murder rate in South Africa today is about four times that of the U.S. and that some 87 percent of South African drivers of every color fear that they will be hijacked sooner or later.[57]

Some may regard these examples as unfortunate exceptions. They may think that Africa holds a majority of more positive and productive regimes that offer freedom, personal security, real participation, dignity, and material well being.   If they believe so, they should read the 1997 book, <u>Out of America: A Black Man Confronts Africa</u>, by Keith Richburg, Hong Kong bureau

118

chief for the <u>Washington Post</u>. He reports knowledgeably about 20 African countries, having spent three years there.

Professor George Ayittey, a native of Ghana, writes that:

"But in many African countries, 'government' as Westerners understand it simply does not exist. These nations are ruled by gangsters, crooks and scoundrels who use the instruments of state to enrich themselves, their cronies and their tribesmen. Thus Western money goes down a sinkhole.

"...in the campaign to liberate Africa from *black* tyrants and thugs, black American leaders are not only latecomers but are often on the wrong side. They have not even mounted a spirited campaign against the enslavement of blacks by Arabs in Mauritania and Sudan. At conferences and summits in Africa, black American delegates laud some of Africa's most ruthless tyrants."[58]

Lastly, we have the depressing fact that sub-Saharan Africa, which comprises 48 countries and 500 million people, had the same gross domestic product in 1991 as Belgium![59] It is the world's poorest region, and a primary cause of this is lack of economic and political freedom - and rampant corruption - according to the annual Index of Economic Freedom of the Heritage Foundation/Wall Street Journal. The report also indicates that Africa's poverty is not due to insufficient foreign aid.[60]

Without question, blacks and other minority-group members in America continue to suffer the indignities and humiliation of being discriminated against. However, to view such discrimination as the *primary reason* for lack of achievement overlooks the fact that American blacks are the most prosperous in our hemisphere - and in the world. Furthermore, discrimination in other cultures has not prevented impressive levels of achievement:

119

Though strongly discriminated against, ethnic Chinese, who comprise only five percent of the population of Indonesia, own about 80 percent of the capital in that country.

Though strongly discriminated against, Jews, who comprised only six percent of the population of Hungary and 11 percent of the population of Poland in the early 1920's, comprised more that half of all the medical doctors in both countries![61]

Why does discrimination occur? It occurs because certain citizens do not understand the importance of *all* of the core values to their personal well being and the well being of society, or - due to their poor early programming or emotional need for scapegoats - they embrace conflicting, alien values. But the fact that such people exist does not diminish the achievements of the majority toward commitment to what is right. Martin Luther King made his mark by courageously admonishing us to be true to ourselves in this regard. It is tragic that many African Americans, as well as many other minority-group and cult members, do not understand or accept - despite our admitted deficiencies - what it is to be an American: both the opportunities and the responsibilities.

Conclusion: This chapter has discussed how we can overcome the effects of poor programming and the drive for immediate gratification in ourselves and others, how we can encourage greater truthfulness in group problem solving, how we can improve the likelihood of creating healthier and more stable families, how we can assist the chronically unemployed and the homeless, how we can rehabilitate many ex-convicts and young delinquents, and the need to distinguish reality from fantasy about Africa.

Chapter 7

THE NEED FOR NURTURING CORE VALUES IN OUR SCHOOLS AND HOW WE WE CAN DO IT

In inflation-adjusted dollars, we spent $2400 per student in 1960 and $6900 per student in 1998. In addition, the student-teacher ratio fell. Yet, what was achieved? Student performance stagnated or declined![1] Why? An important reason is that many practices that are commonplace in our public schools are inconsistent with our core values. Such practices have created problems that would have been non-issues in the first quarter of this century. For example:

Should one-third of our fourth, eighth, and twelfth graders today have an inadequate understanding of the fundamentals of American democracy?[2]

Should the school grades of a would-be doctor, construction engineer, or teacher be adjusted for his or her ethnic identity or difficulties at home?

Should attempts be made to preserve and enhance student self-esteem by overlooking misbehavior and giving false praise against lowered standards?

Should disproportionate representation of a given group in remedial classes automatically signal unwarranted discrimination?

Should our teachers be "morally neutral" for fear of giving certain values preference over others?

If our society is to survive and prosper, the answer to these questions must be "no." And this is true whenever there is a direct conflict between individual interests and the best interests of society. This chapter will document the seriousness of these problems and discuss what needs to be done.

<u>The Erosion Of Standards And Expectations</u>: Dramatic evidence of a negative change in standards is provided by Richard Berman. Fewer than half of one percent of our Army recruits in World War II read below a fourth-grade level; today, the proportion of Americans who cannot read at this level is ten times as high,[3] though a much larger proportion is graduating from our high schools. In 1995, in Gainesville, Florida, high-school English teacher Catherine Berg commented that "I shouldn't have to tell an honors student to put a period at the end of a sentence."[4] And another teacher was dumbfounded when an administrator bragged to him that 75 percent of the school's students were on the honor roll. The implication was clear: give easier tests, reduce passing requirements, and everybody will be happy; the teachers will be heroic, the principal super, and the school a first-class operation - at least on paper.[5]

The 1998 results of the Third International Math and Science Survey showed that U.S. high-school students scored close to the bottom in math in comparison with students in other countries. In addition, 33 percent of our seniors could not compute the price of a $1250 stereo with 20 percent off, and only 11 percent could plot a graph.[6] So, this raises an important question: How well are our young people being prepared for the new world of work? Lincoln Electric still had many positions to fill, after having had to reject a large majority of the 20,000 people who had applied over an 18-month period. And Scott Paper had to screen 14,176 applicants to get 174 new hires.[7] These are but a few of the many indications of the current erosion of standards that started in the late 1930's with "the philosophy of the whole child": the idea that a child should be graded on the basis of her or his achievements relative to his or her potential, and not on the basis of objective standards; otherwise, the child's self-esteem might be damaged.

Imagine what would happen to the quality of performance of doctors, engineers, teachers, and other professionals and their subsequent, real-world self-esteem had their credentials been assessed this way! A glimpse of the possibilities is provided by a 1994 Journal of the American Medical Association study of the effects of racial preference as a factor in admission to medical schools. Fifty-one percent of black medical students failed Part I of the National Board of Medical Examiners tests compared to 12.3 percent of white students. This is important because Part I determines minimum competency in the core areas of medical science. However, it was found that black students with the same entry credentials as white students scored about the same.[8]

Apologists for preferential admissions argue that most of those who fail, initially, will eventually pass after repeated attempts. But should this prospect provide comfort to future patients? Even today's most capable doctors find it difficult to keep up with an ever-growing body of new knowledge and techniques, and prospects are that the pace of change will accelerate further.[9]

And what about desirable student behavior? A 1991 study of fifth and sixth-grade children by John Richters and Pedro Martinez in Southeast Washington, D.C. found that 17 percent had been shot, stabbed, or raped, while 44 percent had observed such violence. Forty-one percent had been mugged or chased by gangs, while 63 percent had observed such activity.[10] Patricia Hersch mentions a 1991 report about 26 percent of 9th through 12th graders admitting that they had carried a club, knife, or gun during the previous 30 days, and a 1993 survey that found that 80 percent of eighth through eleventh graders had experienced some form of sexual harassment (85 percent girls, 75 percent boys).[11]

Much of the problem stems from inadequate parental supervision. But, as Kay Hymowitz points out, our courts are also to blame. There are now court-backed "student rights":

"You don't have to answer a school official if he or she questions you.

"A teacher can't make you do anything that violates your conscience.

123

"If you don't like the way the school makes you dress, you can go to court."

She tells of a high-school senior in New York State who distributed copies of an article that urged students to urinate in the hallways, write graffiti on the walls, and riot upon arrival of the police. The school district was able to suspend the boy, but only after the case had dragged on and been appealed to the state's highest court, *and this took two years!* A teacher at another school claimed that students had made sexually degrading comments about her in the hallway. When asked why she hadn't make a formal report about it, she replied: "Well, it wouldn't have done any good...I didn't have any witnesses."[12] A school district and principal in Half Moon Bay, California were sued by the parents of another student for suspending their son for five days. He had written two English-class compositions: one about torching the school library and beating up the principal; the other about "goin' postal" and pumping seven bullets into the principal. The district and the parents reached an agreement by which the suspension was reduced to two days and the statement of the offense was watered down.[13]

Questionable Preparation Of Teachers: A 1995 survey of 600 experienced teachers about their college-of-education courses produced rather negative responses. Typical comments were: "mind numbing," "shabby psychobabble," "superficial," and "an abject waste of time."[14] In view of such reactions, it may not be surprising that, in 1998, almost 60 percent of those aspiring to teach in Massachusetts flunked the Board of Education's Certification Examination, and that 75 percent of the teaching applicants in Suffolk County, New York failed an eleventh-grade reading comprehension test.[15]

Also, consider the results of a 1997 poll of 900 of the nation's professors of education:

A majority placed discipline and the teaching of grammar, punctuality, and manners at the bottom of their lists.

124

A majority valued process over content, indicating that it is more important to "learn how to learn" than to know the right answer. Yet, they did not see a need for students to master mathematical processes before seeking answers through aids such as calculators.[16]

These responses are in sharp contrast with what parents - as well as students - say they want. For example, in 1997, Greene, Howell, and Peterson collected the very inclusive response data presented below from parents in the Cleveland area:[17]

Percent Of "Very Satisfied" Public School Parents:

Academic Quality	Less than 30%
School Safety	Just over 25%
Discipline	23%
Teaching Moral Values	25%

Lack of Parental Support: A 1997 Wall Street Journal/NBC poll of 2010 people indicates that they placed a large part of the blame for the poor state of U.S. secondary education today upon parents and the quality of family life. Among the specifics enumerated: 86 percent mentioned undisciplined children, 85 percent mentioned the spread of violence and drugs in the schools, 81 percent mentioned lack of parental involvement, and 77 mentioned breakdown of the family.[18] Based upon a survey of 20,000 teenagers and their families, psychologist Laurence Steinberg of Temple University reports that nearly one-third of the students claimed that their parents had no idea of how well they were doing in school, one-fourth said they could take home grades of "D" or worse without consequence, and respondents indicated that only about one-fifth of the parents had consistently attended school programs.[19]

In addition, the presence of a father today is not as likely to support the strict and consistent administration of school discipline as it once did. In fact, we hear about parents who protest the disciplining of their children at school, whatever the reason! Anecdotal support for this diminished role of the father was provided by my uncle, Creed Bates of Chattanooga, Tennessee, who dealt with thousands of young people while serving as principal of a large city high-school for some forty years, starting in 1922. When I asked if he had noted any significant changes during those years, his answer was an emphatic "yes." He said:

"Before the Second World War, if the usual measures failed with a chronic trouble-maker, the most effective threat I could use was: 'I'll call your father.' On the few occasions I had to call, the father would invariably apologize for the imposition upon me and the school, and would assure me that I would not have to call again. Nine out of ten times I didn't have to.

"But after the War, things changed. I found the threat to be ineffective. The typical attitude or response might be characterized by something like, 'Go ahead, call, it'll be fun to see how the old boy handles this.'"

<u>What Needs To Be Done</u>: There are a number of things we can do, and the sooner we start, the better.

Improve The Preparation Of Teachers: A first concern should be the preparation of those who will teach our children. In an extensive study of progress in math by some 2500 students across many states, Rand researchers found that higher teacher salaries, alone, had little impact.[20]

We need to prod school boards to investigate the results of programs like the Cincinnati Initiative for Teacher Education, called CITE. It requires prospective teachers to obtain a bachelor's degree in a science or the humanities first, and then spend a fifth year in the classroom as paid teachers of record under the supervision of experienced-teacher mentors. CITE also offers a two-year program for experienced college graduates who decide upon teaching as a second career.[21]

The AmeriCorps Teach For America Program has placed some 900 non-college-of-education graduates with bachelor's degrees in rural and urban areas that are short of teachers. A subsequent survey found that 75 percent of the principals rated corps members as being superior to other beginning teachers, and 89 percent assessed their intellectual ability as being higher.[22]

Support Successful Programs For Underachieving Students: There are innovative programs that provide much-needed boosts to underachieving students. For example, 100 percent of the 29 inaugural black students in The Love of Learning minority enrichment program at Davidson College went on to college! Program design was influenced by data which indicated that 70 percent of black students had dropped out of college *whether or not* they had been well-prepared, academically, upon entering. Consequently, in addition to providing academic support, Love of Learning provides constant social, spiritual, and emotional support.

The need for such support is confirmed by research studies conducted by Claude Steele of Stanford University. He demonstrated that the scores of female math students on a difficult math test were four times lower than male scores, despite the fact that both groups had equally strong academic records. However, when he gave other groups of similarly qualified students a difficult math test - but indicated that men and women had done equally well on it - female performance went up dramatically. He attributes the first result to the stereotype that women have about not being as good as men with high-level math problems.[23]

Love of Learning recruits middle-of-the class eighth-graders from the local public school system. They must agree to spend the next five Julys at Davidson, in addition to attending twice-monthly workshops during the regular school year. Their summers are really an "academic boot-camp." They get up at 6 am, and are in class from 7:45 until 8:30 pm. The one-month, dormitory programs include live-in counselor-mentors, compulsory evening homework sessions, and lessons in leadership and spiritual development. Addicted or pregnant students are not retained, and parents of the participants must agree to visit their high-school counselors, become aware of program requirements, and participate in quarterly discussions.[24] Due to the success of Love of Learning, Washington and Lee College and Furman now have similar programs, and Presbyterian College and Clinton College have programs for non-black as well as black, low-income students, while the University of the South has one for its black freshmen.[25]

The need for colleges of education and public-school administrators to replace unproven theories and fads with results-based methods is long overdue. Teachers should be encouraged to be innovative, but they should be required to demonstrate, via controlled experiments, that an innovation produces better results than current methods before it is permitted to displace them. For example, "Direct Instruction" has been a highly successful approach since 1977. Children taught with it have excelled in both academic scores and in measures of self-esteem. Direct Instruction requires teachers to tell students what they need to know, drill them for retention, reward them for right answers, and immediately correct wrong ones.[26]

Another successful program, "Success For All," was developed in 1986 by Robert Slavin. The American Institute for Research has identified it as one of only three school-reform programs whose results have been backed by sound research. It was adopted by a majority vote of the teachers in each of 1700 elementary, Title 1 schools in 1999. Success For All requires reading classes for all students at the same time, so that they can be grouped in classes of 15 each on the basis of ability rather than age. This is made feasible by having all school staff members - even librarians and gym teachers - teach reading, simultaneously, by means of a precisely prescribed set of procedures. The children are tested regularly to determine when they are ready to move to the next skill level. Those who are not receive 20 minutes of remedial tutoring a day until they are ready. Success For All is now developing programs for teaching math, science, and world culture.[27]

Enhance Motivation: Psychologist Henry Pennypacker recommends:

The establishment of an incentive plan to encourage young, adult, male, college-trained blacks to assume positions of authority in the ghetto schools;

the installation of a "token economy" in the school setting whereby all lunches, free time, and other privileges (such as participation on sports teams) would be purchased with tokens earned through academic achievement;

that the payment of welfare funds be made contingent upon a child's school attendance: so many dollars per child per day in school.[28]

William Buckley, Jr. has similar thoughts. In 1988, he observed that "If it is true that there are about 25 million people in America who are functionally illiterate notwithstanding our compulsory school system and the world's highest per capita expenditure on those schoolchildren, then something more basic is wrong." It is time, he suggests, to apply the following remedies:

"The student who, at the end of the first grade year, does not know how to read, yields every afternoon of the week to his teacher. The teacher divides the time spent...between mowing the lawn, scrubbing the latrines and practicing reading. The moment the child passes a reading test, he is released from conscript duty.

"I.D. cards will be standard equipment among children. Any student under 13 is not permitted inside a movie theater until he passes through a ticket office and reads a couple of lines of print flashed on the wall.

129

"No 16-year old applying for a driver's license need do so without giving ample evidence that he can read."[29]

Support Successful School-Reform and School-Choice Programs: Residents associated with 34 schools in Ascension, Jefferson, and St. James Parishes in Louisiana have learned that school reform can work - despite the fact that Louisiana has America's highest illiteracy rate, the highest percentage of children living in poverty, and among the highest rates of unemployment, teen pregnancy, high-school dropouts, and juvenile delinquency.

Reform started with a Shell Foundation-supported study: Tulane University researchers interviewed 50 teachers and administrators to determine why a number of previous reform attempts in the state had failed. They identified four major barriers:

> Overly centralized decision making, with little input from the schools.

> Undue influence on decisions by politicians, special-interest groups, and the media.

> Such proliferation of state-level organizations dealing with public education that achieving a consensus about any program had been virtually impossible.

> Inadequate funding by the state.

The next step was to establish the Louisiana Alliance for Education Reform, formed in 1992-1993 and housed at Tulane to devise a viable reform effort. Here are some highlights of the on-going program:

> When a school signs on with the Alliance, teachers, administrators, and parents attend 26 full-day workshops over a three-year period. They learn to engage in effective strategic planning, goal setting, and teamwork.

Members of the business community and local government are invited to participate in strategic planning. As a result, important outsiders learn of the schools' strengths, needs, and problems. This has resulted in support from many corporate financial sponsors and volunteers. For example, one company gives some 20 hours per week to repairing donated computers, salvaging parts, and training teachers.

Teachers, and some 100 students from a school that had serious disciplinary problems, were trained by The Center for Dispute Resolution in New Mexico in the art of mediating disputes and fights.

After-school and peer tutoring programs have been established.

A suspended student is not sent home - he or she must spend the day at school working with a parent, a teacher, and a law-enforcement officer. This has had a salutary effect upon both attendance and in-school behavior. After this approach had been used for a year at one school, suspensions dropped from 500 to 190 and expulsions dropped from sixteen to four.[30]

In addition to motivating students better and providing productive reforms, we need to pay careful attention to on-going experiments with school choice based upon the issuance of school vouchers. Initial findings in Indianapolis, Milwaukee, New York City, and San Antonio are encouraging. Paul Peterson reports that:

"Low-income families receiving vouchers are pleased with their children's school, even when the grants amount to less than half what the public school spends. Voucher students are more apt to stay in school, learn more, and earn their high-school diploma."[31]

Whereas, over 50 percent of the parents in two of the cities surveyed gave their voucher schools an "A," only 16-26 percent of them gave the same grade to the public schools their children had attended previously. And - despite the opposition of many teachers' unions to the use of vouchers - *over half of the teachers in central Milwaukee send their children to private schools!*[32]

More recent evidence is provided by Professor Jay Greene of the University of Houston and Paul Peterson, director of Harvard's program in education policy and governance. Based upon their carefully designed analysis, they found that - after 3-4 years in the Milwaukee choice program - the reading scores of low-income minority students who received vouchers were 3-5 percentage points higher than those of comparable public-school children; math scores were five points higher for third-year students and 12 points higher for fourth-year students. They also determined that this result was *not* due to the fact that poorly performing students left the choice schools after two years; thereby, leaving a more selected group of third- and fourth-year students.[33] In a subsequent review of the same data against a more demanding standard, researcher Cecilia Rouse was surprised by the magnitude of the math gains. She indicates that "Her findings, confined to one program in one city, absolutely support the need for more school-choice experiments."[34]

The Cleveland area was the site of the first state-funded program that gives low-income households a choice of both religious and secular schools. In 1997, Greene, Howell, and Peterson collected extensive data from area parents. They found that the demographic characteristics of the new choice-school parents were similar to those of the public-school parents, and that many more of the new choice-school parents were "very satisfied" with various aspects of their schools:[35]

	Percent "Very Satisfied"	
	Public School Parents	New Choice Parents
Academic Quality	Less than 30%	63%
School Safety	Just over 25%	Nearly 60%
Discipline	23%	55%
Teaching Moral Values	25%	71%

A 1997 statistical analysis by Derek Neal of the University of Chicago revealed that students from disadvantaged urban communities performed much better in Catholic schools than in public schools, and a Phi Delta Kappa/Gallup Poll found that vouchers are favored by 55 percent of public-school parents.[36] In addition, in 1998 Harvard's Kennedy School of Government found that 1200 below-poverty-level children, attending second through fifth grades in private schools on vouchers, averaged six points higher in standardized math tests, and four points higher in standardized reading tests, than their public-school peers.[37]

The Feasibility Of Higher Standards

Governor George Bush observes that: "In Texas we have found that when you raise the bar, people rise to the challenge."

This comment was prompted by the fact that little more than half of the state's students passed the Texas Assessment of Academic Skills test in 1994, used to identify low-performing schools. However, by holding back students who failed, more than 75 percent passed it in 1998!

Source: Jodie Morse, "The Test of Their Lives," Time, February 15, 1999, page 56.

Note: When a tenth grader failed the test, she or he could take remedial courses and summer schools. This afforded the student eight additional chances to pass during the following two years.[38]

Chances are that one of the most important outcomes of choice programs may be the reform of our public schools. Paul Peterson, a Harvard researcher, notes that when a private offer of scholarships to all of the students in an Albany, New York school was made, the local officials undertook sweeping reforms.[39] And June Kronholz reports that the advent of charter schools in Mesa, Arizona has provoked impressive responses from the school district:

> Parents no longer have to wait in overnight queues to enroll their children in one of only two back-to-basics-curriculum schools - Mesa has now opened two new ones.
>
> Mesa had only accepted youngsters who attained 5 $1/4$ years by September, but began to accept five year-olds after the charter schools showed the way.

Mesa is establishing special-program and so-called "theme" schools.

And, now, all Mesa school employees - from bus drivers to principals - must attend customer-service workshops!

Kronholz also reports that Eric Rofes, a University-of-California researcher, found that 25 percent of 25 school districts he studied had made significant changes due to the arrival of charter schools.[40]

The National Commission on Governing America's Schools was created by the Education Commission of the States (which had been overseen by all 50 state governors). It made two key proposals in 1999:

Full public-school choice, with each school getting money in direct relation to its enrollment - along with the right to make decisions about hiring, firing, and salaries. Or, more drastically,

Eventually make every public school an independent charter school, with public authorities funding and overseeing the schools, but not directly operating them. Every 4-5 years authorities decide whether or not to renew each school's charter, or let someone else take over its management.[41]

Brookings Institution guest scholar Thomas Toch reports about Edison Schools, a for-profit company that manages some 79 schools. Despite the fact that nearly half of the students come from impoverished families, Edison has improved student performance with a number of innovations:

The equivalent of four extra years of instruction was created by lengthening the school day and year.

Each student's progress is assessed monthly and reported to parents, teachers, and headquarters. Student satisfaction is surveyed annually.

Home computers, linked to school-based networks, are provided.

Performance-based bonuses of up to 20 percent of salary are given to principals.

Reactions to the arrival of Edison in Toledo, Ohio lend further support to the argument that competitive pressure may be the best tool for reforming our public schools. Faced with the prospect of a new Edison school, the local teachers' union joined with local school officials to make many Edison-like changes: they lengthened the school day and year, adopted Edison's highly regarded reading program, and abandoned seniority-based hiring in favor of ability-based hiring.[42]

Opponents of school choice claim that a "creaming process" is taking place; that only the families of high achieving students seek vouchers, because poor people don't want them, or that they don't have the energy or motivation to apply for them. However, experience with applications for School Choice Scholarships Foundation scholarships in New York City has shown this to be a false concern: The average income of applying households was some 30 percent below the national poverty level, only 19 percent of the students scored at or above grade level in math, and minority families were more highly represented than Caucasian families.[43]

Support The Teaching Of Values In School: As we have seen, our core values are being threatened by many negative influences, and our prospects for strengthening their acceptance and influence depend upon what we teach and how we act. Second to the family setting, our schools provide the most important place for teaching and stressing them. Due to this realization, parents, teachers, and other leaders in various school districts throughout the country have begun to meet to seek

136

agreement about which values and goals should be communicated in school.

One such undertaking - PREP (the Personal Responsibility Education Process) - began in 1988 in the St. Louis area and is now part of CHARACTERplus[TM]. It is a cooperative program for kindergarten through 12th grade children that involves 334 schools. It operates on the premise that education is incomplete without an emphasis upon values, and that such emphasis is necessary for democracy's survival. It is designed to encourage children to grow into responsible, contributing, and compassionate adults by stressing the teaching of values in all aspects of the school setting. One of its slogans is: "A child is the only known substance from which a responsible adult can be made."[44]

There has been variation among the school districts as to which values should be stressed. For example, the Parkway-District committee spent three years surveying 1200 adult members before defining a set of core values and deciding upon the specifics of a character-development program. Here are the values it selected:

Personal Values

Accountability - Accepting the consequences of one's actions, as well as the credit or blame for them.

*Honesty - Being truthful (explanation of asterisk given below).

Integrity - Adherence to truth - that which is right, fair, and honorable in all dealings.

*Responsibility - Dependable fulfillment of obligations to one's self and others.

*Respect for Self - Having and demonstrating a positive belief in one's intrinsic worth.

137

Social Values

Abstinence - Voluntarily refraining from an improper indulgence in alcohol, drugs, and sex.

*Caring About Others - Being responsible for the well-being of other people.

Commitment to Family - Being sensitive to and supportive of the needs of the family.

Positive Work Ethic - Performing to the best of one's ability.

*Respect for Others - Showing consideration, appreciation, tolerance, and good manners toward other people.

Civic Values

Equality - All people are entitled to the same rights.

Freedom - The right to choose one's works and actions without infringing on the rights of others.

Justice - Fair treatment.

*Respect for Authority - Showing consideration and regard for people in positions of responsibility.

*Respect for Property - Showing consideration and regard for public property and things belonging to others.

Other school districts developed lists that include some of the above values and added others. For example, six districts (Affton, Kirkwood, Ladue, Maplewood-Richmond Heights, Pattonville, and University City) decided upon the following additional values:

Appreciation of Learning

*Citizenship - Being a responsible and contributing member of society.

*Cooperation - In accomplishing work or play task or goals.

Decision Making - Making wise choices.

Humanity - Believing that people of different cultures, religions, sexes, and races can be equally valuable members of society.

Loyalty

Perseverance - Not giving up, taking a stand.

Self-Discipline - Choosing appropriate behaviors.

Six of the seven districts adopted those items with an asterisk: Honesty, Responsibility, Respect for Self, Caring About Others, Respect for Others, Respect for Authority, Respect for Property, Citizenship, and Cooperation.[45] And it should be noted that this output was not merely the result of a "laundry-list" endorsement by some central office - there was meaningful, widespread involvement. People in each district, after considerable reflection and discussion, made decisions about which values to include, and how they should be communicated and reinforced in their schools.

To further illustrate that consensus about which values to teach is not hard to achieve, a Phi Delta Kappa/Gallup poll of 1306 adults found that 90 percent or more felt that the following values should be taught in the public schools:

Honesty

Democracy

Acceptance of People of different races, ethnic backgrounds

Caring for Friends and Family Members

Moral Courage

The Golden Rule

Civility

Fairness

Industry[46]

In 1996, parents and teachers established a character education program for the mixture of Asian, Latino, black, and white students at Annadale High School in Washington, D.C.. They agreed on the following "seven cornerstones of character":

Caring

Citizenship

Fairness

Honesty

Respect

Responsibility

Self-Discipline[47]

There are other programs, like "Character Counts," "The Child Development Project" in California, "Character First," and " Lesson One." Character First, which has been adopted by some 600 schools nationwide, sells teacher manuals, posters, tapes, and compact disks. It also arranges for volunteer "character coaches" when schools do not wish to use their own staff members.[48] The Lesson One Foundation, founded 24 years ago by Jon Oliver, is a nonprofit, Boston-based organization that provides its "Skills for Life" program to elementary schools. The program has demonstrably reduced school violence through its emphasis upon the development of self-control.[49]

Character education has gained the support of the American Federation of Teachers, the National Education Association, the YMCA, and the American Youth Soccer Organization. The Clinton Administration funded initiatives to establish character-education programs at the state level, and sponsored three White House conferences about the subject.[50] Since 1995, the U.S. Department of Education has given more than $22.5 million to 28 states for the implementation of values programs.[51]

In addition to the obvious advantages such programs provide to counter the negative influences we have discussed, they offer immediate payoffs to the schools that implement them. For example, an independent study of the programs in some 4000 schools of The Jefferson Center for Character Education[52] found:

A 25 percent reduction in major disciplinary problems involving fighting, drugs, and weapons,

a 39 percent reduction in minor disciplinary problems,

a 16 percent reduction in suspensions,

a 40 percent reduction in tardiness, and

an 18 percent reduction in unexcused absences.[53]

Reject Spurious Claims Of Unwarranted Discrimination:

An important obstacle to the well-being of various remedial programs in education and other areas is the illusion that over-representation of minority-group members in them - or their under-representation in higher-level jobs - *automatically* indicates unwarranted discrimination. It is now well-established that:

Certain minority groups have lower general-cognitive-ability scores than certain other groups (see table below), this ability is the best single predictor we have - for all groups - of success with complex learning and performance in all types of higher-level jobs,

these score gaps have remained remarkably stable over the last 60 years, despite dramatic changes in the funding and delivery of educational services and various other remedial efforts,[54]

the predictive accuracy of these scores does not decline with added job experience.[55]

Percentage Who Score Above The Majority
Average On Cognitive Ability
(As Measured by The General Aptitude Test Battery)

Majority	50 Percent
Oriental	45
Mexican American	31
Black	23
Indian	20

Source: Paper by John Hunter (with analytical assistance from John Hawk of the U.S. Employment Service and Ron Boese of the North Carolina Employment Security Commission), "Fairness of the General Aptitude Test Battery (GATB): Ability Differences and Their Impact on Minority Hiring Rates," March 16, 1981.

To illustrate the significance of these differences: few people who score below the top 25 percent in cognitive ability ever become physicians, mathematicians, or scientists;[56] and if we find that 25 percent of whites will satisfy a given higher score level, only 5 percent of blacks will score this high.[57]

Another example is provided by the 1996 rejection of racial preference as a criterion for college admissions in California. In 1998, the number of black freshmen at Berkeley declined by 57 percent from 1997, but the drop in black freshmen was only 17.6 percent for all eight University of California campuses taken together. However, the *dropout rate* for blacks at Berkeley had been 42 percent, compared with 16 percent for whites. Presumably, in the future, blacks chosen by the same objective criteria as whites - though fewer in number - will have approximately the same dropout and graduation rates.[58] As Thomas Sowell puts it, according to Charles Krauthammer, under the racial preference program many blacks who "were perfectly qualified to be successes somewhere else...[were] artificially turned into failures by being admitted to high-pressure campuses, where only students with exceptional academic backgrounds can survive."[59]

The main point here is that we have a sound basis for predicting expected levels of over-representation in various assistance programs and under-representation in elite universities and higher-level jobs. Consequently, until minority-cognitive-score gaps diminish appreciably, we should assume that unwarranted discrimination has occurred *only* when these expectations are adversely exceeded.

There is an important way in which parents can reduce this cognitive-score gap. They can help their children - especially their very young children - to fully exploit their inherited cognitive-abilities potential by providing them with an intellectually stimulating environment. For example, Capron and Duyme found that when comparable children of lower-class parents were raised in upper-class homes, their IQ scores were much higher than when they were raised in lower-class homes. In fact, the rearing circumstances were found to be equal in importance to the presumed genetic influence of the biological parents![60] Another means for reducing the minority-cognitive-score gap is provided by better school attendance, since cognitive- ability scores are influenced by years of schooling.

Show Parents Or Guardians The Evidence And Get Them Involved: Hopefully, the evidence presented so far in this book - and that presented below - will persuade many parents to become more involved with their children's schools and to devote more time and emphasis to their academic progress.

Robert Putnam of Harvard University reports the research-based finding that parental involvement in school affairs has more to do with the quality of educational outcomes than the relative size of the school budget.[61] And Caplan, Choy, and Whitmore stress the importance of parental support of values about learning and effort as primary reasons for the extraordinary success of the children of the poor and dislocated Asian Boat People in the face of serious economic and language handicaps. They found that:

> Family reading time was an important predictor of academic success, whether or not the reading language was English; that these refugee families adapted well, found jobs, and moved out of poverty, due to their sense of personal responsibility and commitment to each other - even though they had dealt with more real trauma and life disruptions than most Americans - white or black - will ever have to face.[62]

Psychologist Laurence Steinberg asserts that we must:

> "Re-establish in the minds of young people and parents that the primary activity of childhood and adolescence is schooling. If we want our children to value education and strive for achievement, adults must behave as if doing well in school - not just graduating, but actually doing well - is more important than socializing, organized sports, after-school jobs or any other activity."[63]

And Fox Butterfield reports some interesting statistics:

> "Although Asian-Americans make up only 2.4 percent of the nation's population, they constitute 17.1 percent of the undergraduates at Harvard, 18 percent at

the Massachusetts Institute of Technology and 27.3 percent at the University of California at Berkeley.

"University of Michigan psychologist, Harold Stevenson, who has compared more than 7000 students in kindergarten, first grade, third grade, and fifth grade in Chicago and Minneapolis with counterparts in Beijing; Sendai, Japan; and Taipei, Taiwan...found no differences in IQ...When the Asian parents were asked why they think their children do well, they most often said 'hard work.' By contrast, American parents said 'talent.'

"Sanford M. Dornbusch, a professor of sociology at Stanford...in surveys of 7000 students in six San Francisco-area high schools, found that Asian-Americans consistently get better grades than any other group of students, regardless of their parents' level of education or their families' social and economic status...Asian-Americans do an average of 7.03 hours of homework a week. Non-Hispanic whites average 6.12 hours, blacks 4.23 hours and Hispanics 3.98 hours."[64]

Further evidence of the need for change is provided by the findings of a 1994 study of immigrant children in San Diego and Miami: At first they did better in school than their American classmates, but their performance declined as they became more Americanized![65]

Prospects: The pressures of school choice, greater parental involvement, and a growing movement toward decentralization of decision making to the local level will prod our schools toward:

The improved preparation of teachers,

enhanced course content and academic standards,

145

more performance-based grading and promotional practices,

performance-based bonuses and better remuneration to attract and retain good teachers, and

the nurturing of sound moral values.

Chapter 8

THE NEED FOR NURTURING CORE VALUES IN POLITICAL LEADERSHIP AND HOW WE CAN DO IT

In this chapter we examine the status of ethics in political leadership - both generally and with regard to the administration of welfare - and we consider many forms of remedial action.

The Self-Serving Culture Of Expediency, Indifference, And Opportunism: How much progress have we made toward more responsible government? Consider the following:

> According to the Army Chief of Staff, there was a 31 percent failure rate on test flights in 1983 for Pershing 2 missiles. Nevertheless, this model was later deployed in West Germany. The same year, the General Accounting Office reported that 25 percent of the Navy's Sidewinder missiles and 33 percent of its Sparrow missiles were "unserviceable."

> A year later, tests of DIVAD, designed to be a fully automatic anti-aircraft/anti-tank gun, revealed one serious problem: despite the $1.5 billion that had been invested in it, it didn't work! This was not surprising to General James Maloney, DIVAD's project chief, who had observed three years earlier that "No computer can handle a jinxing [cleverly evasive] target." Still the Army didn't want to give it up.[1]

The Grace Report: Motivated by such reports, 162 corporate executives and their staffs led by J. Peter Grace went to work for 18 months and produced, by 1984, 2,300 pages of documentation and recommendations relating to our government's gross inefficiencies. Here are some of the gems they turned up:

> The Veterans Administration had been paying $61,250 per bed for the construction of nursing homes,

147

in contrast to an average cost of $16,000 per bed for private nursing homes.

The government had tolerated a 41 percent delinquency rate on amounts owed. Defaulted loans had cost $4.7 billion in 1983.

Overpayment for "means-test" poverty programs had been running about $4 billion per year.

Though government civilian employees had been paid salaries that were comparable to those in the private sector, their fringe benefits were running about 76 percent higher.

Over a three-year period failure to negotiate discounts for high-volume shipments had cost about $530 million, and failure to keep money confiscated from criminals in interest-bearing accounts had cost about $50 million.

Many top government bureaucrats refused to name congressional culprits. As one assistant secretary put it: "Long after your report is forgotten, we'll have to deal with these committees in Congress, and it would be suicide for us to cooperate with you."[2]

Things Have Not Gotten Better: Surely, you must think, the Grace Report prompted far-ranging changes. Unfortunately, it didn't! For example, Paul Harvey reported in 1991 how Anchorage Alaska was in real trouble with the Government:

The National Clean Water Act, as amended in 1987, required that cities with only primary sewage treatment plants would have to remove at least 30 percent of any organic material from their sewage. However, Anchorage had a problem with this - it had no organic material in its water!

The EPA's solution for Anchorage? The city should dump fish viscera and other organic garbage material into the system so that it could take 30 percent back out.[3]

In 1992, Secretary of Defense Dick Cheney indicated that $9 billion of largely obsolete materials - at least $7 billion more than could ever be used for all-out war - was being stockpiled at considerable annual expense. Pentagon leaders wanted to sell the stockpile, but the Armed Services Committee wouldn't let them.[4]

Despite the publicity given these post-grace-Report events, little change occurred. Kevin Phillips tells of a general who was flown from Italy to Colorado with only his cat and one aide at a cost of $116,000. Then, he illustrates the process of irresistible expansion in the Washington establishment: In 1957, personal staffs for each House member comprised five aides with a salary budget of $20,000. By 1976, this had climbed to an allotment of 15 assistants with a salary budget of $255,000. And total staff personnel for both House and Senate experienced an explosive growth during the 1960-1990 period: from 6,255 to 20,000![5]

Featherbedding At Sea

It's cheaper for a logging company in Alaska to send logs to Korea than to Olympia, Washington, while Canadian companies can do it at world market prices in state-of-the-art ships.
Why? Because the 1920 Jones Act requires maritime commerce in the U.S. to be on U.S.-built, U.S.-owned, U.S.-operated ships that are manned by U.S. crews. It is estimated that the U.S. economy would enjoy about a $2.8 billion gain, and our national-security shipping needs would be better served, were the act to be removed.

Why hasn't it been removed? Good question. One reason is that seven maritime unions gave almost $1.8 million to congressional candidates prior to the 1996 elections, and three of the top ten PAC givers in 1994 were maritime related.

Source: Review And Outlook, "A Washington Tale," The Wall Street Journal, October 5, 1998, page A30.

Recent polling responses reveal the extent of disenchantment on the part of the public:

Do public officials ignore what ordinary Americans think? (35% said yes in 1952, compared to 60% in recent years)

How many politicians are crooked? (the percentage saying "quite a few" or "all" has more than doubled from the 1950's to 53% in 1997)

Is government run for the benefit of a few big interests instead of the benefit of all the people? (29% said yes in 1964, compared to 74% in 1997) How much do you think you can trust the government in Washington to do what is right? (the percentage saying "most of the time" or "just about always" has dropped from about 72% in 1958, to about 21% in 1997)[6]

Interesting Survey Finding

"The least moral occupations in America include crime bosses, drug dealers, and Congressmen."

Source: An anonymous survey of a random sample of 2000 adult Americans reported in James Patterson and Peter Kim, The Day America Told The Truth. New York: Prentice-Hall Press, 1991, page 237.

The Buying And Selling Of Influence: In 1991, lobbyists challenged James Thurber's guestimate of some 80,000 lobbyists in Washington, claiming the figure to be more like 10,000. When Thurber undertook a more thorough-going survey, he came up with an improved estimate of 91,000. In response to all of this, Phillips observed that:

"The capital supports a growing, well-to-do elite of lobbyists, lawyers and other influence peddlers, while America's middle class has suffered from stagnant incomes and shrinking opportunities. In an ominous number of ways, in fact, Washington has come to resemble the parasitic capital of a declining empire..."[7]

Tony Bouza cites a 1995 study of the Consumer Federation of America and Common Cause that found that one fifth of the members of state legislatures who serve on committees that regulate the insurance industry were also involved with the industry as employees, accountants, lawyers, or in other capacities.[8]

Letter To Bob Dole's Presidential Campaign

(From An Individual Who Had Been Made An Envoy To The Netherlands After Giving $100,000 To The Republican Party)

"I know I can't afford enough to get Italy, but how much would I have to give for New Zealand? Could you please send me a complete price list?"

Source: Tony Bouza, The Decline And Fall Of The American Empire. New York: Plenum Press, 1996, page 85. Copyright (c) 1996 by Tony Bouza. Reprinted by permission of Perseus Books Publishers, a member of Perseus Books, L.L.C..

In 1996, after a strong Republican pledge to cut the fat from our expenditures, we saw continuing support for the construction of logging roads for timber companies (so they can cut government timber at below-market prices), and other items, such as:

$2 billion to help keep electric rates low for the people in top-drawer resorts like Aspen and HiltonHead,

151

$3 million per ship to owners for making no-longer-wanted ships available in wartime[9]

Required by Our 1872 Mining Law

Giving away 248 acres of Nevada land that hold an estimated $110 million in gold reserves for $620.

Giving away 1793 public acres with an estimated $9 billion in gold assets to a Canadian company for $8965.

Giving away 6000 other acres of Western land estimated to hold $15 billion in exploitable resources.

In the meantime, Congress has rebuffed all attempts to'exact fair royalties for the taxpayers from its corporate patrons!

Editorial: The Gainesville Sun, May 15, 1997, page 10A.

Sweet Deal

"Whether they sell sugar from their holdings in the Everglades or from their mill in the Caribbean, the Fanjuls are guaranteed a U.S. price that is more than double anywhere else in the world...that means they collect at least $60 million a year in subsidies.

"The subsidy has...helped create an environmental catastrophe...[that] will cost anywhere from $3 billion to $8 billion to repair...Growers are committed to pay up to $240 million over 20 years for the cleanup. Which means the industry that created much of the problem will have to pay only a fraction of the cost to correct it."

Special Report: Corporate Welfare. Time, November 23, 1998, pages 81-82.

T.J. Rodgers, president of Cypress Semiconductor, comments about the special tax credits that Congress gives to ethanol producers, along with a 54 cents per gallon exemption from federal excise taxes. He points out that in September, 1996, the Republican chairman of the House Ways and Means Committee tried to have the exemption reduced from 54 to 51 cents to save taxpayers some 1.8 billion dollars over a seven-year period. However, Leader Bob Dole - whose campaign committees and foundations had received more than $200,000 from the leading ethanol producer - helped persuade House Speaker Gingrich to keep it at 54 cents.

Rodgers quotes Republican Representative and House Majority Leader Dick Armey as saying, after the defeat of an attempt to kill the Market Promotion Program failed, "I wonder about our commitment to deficit reduction if we cannot take Betty Crocker, Ronald McDonald and the Pillsbury Doughboy off the dole."[10]

On Peddling Influence

Lee Iacocca, former CEO of the Chrysler Corporation, observed that "If a CIA agent quit one day and went to work for a foreign intelligence service the next, we'd call it treason. But when U.S. trade officials, sworn to protect the economic interests of the country, defect in droves to the Japanese, we don't even bat an eye."

Source: Harvard Business Review, November-December, 1990, page 184.

According to Schatz and Denman, despite the fact that:

Seventy percent of American voters do not want nuclear plants to be taxpayer-funded,

> ninety percent of utility chief executive officers don't want them built at all, and

> all reactor orders given over the last 23 years have been canceled,

Corporate supporters of the federal Light Water Reactor Program - such as General Electric, Westinghouse, and Asea Brown Boveri/Combustion Engineering - have managed to squash attempts to eliminate its funding. From 1992-1996, taxpayers sank more than 275 million dollars into the program, and another 39 million was budgeted for 1997.[11]

Donald Barlett and James Steele describe how the Seaboard Corporation, a giant, agribusiness company with headquarters in Merriam, Kansas, has played the corporate-welfare game to the detriment of community well-being. For example, to induce the company to restart a pork processing plant, the town of Albert Lea, Minnesota gave it a $2.9 million, low-interest loan; a special deal with its sewer bill; graded and paved employee parking lots; and later - when the company threatened to leave town - an additional $12.5 million in incentives.

In return, Seaboard paid $4500 per year (less than the plant's 1983 wage) to imported Hispanic laborers who couldn't afford the local cost of living and usually ended up on welfare. Then, when the work force became unionized and upped wages to within $3100 of the 1983 level, the company left for Guymon, Oklahoma, because Guymon had come up with an incentive package worth $21 million. This left the town of Alber Lea with displaced workers that Minnesota paid $700,000 to retrain and relocate.[12]

Another welfare game involves the setting up of a foreign sales corporation in one of 32 countries, including Jamaica, Barbados and the U.S. Virgin Islands. Then the company can channel its export paper work - not necessarily its physical exports - through the offshore office, and avoid some 15 percent or more in federal income taxes on a portion of its export profits. Donald Barlett and James Steele report that this single "game" has cost U.S. taxpayers more than $10 billion in this decade, alone.[13]

During the dark days of the Depression, the Export-Inport Bank was established to create jobs by offering loans, grants, and long-term guarantees to exporters. Though times have changed dramatically, the bank lives on. U.S. taxpayers were billed some $4.3 billion during the 1993-1997 period to help "needy" companies, such as AT and T, Bechtel, Boeing, Caterpillar, Foster Wheeler, and Westinghouse.[14]

Quid Pro Quos

"The business of politics consists of a series of unsentimental transactions between those who need votes and those who have money...a world where every quid has its quo"

Don Tyson, Senior Chairman of the Board, Tyson Foods

Source: Reported by Molly Ivins of the Fort Worth Star Telegram, "It Makes a World of Difference," in The Gainesville Sun, May 16, 1997.

What Needs To Be Done: What is needed seems clear: able and conscientious people of principle who can afford to serve the public without fear or favor. The present political climate prevents recruiting such people and properly nurturing them when they get into office. We seem to have reached the point where we must choose from four types of candidates:

Wealthy individuals who can outspend their rivals, but may have little relevant training and experience and little real knowledge of mainstream Americans.

Those who have the flexibility and savvy of the professional politician, but are quite willing to sell their votes to the highest bidders.

Honest, but immature, risk takers who are willing to mortgage all they own, and then some - including the financial future of their families - to get into office.

Honest and competent, but preoccupied, incumbents who are so caught up in the endless and time-consuming money-raising game, that they have begun to slight their real duties and obligations.

Increasingly, the most desirable prospective candidates - concerned, experienced, mature, and able leaders, who might be drafted into doing a turn or two in public service - are, understandably, not willing to mortgage their souls or financial futures. To a certain extent, term limits would help. But this still leaves excessive fund-raising and spending requirements and the temptation to play too closely with special-interest groups. Perhaps, a 1996 poll of voters provides the answer. It indicated that 65 percent advocated banning all private contributions and providing federal funds for Congressional and presidential campaigns.[15]

Let's expand upon this idea. Bona fide candidates - those who secure a prescribed number of valid signatures - would be permitted to spend only the allotted public funds on their campaigns. Newspapers, radio stations, and television stations would be required to donate public-service space or time to candidate presentations, debates, question-answer sessions, and discussion panels - with all official candidates being afforded the same opportunity for equal exposure. Hopefully, this would discourage the use of political consultants for insulating their candidate-clients from real scrutiny and for maliciously smearing their opponents. Interestingly, a poll of 200 such consultants in 1998 found them to be almost unanimous in seeing nothing wrong about the low-content, negative campaigns they had devised.[16]

To help obtain more competent and responsible government, we should require that all voters be literate in English and not in prison, and encourage communities to use Search Conferences (discussed later in chapter 10) to provide useful guidance to their elected leaders and governing bodies. In addition, voters and conscientious representatives should have improved opportunity to review and reject questionable legislation from the past. This can be facilitated by requiring that various appropriations expire by a certain date unless they are renewed after due public consideration.

With regard to immigration policy, our founding fathers had good reason to believe that the right of all humans to liberty should not include the right to be a citizen wherever one pleases, if one does not share - or aspire to share - certain core values with those already there. We need to review our criteria for immigration to America with this in mind. In addition, those from other cultures who do meet relevant requirements still face a period of assimilation. If undue concentrations of them are permitted in any one area, we not only retard the assimilation process, we run the risk of converting the present residents to a minority role, both socially and politically. Consequently, it seems reasonable to forbid new immigrants to settle in overly concentrated immigrant areas for at least a certain number of years.

Lastly, we must find ways to deal with the gamesmanship and resulting social costs that are deviously imposed upon small towns like Albert Lea and Guymon by large corporations. They promise benefits that prompt "bidding wars," move in and reap the benefits, and then demand "blackmail" payments for not leaving. One interesting proposal: end this game through the passage of a federal excise tax on all such location incentives that would be equal the value of the incentive.[17] A less drastic remedy has been enacted by Minnesota: when a company seeks an economic-development subsidy, it must indicate how its project will benefit the community in both jobs and wages.[18]

Misdirections In Welfare: Whether or not one defends the present welfare system depends upon how she or he answers a

157

basic question that was discussed in the Introduction: Does poverty cause most crime and irresponsible behavior? If poverty is the real culprit:

> Why are crime rates for our teenagers three times what they are for older adults who often have dependents and no one else to support them?

> Why are American crime rates significantly higher than those of many countries that have larger portions of their populations suffering extremes of poverty with little, if any, public assistance?

> And how can so many "boat people" and other immigrants who come here destitute - not knowing our language or customs - succeed so well in obeying our laws and in educating and supporting themselves?

The opposing argument appears more likely to be valid: that negative characteristics like poor education and weak self-control - along with the absence of values about respecting others and honestly earning one's way - are the primary causes of impoverishment for those who are not mentally ill or seriously disabled.

From Rationality To Rewarding Undesirable Behavior: Gertrude Himmelfarb, Professor Emeritus of History at the Graduate School of the City University of New York, observes that:

> "There was a time, and in the not so distant past, when moral concerns did run through public policy...Liberals and conservatives, radicals and socialists...were agreed on the principle that any measure of relief...had to justify itself by showing that it would promote the moral as well as the physical well-being of the recipients...the character not only of those receiving relief but also of those not receiving relief, the independent laboring poor as well.

"This was the rationale behind the principle of 'less-eligibility,' which was the basis of the Poor Law reform of 1834. This principle stipulated that the condition of the 'able-bodied pauper'...be less 'eligible' - that is, less desirable, less favorable - than the condition of the independent laborer...Also that he [the less-eligible] receive it in such a way as to make pauperism less respectable than work - to 'stigmatize' it, as we now say disapprovingly."[19]

Consistent with this philosophy, homeless men were required to chop wood or do other chores to earn food and lodging. Charitable organizations demanded abstinence from drugs or liquor - along with commitment and tangible efforts toward self-improvement - as conditions of continuing support. Interestingly, Abraham Lincoln subscribed to this approach. In response to his debt-ridden brother's request for $80, he offered the following proposition:

"Go to work 'tooth and nail' for somebody who will give you money for it...I now promise you that for every dollar you will, between this and the first of May, get for your own labor either in money or in your own indebtedness, I will then give you one other dollar...you will soon be out of debt, and what is better, you will have a habit that will keep you from getting in debt again."[20]

Years ago, illegitimate child-bearing bore a definite stigma. First aid to destitute mothers and their children was reserved for those in "suitable homes"; that is, only the homes of deserving widows - not those with illegitimate children or absent fathers. One observer prophetically expressed the prevailing sentiment in 1914: "To pension desertion or illegitimacy would, undoubtedly, have the effect of a premium upon these crimes against society." Until the late 1930's, this policy was closely adhered to. Only 3.5 percent of Aid for Dependent Children (ADC) recipients were illegitimate in 1937.

But, then, administrators began to see this suitable-homes policy as being "irrational." Why should the children of unmarried or deserted mothers be discriminated against? So, the policy changed, and the "absent-father" rate jumped to 30 percent in 1940, and to 64 percent in 1960.[21] The proportion of applicants who were eligible to be on the dole increased dramatically. It went from about 33 percent in the early 1960's to 90 percent in 1971.[22] And the illegitimate teenage birth rate soared from 15 percent of all teenage births in 1960, to 75 percent in 1995![23] For some two decades now, a strong correlation has been found between the amount of welfare payments in various states and illegitimate birth rates.[24]

Maggie Gallagher tells us that thirty-three percent of the Tipton High School senior-class girls in Tipton County, Indiana were pregnant or already unwed mothers in 1996, despite the fact that this is a rural area of churchgoing families where only some five percent of the households are below the poverty level. In addition, she reports that 55 percent of today's teenage girls say they will consider having a child out of wedlock. She concludes that "Giving subsidies and special legal protections to children who have children is not just a waste of taxpayer money, it's a form of child abuse for both mother and child."[25]

In effect, we have created an incentive system that encourages those on welfare to have children they shouldn't have. Fifty-three percent of welfare funding today is spent on families formed by births to teenagers and these children tend to be troubled. Their preschoolers have more behavioral problems than those born to older mothers, and their adolescents experience higher rates of grade failure, delinquency, incarceration, and early pregnancy.[26] The dysfunctional families that result usually end up in ghetto housing units that are characterized by rampant drug dealing, violence, rats, filth, and dilapidated structures.

The abandonment of responsible accommodation has also occurred in another arena. Judges in some jurisdictions - unconcerned about discriminating between irresponsible or incompetent vagrants and the unavoidably homeless - have ordered cities to provide shelter for anyone who asks for it. Consequently, despite significant economic growth at all wage levels during the 1980's and the fact that federal housing

160

subsidies rose over 50 percent in real terms, new shelter beds were immediately occupied as they grew in number from 98,000 to 275,000! And there was no real reduction in the available homeless population. In fact, a 1988 survey in New York City showed that 90 percent of the families arriving at the shelters were already receiving welfare benefits.[27]

When we take this type of free or subsidized accommodation into account - as well as welfare payments, state taxes, food stamps, and other benefits - *we find that many poor people are actually penalized for working more.* This fact is documented by the findings of the Cato Institute:

A Hawaiian welfare mother with two children can receive as much as $36,400 per year (which is the equivalent of $17.50 per hour - more than three times the minimum wage).

In 46 states, recipients get the equivalent of $7.16 per hour.

Twenty-one states provide individual welfare payments that exceed 150 percent of the poverty level (and this is more than the national average salary for a secretary in 29 states, the average for a teacher in nine, and the average for computer programmers in six).[28]

Admittedly, achievement in this world is easier for some than for others. However, the only way for society to generate the goods and services it needs is for it to give higher priority to rewarding members for their positive achievements, rather than for their desires, excuses, or disabilities. But this basic concept is being violated every day. If we persist in our present course, we will be stuck with a system that flies in the face of hard realities about economic capability and human motivation. We will also be at odds with a fundamental value of our founding fathers: that all who aspire to the freedom and privileges of first-class citizenship must be accountable for their behavior.

Vannevar Bush, Eminent Scientist, Founder and Former Head
of Office of Scientific Research and Development

"A people bent on a soft security, surrendering their birthright of individual self-reliance for favors, voting themselves into Eden from a supposedly inexhaustible public purse...scrambling for subsidy, learning the arts of political log-rolling and forgetting the rugged virtues of the pioneer, will not measure up to competition with a tough dictatorship."

Source: Speech, 1949. Reported by Constance Bridges in Great Thoughts Of Great Americans. New york: Thomas Y. Crowell Company, 1951, page 271.

Further Flight From Personal Responsibility: Since a majority of our policy makers now assume that poverty is almost always due to circumstances beyond the control of the individual, they classify substance abusers as being "disabled" in the same sense as the physically handicapped, and they regard virtually all unmarried mothers as being unfortunate "social victims."[29] George Will discusses how this dilution of personal responsibility has now invaded the workplace - why "you have a right to be an obnoxious jerk on the job." He points out that the Americans with Disabilities Act of 1990 is being construed to protect workers with "mental disabilities," such as:

Oppositional Defiant Disorder (includes negativistic, defiant, disobedient and hostile behavior toward authority figures - a tendency to lose one's temper, to be touchy and spiteful, and to deliberately annoy people).

Anti-Social Personality Disorder (includes a tendency to disregard the rights of others and to be callous and cynical, as well as possess an arrogant and inflated self-appraisal).

162

Histrionic Personality Disorder (includes inappropriate sexually provocative or seductive behavior, attention-seeking, and excessive emotionality).

Narcissistic Personality Disorder (includes being boastful and pretentious and interpersonally exploitative).[30]

In other words, the rights of certain individuals are pushed to an extreme, without regard to the rights of fellow workers, the demands of teamwork, and the productivity needs of the organization.

Resulting Decline In The Quality Of Welfare Recipients: Past studies have shown that the hard-core unemployed are usually functionally illiterate and their work habits are bad. Many have the attitude that work is for "squares" and that pimping and running numbers are more rewarding pursuits.[31] Many of them are also classified as "culturally deprived" (an additional handicap). Those in this subgroup tend to be slow learners, have short attention spans, believe that others are always responsible for their misfortunes, use physical force to settle disputes, and find it very difficult to defer the immediate gratification of their desires. In view of their intellectual deficit, they are even harder to resocialize with skills and different values.[32]

Society's interests were not helped when, in effect, the Supreme Court held our vagrancy statutes to be Unconstitutional in 1972 due to their vagueness and restrictions on personal freedom (see Papachristou v. City of Jacksonville). With this declaration about vagrancy, many of the culturally deprived became street people. Vagrancy had become a Constitutional right! Now, many of them sleep on our walkways and urinate and defecate on our streets, as some of us wonder what counter-balancing concern has been given to the normal rights and sensibilities of the majority? Just how valid is the assumption that such behavior, on the part of most of these street people, should be overlooked because they are assumed to be the victims

163

of a cruel environment - as opposed to being unwilling or unable to submit to the normal requirements of an organized society.

I say "most of these street people," because there are those among the homeless and deprived who care and are deserving. But they are outnumbered by those who don't care and are undeserving. In effect, our welfare policy makers have violated what we know to be the requirements for successful rehabilitation. They have helped to create an ever-expanding culture of social pathology.

We now know - based upon a wealth of experience - that for rehabilitation to succeed, participants must satisfy the following requirements:

> They must be conscientious volunteers who are serious about wanting to improve their circumstances and are willing to commit to literacy classes, skill training, or some other improvement program.

> They must give up drug and alcohol abuse and observe certain rules about punctuality, dependability, and appearance.

> When necessary, they must be willing to start at the bottom and work up.

> They must accept the idea that - beyond a basic subsistence level - they will be rewarded for the consistent discharge of their work responsibilities and for their special achievements. This last requirement is valid in terms of psychological theory, and it is consistent with an article of the UN declaration that states: "It is the duty of able-bodied persons to support themselves and to contribute to the common good..."

To the extent that one is either unable or unwilling to satisfy these requirements, she or he should be subject to certain constraints. It is against the interests of society to permit one to enjoy the privileges of unfettered citizenship without meeting its responsibilities. Those who are able-bodied, but unwilling or unable to make or honor the necessary commitments, should be housed in supervised dormitories with minimum levels of comfort, and made subject to curfews. They might earn "merit points" through work (as well as demerits for misbehavior) with which they could gain or lose certain privileges and comforts.

Stop Non-Productive Spending: The indiscriminate throwing of money at the poor is worse than useless; it creates even more dependency, crime, and destitution. We must never lose sight of the critical role of values in determining behavior. For example, the role of parental values in determining the well-being of young people is dramatized by recent research findings about poor families that were tracked over extended periods of time. Susan Mayer found that substantial increases in income do not, in themselves, significantly improve the lot of the children: illegitimacy, teen-childbearing and high-school dropout rates go down only slightly, and the average number of years of schooling rises very little. In addition, more young men were idle and more young women became single mothers in high-welfare-benefit states than in low ones.

As Mayer points out - *once basic material necessities are satisfied* - parental skills, diligence, honesty, reliability, and good health are far more important than money to the well-being of such children. Reading to them, taking them to the library to interest them in books, and taking them on outings to zoos, museums, and state parks are not expensive activities - yet, they are far more important to the proper development of children. They are clearly superior to buying the latest toys or clothes or providing expensive food, TV sets, cars, and housing.

In addition, temporary payments to those parents in distress through no fault of their own; treatment for their mental illness or other health problems; and support groups to offer them encouragement can make a big difference to their well-being, as well as that of their children.[33] And we should not forget the key role that the Earned Income Tax Credit - which returns a portion of taxes to the working poor - has played. Timothy Smeeding, Director of the Center for Policy Research at Syracuse University, regards it as "our most effective federal program for leading low-income families on a path toward true economic independence." In fact, it raised 43 million Americans above the poverty line in 1998.[34]

Implement Governmental Specifics That Work: We need to reestablish the validity of anti-vagrancy laws. One-fifth of the homeless are ex-patients of mental hospitals and many of them need to be returned to appropriate facilities. Others need to have their medications reviewed and supervised by shelter administrators or other facility personnel. Better yet, they should have access to the type of psychosocial rehabilitation that was discussed in Chapter 6. Eighty percent of the homeless have tested positive for substance abuse and many - along with a majority of the hard-core unemployed - are illiterate and have poor work habits and attitudes. They need to be counseled and steered into programs like those of St. Vincent de Paul Village and America Works (discussed in Chapter 6).

According to Robert Rector, Wisconsin already incorporates many of these ideas in its welfare programs:

> First, the state seeks to discourage unnecessary welfare enrollment. A program called "Self-Sufficiency First" counsels new applicants about the negative effects of welfare dependence and provides short-term aid (such as for car repairs) to help people avoid the need to enroll. And it requires those who must enroll to start working immediately in private-sector or community-service jobs.

> Second, those who cannot find a job within a few weeks are required to do community-service work as a condition for continuation on welfare. Also, they are subject to a "Pay After Performance" rule: Welfare checks are reduced by the amount of work they fail to perform (or the extent of their failure to attend prescribed classes or pursue supervised job searches). In other words, the state has virtually eliminated the opportunity for able-bodied individuals to be "free riders."

Third, state bureaucrats are motivated to implement the program efficiently, because offices that don't measure up are replaced by outside contractors.

How successful have these efforts been? Assuming that many former welfare recipients have not merely fled to other states, the following data are impressive: During the past 10 years (since 1987), Wisconsin's caseload for its Aid to Families With Dependent Children program (AFDC) dropped by more than 50 percent, while national case loads rose more than 35 percent. Welfare rolls dropped by 80 percent or more in 28 of the state's 77 counties. And total day-care and training costs declined, while they have nearly doubled nationwide.[35] Lastly, since 1991, the teen pregnancy rate dropped faster than the national decline. An important reason for this may be Wisconsin's policy of not automatically giving a larger welfare stipend for an additional illegitimate child.[36]

A similar success story is provided by Michigan. First, Governor John Engler ended a General Assistance program that gave welfare benefits to single, able-bodied adults. Then, he led the way in modifying the state's Aid to Families with Dependent Children (AFDC) program so that, in order to continue to receive benefits, recipients would have to find work, enter a training program, or do community service. As a result, AFDC fell from 229,000 in 1992-93 to 162,000 in 1996-97, and the budget for the Family Independence Agency fell by $164 million in one year! In addition, the state stimulated the creation of new businesses by relaxing many regulations in "Renaissance Zones" in certain depressed neighborhoods, and it exempted companies grossing less than $250,000 from a special value-added, business tax. Consequently, Michigan has become a leader in economic growth, having gained some 460,000 new jobs between 1991 and 1996.[37]

Since 1994, Minnesota's program has helped to cause a 35 percent increase in the employment of its welfare recipients - by requiring them to work, while initially supplementing low pay.[38] And Nancy Johnson reports the effects of welfare reform nationally: between 1994 and 1999, case loads had declined an average of 45 percent, and some 60 percent of welfare mothers had become employed.[39]

Dwight Morrow, Distinguished U.S. Senator

"As I get older...I become more convinced that good government is not a substitute for self-government."

Source: Reported by Constance Bridges in Great Thoughts Of Great Americans. New York: Thomas Y. Crowell Company, 1951, page 192)

We need to distinguish irresponsible pregnancies on the part of "advantaged" teen mothers from those of teen mothers who were exploited by older males. The latter are more deserving of the label "social victim" and should be treated accordingly. A Washington State study in 1992 underscores the need for this distinction: Sixty-two percent of 535 teenage mothers had been raped or molested prior to becoming pregnant, and the average age of the male involved was 27.4 years.[40]

For those who are deserving of welfare support, three important policy changes are needed:

1) We need to reduce a disincentive to self-improvement and working by requiring that food-stamp purchases, and other benefits, cover only essentials,

2) we need to follow Wisconsin's example in not giving automatic welfare increases for additional illegitimate children, and

3) we need to maintain the purchasing power of the minimum wage for regular, qualified workers.

Properly Use Minimum Wages And Subsidies: In the latter regard, consider the following figures: In 1996 dollars, the $1.60 1968 minimum-wage figure was worth $7.28, but this dropped to $4.27 by 1989 when the minimum wage was $3.35. It climbed back to $4.75 in October, 1996 with an increase to $4.75, and the 1997 boost to $5.15 equaled about $4.89 - way below the 1968 value of $7.28![41] Clearly, we need to do a better job of maintaining a given floor.

The theoretical argument against raising the minimum wage is that this increases unemployment, especially for inner-city teenagers. However, according to Mark Weisbrot, research director at the Preamble Center For Public Policy, a 1998 study that employed four different approaches could find no job loss due to the minimum-wage increases in 1996 and 1997.[42] And Robert Murphy adds that the unemployment rate for black, male teenagers actually fell from 37 percent in 1995, to 36 percent in 1997.[43] On the other hand, Bruce Bartlett reports a study of the 1996 increase that claims a 2 percent reduction in overall teenage employment and a 10 percent reduction for black teenagers for each 10 percent minimum-wage increase.[44]

But Richard Berman raises a different objection. He asks if a minimum-wage increase can really help entry-level applicants, given the estimate that 85 percent of unwed mothers are illiterate and that 70 percent of the unemployed fall into the lowest literacy level.[45] A more plausible question might be: "Why penalize qualified persons because there are many who are unqualified?" We have ample historical evidence of the willingness of employers to exploit qualified workers whenever economic conditions permit it. Why not make additional minimum-wage exceptions to accommodate those who refuse to try to become literate, to part-time teenagers, and to participants in legitimate training programs?

There is also the cost to taxpayers of keeping marginal workers on welfare, versus the "subsidy" part of paying a minimum wage. E.S. Savas reports that Mayor Giuliani has saved New York City about $60 million - compared to what would be paid union members in equivalent positions - by placing more some 35,000 welfare recipients in his Work

169

Experience Program. They work at minimum wage for enough hours each week to earn their welfare stipend, and the positions they fill are created solely through attrition, not through the layoff of union members. Savas proposes that:

> "No make-work jobs should be created. If excess workers are available under workfare, then the level of public services could be increased, giving taxpayers more for their money: Schools that are now cleaned only once a week could be cleaned two or more times a week; welfare workers could patrol the streets to find and fix potholes before they get bigger. The basic municipal work forces in many fields could be comprised primarily of welfare workers. And these wouldn't have to be dead-end jobs: Like any good employer, public agencies should provide training to prepare workers for higher-level jobs. Of course regular employees would supervise and instruct the welfare ' workers."[46]

Economist Edmund Phelps proposes that the government pay a subsidy to private-sector employers for each low-wage, full-time worker, so that the employee would receive above-poverty-level income; certainly more than the level of welfare benefits. And the amount of the subsidy would decline with each increase in the employee's hourly rate.[47] Minnesota is already experimenting with this subsidy idea in Minneapolis and other areas. A welfare recipient continues to receive a portion of the benefit check until paid earnings reach 140 percent of the poverty level. In August 1997, after 18 months, some 52 percent of the long-term welfare recipients had obtained paid employment and almost 30 percent had incomes above the poverty level.[48]

The number on welfare, nationally, dropped 44 percent from 1994 to 1999. But this means that those who can move off of welfare easily have done so. What about the others? The federal government is providing additional help for tougher cases by providing funding to:

Help long-term welfare recipients in high-poverty areas move closer to available work, provide transportation to low-paid workers who do not have access to public transportation,

extend the tax credit to businesses that hire people off welfare.[49]

Create Productive, 24-Hour Environments: With regard to seriously disadvantaged children, when we place them in foster homes or communal facilities, we often create as many problems as we solve. Craig Shealy observes that:

"...Unless an infant is removed from its home shortly after birth, the emotional bond between infant and parent will likely grow in strength. The stronger (and healthier) the bond, the more consequential is its severance likely to be, and the more difficult it becomes to establish an equivalent emotional connection with a surrogate parent.

"...Some children and youth who have experienced...physical or sexual abuse, exploitation, humiliation, and rejection still remain fiercely loyal to their family of origin, often clinging tenaciously to the hope that things at home can be put right."[50]

Therefore, whenever feasible, our goal should be to guide and supplement parental and extended-family influence rather than remove it altogether. We must provide single parents on welfare with guidance, safety, and support, as well as responsibilities. And we need to create 24-hour environments for them that are positive and safe.

Perhaps, the best way for doing this would be through a team approach that would tap the coordinated efforts of representatives of child and family services, charitable agencies, the schools, and law enforcement agencies. They could create a superior facility for single mothers or fathers and their children to live in - one that would provide food service, laundry service, day care, recreational activities, and professional staff to coordinate activities and help to oversee the children. In addition, the children - as well as young, single parents - could receive guidance, security, and membership in mutual-support groups.

Single parents would also have guilt-free time for work, job training, and an improved social life, and they could spend more quality time with their children, as well as assist, part-time, with the on-going work of the facility. They could also select representatives to serve on an oversight board of directors, and extended-family members could be invited to participate as volunteers. Such an environment would better satisfy a need that is often neglected: the need children have for order and external structure as means for developing constructive values and self-guidance.[51] And all of this should be cost-effective for taxpayers, since such a coordinated program would eliminate overlapping welfare services, conserve agency personnel, and, presumably, be supported in part by a portion of each tenant's welfare check. James Wilson goes even further by recommending that young, unmarried mothers be *required* to move into such a facility as a condition of receiving public assistance.[52] The opportunity for skill upgrading that would be afforded is of particular importance in view of the report by the Washington Literacy Council that 85 percent of our unwed mothers are illiterate.[53]

Matt Kelley tells us about an interesting, government-subsidized, variation of the above approach called Hope Meadows. It is designed for children in state custody, and is now operating on an abandoned Air Force base in Rantoul, Illinois. Families get free housing, and one foster parent gets $18,000 per year for staying home and caring for the children. Retired people, whom the children refer to as grandpa and grandma, are lured to Hope Meadows by reduced rents in return for working with child-welfare workers and community volunteers to do such things as reading to the children and serving as school-crossing guards. Residents report that the program is working well, and when it reaches its capacity of 40

172

children, is expected to require about half the $30,000 per year it takes to raise a child in a group home.[54]

The problems of ghetto housing are being solved by people like William Lindsey in Fort Lauderdale, Florida. As with the founders of other successful programs, he is convinced that effective rehabilitation requires specific commitments from the beneficiaries. He establishes Resident Councils to assist in screening applicants for housing and in setting the rules and policies for the projects. He also helps deserving residents with starting small businesses. When he first arrived and began to clean up around the units, tenants would ask him what he was doing. He'd tell them: "The first time I'm cleaning it up for you. The second time, I'll be cleaning it up for the new tenant."

He calls this approach the "Oasis Technique": identifying responsible resident leaders and then helping them create islands of stability. He asserts that "Public housing must be a privilege. You don't get in just because you're poor. You get in because you are poor and willing to accept responsibility."[55]

In one of the worst drug-dealing neighborhoods in Los Angeles - which had experienced regular drive-by shootings - police launched "Operation Cul-de-Sac." They first surveyed 563 people for approval and support. Then, they erected a barricade and established street patrols with the cooperation of Neighborhood Watch groups. Within a year, crime in the area had dropped 12 percent and drive-by shootings had declined 85 percent![56]

Conclusion: The evidence presented in this chapter underscores what was stressed in Chapter 1: Individual responsibility for one's behavior is an absolute prerequisite for the proper functioning of a free society. Those who are unwilling or unable to satisfy this requirement cannot legitimately expect to enjoy the same benefits and degree of personal freedom as those who do satisfy it. On the other hand, those who are willing and able to work, and learn, and develop, should not be economically penalized, in comparison with those who are unwilling or unable to do so.

173

Chapter 9

THE NEED FOR NURTURING CORE VALUES IN THE ADMINISTRATION OF JUSTICE AND HOW WE CAN DO IT

Most of us enter adulthood thinking that the primary purpose of the criminal-justice system is to seek justice based upon a search for truth. However, we quickly become disillusioned. We see the system nurture an unduly drawn-out and highly expensive game - one in which, more times than not, the primary goal of the defense attorneys, and the judicial technicians involved, is to thwart - rather than facilitate - the achievement of common-sense justice. Supreme Court Justice Byron White observed that: "Defense counsel need present nothing, even if he knows what the truth is...If he can confuse a witness, even a truthful one, or make him appear at a disadvantage, unsure or indecisive, that will be his normal course,"[1] and Richard Wasserstrom, a legal philosopher, described lawyers as "amoral technicians."[2] In fact, at present, only our military courts do not tolerate defense-attorney attempts to knowingly mislead a jury.

The ethical responsibility of the prosecutor is quite different. She or he is concerned with both convicting the guilty and acquitting the innocent, and must always disclose any information that is helpful to the defendant. In other words, the prosecutor is not free to employ tactics that produce an unfair conviction.

Diminished Personal Accountability: Increasingly, we hear about repeat criminals who laugh at conventional morality and the "understanding" justice system. For example, during the Los Angeles riots - due, presumably, to the beating of black Rodney King by white police - two young men pulled an innocent truck driver from his seat, crushed his skull, and did a victory dance over his body. They were successfully defended in court on the

175

grounds that one cannot be held accountable for getting caught up in the excesses of widespread violence! And John Miller tells us about a new "cultural" defense in his book, The Unmaking of Americans. A Chinese immigrant killed his wife with a hammer for adultery. The defense argued that this was quite understandable, given Chinese attitudes about infidelity. Consequently, the husband received five years probation and not a day in jail. Miller adds that a similar "cultural" defense was used to reduce charges in several child abuse, kidnapping, and rape cases, and that the Equal Employment Opportunity Commission successfully sued employers for requiring immigrants and others to speak English at work![3]

The "exclusionary rule" has the commendable purpose of protecting citizens from illegal search and seizure, by excluding from a trial any evidence so obtained. Yet, the mandatory application of this rule in recent years has left many law enforcement officers in a quandary. For example, In 1996 a federal judge refused the admission of 80 pounds of cocaine and heroin as evidence. It had been obtained during the arrest of a drug courier. The judge ruled that the police had no right to search the courier's out-of-state car in an active drug area, despite the fact that men were hastily loading it with bags in the middle of the night, and the men had run away when the police approached them.[4]

In addition, personal accountability has been diluted by our bankruptcy courts. According to Diana Bork, courts now tend to accept a debtor's assertions at face value. They do not require any minimum showing of need or minimum level of remaining debt; nor do they require an independent review of assets, income, or future ability to pay. Consequently, courts are often conceding more than is necessary, by granting Chapter 7 relief from all dischargeable debt - rather than requiring more demanding Chapter 13 - despite the fact that most debtors are able to handle some repayment, though they may not be able to discharge all of their obligations on time.[5] Partly as the result of this leniency, the number of U.S. bankruptcies, as of June, 1998, was four times that of 1985 according to the Administrative Office of the U.S. Courts. And these bankruptcies cost U.S.

business some $40 billion annually according to the U.S. Chamber of Commerce![6]

Justice For Whom?:   We have now become the most litigious nation in human history.[7] We have three times as many lawyers per capita as Great Britain, our tort claims are ten times higher, and our product liability claims are a hundred times higher.[8] There was a time when the fees of lawyers were capped to offset the potential for abuse that their limited numbers and licensed position gave them.   Today, they have priced themselves out of the reach of many Americans. This fact is impressed upon us when we learn that, typically, we will be required by law to pay an attorney a set percentage of the value of an estate to have a will probated, regardless of how little legal work is required.

Even when a lawsuit is groundless, each party must pay its own attorney's fees. This has set the stage for a kind of "legal blackmail": a complainant, egged on by an attorney with a contingency-fee agreement, threatens someone with a frivolous suit, but is willing to settle out of court for less than that person's anticipated legal fees.   The unscrupulous complainant gets a wind-fall and the immoral attorney gets a 30-40 percent fee for little, if any, legal work.

Such games so overload the court system that we have instituted plea bargaining, whereby guilty pleas are traded for reduced sentences. This is also quite profitable for attorneys, because they get their fees without having to prepare for a trial. According to Douglas Smith, as early as 1985, over 85 percent of all felony convictions were the result of plea bargaining.[9] As a result, everyone seems to win but the victims of crime and society at large: docket space is freed up for judges and their support personnel, criminals get off easy, and lawyers enjoy financial windfalls. It's as if regard for the victims and the dispensing of justice are of secondary importance.

Misdirections In The Rehabilitation Of Criminals: In Chapter 5, we discussed how one's behavior is the result of a genetic predisposition interacting with one's environment.   At one extreme, constructive environmental influences - both early and late - are minimal for those who are genetically predisposed toward the criminal personality profile presented in Chapter 4.

Recall our discussion there of how Yochelson and Samenow started an intensive, long-term individual counseling and group therapy/learning program for some 255 volunteer, criminal-personality individuals who wanted to turn their lives around. The group meetings lasted four hours per day, five days per week, for a year. And these were hardly self-justifying or "therapist-snowing" bull sessions. Each participant had to keep a daily record of his thought processes, report these to the group, and relate them to various dysfunctional thinking patterns, as well as, to what he had learned that day. Yet, such heroic efforts were not very fruitful. Only 30 of the prisoners completed the rigorous program. And then, only ten could be counted as successes several years later. And these ten had to behave almost saint-like to achieve this level of success. They could not deal with everyday moral gray areas or fine circumstantial discriminations. One slip off a carefully prescribed straight and narrow path was like a "cured" alcoholic attempting one drink.

Unfortunately, most rehabilitation program designers have ignored such realities. They need to consider the sobering review of all rehabilitation research for criminals - some 231 studies between 1945 and 1967 - that was made by sociologist Robert Martinson. He reviewed all of the approaches: educational and skill improvement, individual and group counseling, milieu therapy, medical treatment, intensive supervision in the community, individual psychotherapy, and shorter sentences. All were programs for mixed groups of criminals and *none of them appreciably reduced relapse into crime*.[10] However, as we will see, a number of these approaches were not used properly. Furthermore, our legislators need to become aware of such findings. Not too long ago, evidence of an offender's past crimes was admissible in a trial. Now, laws require that such evidence be routinely excluded. Needless to say, this is a real boon to career criminals, for any criminologist today will confirm the likelihood of repeat performances on the part of hardened veterans.

Employers Put On The Spot: Given the current odds against genuine rehabilitation for many of our criminals, the present interpretations of "job relatedness," that the federal Equal Employment Opportunity Commission uses to permit discrimination in employment, is unrealistically narrow. For example, a just-paroled embezzler may be denied a bookkeeping job, but a hotel cannot refuse to give the job of bellman to an applicant who had been convicted of receiving stolen goods, despite the fact that the job provides access to guest rooms and valuable personal property. Consequently, the Commission has created a real conflict of interests. On the one hand, it wants to assure that those who have been convicted of, or charged with, serious crimes are not forever barred from gainful employment; on the other hand, it seriously hampers employers from meeting their moral and legal obligations with regard to the safety and welfare of their customers and employees. In other words, employers are liable to being sued by aggrieved parties if they do hire such people, and they are liable to being sued by former criminals if they don't![11]

What Needs To Be Done: Judge Harold Rothwax of New York City proposes a means for avoiding the arbitrary and often irrational use of the exclusionary rule:

"Make the exclusionary rule *discretionary instead of mandatory*. If it was at the discretion of the judge, there could be a test of reasonableness. A judge could consider factors such as whether a police officer acted with objective reasonableness and subjective good faith."[12]

With regard to bankruptcies, courts should automatically conduct an independent review of a filer's assets or, at least, permit creditors to call for such a review, and they should deny Chapter 7 relief when a multiyear repayment plan under Chapter 13 is feasible. In addition, every filer who satisfactorily completes such a Chapter 13 plan should be rewarded by having the bankruptcy notation removed from his or her credit report earlier than had it been a Chapter 7 action. And federal limits should be placed upon the amount an individual can shield from creditors. Presumably, the only defensible intent of such shielding is to provide for necessities - not luxuries or the maintenance of a prior standard of living.[13]

With regard to unwarranted legal costs, Andrew Thomas notes that we are the only nation in the world that requires a defendant in a groundless law suit to pay his or her attorney's fees.[14] We need to adopt a "groundless loser pays" rule by which the capricious losing party must pay the winning party's fees, in addition to any judgment that was awarded. The judge or jury might be made responsible for determining the extent of "groundlessness," as well as fairness-in-size, of the fees to be reimbursed. This approach would ease our court-overload problem, better protect deserving poor people from the drain of high contingency fees and, hopefully, reduce our dependence upon plea bargaining - except when it involves the only means for obtaining information about accomplices. And judicial productivity might be publicized, as an additional means for easing the overload problem. A study by the National Center for State Courts found that judges often prove capable of handling more cases when the pace of litigation in their courts is made known.[15]

To curb greedy lawyers and protect people from unwarranted penalties, we should consider placing caps on punitive damages, as opposed to demonstrated damages. Alternatively, we might give serious consideration to the idea of replacing juries with carefully selected panels of judges for cases involving complex, legal issues. And we should make it possible for all relevant data, including past convictions, to be made available to them. In addition, it would materially and emotionally benefit victims - and provide a good lesson in accountability - to require criminals to pay restitution for the damages they inflict. If such civil claims were processed by the same courts, the only additional work involved would be the evaluation of evidence presented by the victim-claimants as to the extent of damages suffered.

With regard to rehabilitation, our only recourse at present for those with a criminal personality (see Chapter 4) is to restrain their freedom when they become chronic offenders, and then segregate them in prison from those who can benefit from useful interventions. Some will argue that such non-rehabilitative "warehousing" is too expensive; that release is cheaper than imprisonment for society. But Harvard economist Steven Levitt shows that this is a serious misconception. His empirical analysis found that:

An average of some 15 crimes per year are eliminated for each prisoner locked up,

and an average estimated net benefit to society of $23,900 per prisoner, per year, is realized, after taking into account the cost of incarceration.[16]

Additional data on the likely role of deterrence are provided by Morgan Reynolds, director of the Criminal Justice Center at the National Center for Policy Analysis. Using 1993 as a reference point, he reports that:

As the probability of imprisonment for murder has increased 53 percent, murders have decreased 30 percent.

As the probability of imprisonment for rape has increased 12 percent, rapes have decreased 14 percent.

As the probability of imprisonment for robbery has increased 28 percent, robberies have decreased 29 percent.

As the probability of imprisonment for burglary has increased 14 percent, burglaries have decreased 18 percent.[17]

Appropriate programs for segregated criminals with more normal genetic endowments are particularly successful - if attempts at remedial action are made early enough - for things start to "jell" at an earlier age than most of us realize. When most normal, young people are deprived of proper early guidance and are exposed to environments that consistently give them feelings of worthlessness and hopelessness, they stop making an effort to "fit in" and "do the right thing." They often kick over the traces - and even resort to violence - to vent their frustrations and achieve some kind of attention or recognition out of nothingness. Although important changes can still occur after such deprivation, the task is not as easy as many enthusiasts would have us believe.

This need for early intervention is supported by the findings of a survey of 780 police chiefs of both large and small cities. Ninety-two percent agree that we can sharply reduce crime by committing more government money to programs that help young people get a good start in life; that a higher, current investment will more than pay for itself later on in reduced crime, welfare, and other costs. For example, crime dropped 75 percent in targeted neighborhoods of Lansing, Michigan, after a youth development program was launched in a new community center by police, local schools, and a social service agency. And delinquency was reduced 91 percent in Syracuse, New York by the provision of parent-training home visits, early childhood education, and nutritional, health, safety, and other services that commenced, prenatally, and continued until the children reached elementary-school age.[18]

Psychotherapy can be quite effective for groups from which inappropriate individuals have been eliminated,[19] and success has been achieved in recent years with an approach called "behavior modification" (which utilizes the tools of Behavior Management discussed in Chapter 6). It rewards desirable responses and, to a lesser degree, punishes undesired responses - and then provides for follow-up oversight to encourage good decision making and positive personal associations. It is most effective when it is coupled with collaborative goal setting to give clients a sense of goal ownership.[20]

Such an approach underlies the impressive results being achieved by programs like those of Father Joe Caroll of St. Vincent de Paul Village in San Diego and Dr. Mimi Silbert of the Delancey Street Foundation in San Francisco (see Chapter 6).

However, as was also pointed out there, these programs will not work for everyone. They require voluntary application; mature, conscious self-analysis of one's condition; and long-term commitment to meaningful goals and hard work. We have every reason to believe that many more-normal, first offenders would respond quite favorably to them, were they not mixed indiscriminately with hardened, criminal-personality-type individuals. Chances for success are also diminished when there are not enough trained support personnel. The client loads of probation officers, social workers, and counselors are already excessive. Too often, quantity overrides quality as the main factor that drives case-load assignments.

The time is long overdue for putting such workers on a salary-plus-incentive basis, whereby they would be paid a certain fee for each case that remains successfully closed for three months - then receive smaller fees (for several six-month periods) for continued closure. This approach would not only assure adequate pay and protection against case overload and make-work clerical procedures, it would help to attract new talent. And it would be economically feasible because genuine rehabilitation or removal from welfare support would save taxpayers many times the "commissions" involved.

In another vein, Andrew Thomas discusses the unfortunate demise of constructive prison labor. Having reviewed the history of its usage, he writes that:

> "Work gave the inmate direction and discipline, eating up otherwise idle time and showing him the fruits of productive, properly channeled labors. Inmate work also provided a handy system of funding the new, expensive institutions by requiring prisoners to pay for their keep."[21]

The value of prison labor is supported by research conducted by the U.S. Bureau of Prisons. Only 6.6 percent of those federal inmates who had been employed in prison industries had violated their parole or been rearrested within a year of release, while 20 percent of those who had not been employed were rearrested.[22] And additional evidence is provided by the experience of PRIDE Enterprises, a non-profit Florida company that started training and employing prison inmates in 1985. By 1998, PRIDE was employing 4000 prisoners in 51 operations - from making eyeglasses to data entry. Less than 13 percent of these inmates have landed back in prison after release, compared to a national rate of some 60 percent.[23]

By the turn of the century, prison labor had become a powerful competitor of certain private-sector industries. Seeing it as a threat to the earnings and job security of their lower-skilled workers, unions leaned on their political representatives to effectively outlaw the sale of prison-made goods. However, in today's global economy, many of the jobs in question have been lost to low-paid foreigners, anyway. Yet, 90 percent of American inmates remain unemployed.[24]

By repealing our current laws against the use of prison labor, we could bring these jobs back home and reap the documented rehabilitative advantages of such labor, in addition to helping with the high costs of maintaining our prisons. Furthermore, as Andrew Thomas observes: prisoners would be somewhat relieved of the boredom and brutality of modern prison life, crime victims could more readily realize restitution by garnishing a portion of an inmate's wages, and we could more fully utilize the prison cells we have by employing prisoners in round-the-clock shifts.[25]

Chapter 10

THE NEED FOR NURTURING CORE VALUES IN BUSINESS AND HOW WE CAN DO IT

Ethical behavior in business can be much more challenging than in everyday life - and ethical behavior in international business can be even more challenging. Chester Barnard, an experienced chief executive, presents some examples of complications beyond the simple dictates of personal-relations ethics:

A workman promoted to supervisory duties discovers that his or her loyalty to a former fellow worker is of a radically changed character,

the issue of destroying edible food stocks to maintain farm prices,

the thrust to merge with competitors to improve one's ability to survive, versus sincere commitment to the virtues of open competition,

the idea that serious accidents should be prevented at any cost, versus the hard reality that the costs of intensive inspection, testing, and policing may preclude the survival of the organization in the short run.

Barnard concludes that much public misunderstanding has been created by lack of appreciation of the moral elements involved in specialized activities.[1] On the other hand, some business people give unqualified support to the idea of unrestrained free-enterprise, and have nothing but contempt for bigness and inefficiency in government. Their position would make more sense if three important conditions could be satisfied in the real world:

185

1) We could be less concerned about the fate of dependent children and others who cannot provide for themselves through no fault of their own.

2) We would have nothing to fear from an unrestrained concentration of power in the hands of politicians and bureaucrats.

3) We could actually fulfill the requirements for perfect competition: complete knowledge on the part of consumers and producers, uninhibited market access for all, and complete mobility for labor and other resources.

With regard to Condition 1, it is fortunate that most citizens have troubled consciences over the idea of indiscriminate cutbacks in funding for those who honestly cannot fend for themselves. Thank God that they are not yet prepared to let them suffer and die in the streets.

With regard to Condition 2, experience has taught that we have much to fear from the unrestrained concentration of power in the hands of dictators and bureaucrats. To avoid such concentration, we pay a price in inefficiency: we make most government activities subject to multiple political masters, conflicting interest-group demands, and leadership turnover that is usually based more upon political qualifications than bottom-line performance.

With regard to Condition 3, the extent to which we are unable to create perfect competition is indicated by:

the recurrence of price-fixing attempts,

the willingness to rape our unprotected natural resources,

the many attempts to drive competitors out of business through restraint-of-trade practices, such as restriction-of-competition agreements, the tendency to misrepresent products and services,

the incidence of insider market trading,

the exploitation of child labor and the disadvantaged,

the tendency of special-interests business groups to promote legislation that discriminates against their competitors, and

other "unfair" practices.

Business Ethics In The News

"The General Electric Company, which was convicted in a jury trial of overcharging the Army for a battlefield computer system, agreed yesterday to pay one of the largest fines ever assessed for defrauding the Defense Department. G.E. will pay $16.1 million in criminal and civil penalties.

"The Northrop Corporation agreed to pay $17 million for falsifying test data on components of the cruise missile and the Harrier jet.

"The largest military fraud settlement was reached in 1988, when the Sundstrand Corporation paid $115 million for over billing the Government for military hardware."

Source: Barnaby Feder, "G.E. to Pay $16.1 Million Fine for Pentagon Fraud," New York Times, July 27, 1990, pages A1, D2.

Arthur Schlesinger, Eminent Historian, On
Freedom Versus Regulation

"The individual freedoms destroyed by the increase in national authority have been in the main the freedom to deny black Americans their elementary rights as citizens, the freedom to work little children in mills...the freedom to pay starvation wages...the freedom to pollute the environment - all freedoms that, one supposes, a civilized country can do without."

Source: Arthur Schlesinger, Jr., The Cycles Of American History. Boston: Houghton Mifflin, 1986, page 248)

In other words, when we enter the real world, we see a clear-cut need for regulation and business ethics to help correct an otherwise "tilted playing field" and the inhumane demands of imperfect enterprise. To further illustrate this need:

We see doctors, for-profit hospitals, and undertakers who pretend that seriously ill or emotionally distraught clients really do have an opportunity to negotiate fees, dispassionately, and to diligently shop around as a basis for making informed choices.

We see many top managers who decry the loss of a "work ethic" on the part of their workers, as their own behavior makes it clear that large salaries, bonuses, stock options, and other perks are prerequisite to their performance.

And we often see companies close down factories and lay off workers without regard to the social costs involved, due to greed rather than economic necessity.

With regard to the last point, many insensitively implemented "downsizings" have backfired. A 1993 survey of

451 companies which had hoped to raise profits by cutting back their staffs found that only 46 percent had done so within two fiscal years. And more recently, Wayne Cascio and his colleagues examined the experience over 15 years of Standard-and-Poor-500 companies that had downsized *without other changes*. They found that these companies had never outperformed other companies during that period of time.[2]

What's more, David Noer, a vice president of the Center for Creative Leadership, estimates that some 75 percent of the Fortune 500 companies have been affected by "layoff-survivor syndrome" - rising stress and anxiety accompanied by declining loyalty, teamwork, and creativity - as more than a third of the remaining personnel furtively seek other employment.[3] Undoubtedly, callous employers have helped to create the responses presented in the box below.

Percentage Of People Who Claim (Anonymously) That They Live By These Contemporary Commandments

Percent

I will steal from those who won't really miss it 74

I will procrastinate at work and do absolutely nothing one full day in five. It's standard operating procedure   50

Source: An anonymous survey of a random sample of 2000 adult Americans reported in James Patterson and Peter Kim, The Day America Told The Truth. New York: Prentice-Hall Press, 1991, pages 25, 26.

For the most part, such negative effects are caused by employees who feel that top management doesn't care about them; that they are expendable. Often, they are not consulted about what is going on, no effort is made to help retrain and/or

189

•

relocate those being terminated, and work loads tend to increase for those who remain - with no change in pay.

Hypothetical Note From Teamster President Carey to
UPS President Kelly

"Dear Jim, We Teamsters get a good laugh out of your call for openness and democracy. You might want to throw your mind back to the last contract talks, in the fall of 1993. There we were, bargaining away in good faith and a spirit of openness, except UPS management had one big dirty secret. You were planning to raise the weight limit on packages, from 70 pounds to 150 pounds. Jim, that's three times the 50 pound limit that was in effect when you and I were driving UPS trucks...

"You haven't raised the part-time $8 an hour starting wage in 15 years and you want to freeze it for another five...

"Oh, and you want to have our people in your UPS health plan. That's rich, considering you barely recognize work injuries as a problem and have even made it impossible for OSHA to collect data on how you are hurting your workers...

"Now, in your health plan, you demand that health insurance kick in only after six months. In other words, the bulk of your employees won't have any health coverage. And we do know that the injury rate at UPS in 1996 was 33.8 per 100 workers, based on a 2,000 hour working year. That's two and a half times the industry average."

Source: Alexander Cockburn, "'Dear Jim': What Ron Carey Should Tell The Boss of UPS," The Wall Street Journal, August 14, 1997, page A13

Confidence in business and its leadership fell from around 70 percent in the late 1960's to about 15 percent in 1986. Seventy percent of those polled felt that executives had not behaved ethically.[4] And for good reason. Amitai Etzioni reports that, between 1975 and 1985, two-thirds of our Fortune 500 companies were convicted of crimes ranging from price fixing to the illegal dumping of hazardous wastes.[5] And Marshall Clinard notes that by 1989 the costs of corporate crime had exceeded those of street crimes by as much as 65 times.[6] As for future prospects, Rushworth Kidder reports a Shearson-Lehman poll that found that 40 percent of 18-19 year-old yuppies feel that corruption and deceit are important means for getting ahead.[7] And 66 percent of a random sample of high-school seniors in 1990 said they would consider lying to achieve an important business objective.[8]

Inadequate Regulation: Consider the billions of taxpayer dollars - some estimates say more than $150 billion - that have been required to replenish depositor losses due to the irresponsible behavior of the government, and the often reckless and dishonest behavior of savings and loan company officers, that resulted in some 4000 bank fraud prosecutions in the U.S.. A government cannot guarantee the safety of every savings account up to $100,000 and reasonably expect depositors to subject banks and their managements to the same careful scrutiny that they exercised before the advent of insured accounts. The removal of adequate regulation was an open invitation to greedy opportunist to offer unjustifiably high interest rates to attract deposits, take unwarranted risks with questionable ventures, and squander much of the money by paying themselves and their cronies exorbitant salaries and perks - knowing that taxpayers would have to pick up the pieces at the end of the ride.

Unwarranted Compensation: Many U.S. corporate leaders face a growing credibility problem. They have garnered unbelievable compensation packages through the creation of rubber-stamp boards of directors, rather than through personal,

191

bottom-line contributions to their organizations - and this has been documented. Shawn Tully looked at the compensation of 200 chief-executive officers and found that at least 43 had received increases in 1990 in the face of reduced profits for their companies.[9] And other studies show that it is more the exception than the rule that CEO pay is related to corporate performance.[10]

Gilbert Amelio Cried All The Way To The Bank

"During his 17-month tenure as head of Apple Computer Inc., the company racked up losses totaling nearly $2 billion. But when the board ousted him last summer, Mr. Amelio walked away with severance pay of $6.7 million, in addition to his $2 million in salary and bonus for the year ended Sept. 26."

Source: Joann Lublin, "Pay For No Performance," The Wall Street Journal, April 9, 1998, page R1

Christine Gorman found that, by 1989, executive pay and bonuses had jumped 120 percent, while the wages of factory workers had risen only 80 percent.[11] And Joann Lublin reports that median CEO compensation rose 10.4 percent in 1995 and 5.2 percent in 1996, while overall U.S. wages and benefits rose 2.8 percent in 1995 and three percent in 1996. Lublin also observes that ex-CEO's continue to receive about the same cash compensation when they step down to chair the board, though they have fewer responsibilities and often put in fewer hours.[12]

The Wall Street Journal estimates that big-corporation CEOs had gone from making about 44 times the average American salary in 1965 to some 212 times in 1995...a development that Nell Minow characterizes as being of "Marie Antoinette proportions." This prompted some Congressmen in 1996 to propose tax breaks for businesses that would have capped the pay of their top executives at 50 times that of their lowest-paid job.[13]

Since then, we have had even more dramatic examples of "overkill." For example, Gary Strauss reports that Linda Wachner, chairman of the Warnaco Group, received a salary of $2.7 million in 1998 - plus a $6 million bonus and $358,000 for sundry expenses - despite the fact that the average total return on the organization's stock that year (10.4 percent) was about half the return (21 percent) on Standard and Poor's 500 stocks. In addition, the compensation committee granted her $6.5 million in free Warnaco shares, and she reaped $76 million by exercising preexisting options![14]

Wal-Mart's Founder on CEO Pay

"A lot of what goes on these days with these overpaid CEOs who're really just looting from the top and aren't watching out for anybody but themselves really upsets me. It's one of the main things wrong with American business today," Sam Walton.

Source: Time, June 15, 1992, page 52.

Deception And Exploitation: Consider the dramatic defection in 1996 of Jeffrey Wigand, former vice president for research and development at Brown and Williamson Tobacco Company. He claims that the tobacco industry had withheld vital health-related information from the American public; especially, long-held knowledge that nicotine is addictive. He also asserts that Brown and Williamson top managers refused to drop coumarin, a lung-specific cancer-causing agent, in the face of clear-cut evidence about its harmful effects.[15] Subsequently, in March 1997, the Liggett Group broke ranks by conceding that tobacco is addictive and that the company had known this all along.[16]

Anonymous Responses Of Bosses and Workers

	Percentage of Managers Who Agree	Percentage of Workers Who Agree
Who works harder?		
Workers	43	60
Managers	31	18
Who is more ethical?		
Workers	37	37
Managers	13	9
Who is more greedy?		
Workers	10	15
Managers	61	53
Who is more trustworthy?		
Workers	32	40
Managers	14	14
Who takes credit for Another's work?		
Workers	18	23
Managers	50	58
Who cares most?		
Workers	26	41
Managers	29	24

<u>Source</u>: An anonymous survey of a random sample of 2000 adult Americans reported in James Patterson and Peter Kim, <u>The Day America Told The Truth</u>. New York: Prentice-Hall Press, 1991, page 149.

Presumably, the role of labor leaders is to champion the welfare of workers, not exploit them. Yet, Tony Bouza reports that some 400 Teamster officials had been ousted by 1995 due to charges of corruption, and that 50 locals and one joint council had been put under RICO (Racketeer Influenced and Corrupt Organization Act) trusteeships. In addition, federal authorities had listed three other national unions as being controlled by mobsters: the International Longshoreman's Association; the Hotel, Restaurant Employees, and Bartenders International; and the Laborers International Union of North America.[17]

Equally discouraging are changes in the aspirations of our future leaders. Eighty percent of the university students polled during the 1960's indicated that "developing a meaningful philosophy of life" and "doing something good for society" were their most important objectives. By the 1980's, nearly 80 percent had shifted their top priorities to "making money" and "being successful."[18] And by 1989, a poll of 1093 high school seniors revealed that some 66 percent admitted that they would lie to achieve a business objective, 67 percent indicated that they would pad their business-expense reports, and 59 percent said "yes" or "maybe" to facing six months probation for making 10 million dollars on an illegal deal.[19]

"I WANT YOU TO KNOW THAT I THINK GREED IS HEALTHY.
YOU CAN BE GREEDY AND FEEL GOOD ABOUT YOURSELF."

(Excerpt from Ivan Boesky's University of California commencement address before he received a three-year prison term for inside trading)

Source: Harvey Bunke, "Should We Teach Business Ethics?" Business Horizons, July/August 1988, page 5.

Questionable Payoffs Abroad: A 1976 report of the Securities and Exchange Commission indicates that over 400 corporations, including 117 of the top Fortune 500 companies, admitted to making more than 300 million dollars of payments abroad between 1974 and 1976 that were either questionable or illegal. For example, the prime minister of Japan was forced to resign in 1974 due to an alleged payoff from Lockheed. And the company admitted in 1975 to having paid some $22 million to foreign officials and politicians over the preceding five years.[20]

Reactions to these developments prompted passage of the Foreign Corrupt Practices Act of 1977. It outlaws the bribing of public officials to gain business advantage, but permits the making of "grease payments" - commonly required in many cultures - to expedite the performance of routine functions, such as the processing of paperwork and the provision of various public services. Presumably, many governments pay such functionaries marginal wages in anticipation of their "grease income," just as many U.S. restaurants pay very low wages to waiters and waitresses in anticipation of their income from tips.

In addition, as Hoffman and Moore point out, many foreign nationals have a Non-Western view of bribe-taking due to their felt grievances:

"The Europeans and North Americans have been taking advantage of us for decades, even centuries. The multi-nationals establish a joint venture and then strip the local company bare through transfer pricing, management fees, and royalties based on a percentage of sales rather than profits. They have no interest in the profitability of the company or its long-term development."[21]

These practices, on both the domestic and international scene, largely reflect the values of top managers, because they are the ones who play the most important role in the development and maintenance of organizational cultures. But such practices are not the inevitable product of a democratic and enterprise-oriented culture. Consider, for example, the following information about the Australia of the 1970's:

Do Australians Need A Lesson In Greed?

Bernard Sloan, copy chief of a New York advertising firm, encountered the following surprises while living in Australia:

* The bank did not return his canceled checks; a bank teller explained that his check stubs would serve as evidence of expenditures for tax purposes.

* He was not required to pay a deposit on returnable bottles; Aussies return them without monetary reward.

* Prices for soft drinks and meat pies were the same in a stadium as in a street shop.

* Packaged goods were sold in containers of uniform size and shape. A company executive asked him: "If it isn't a saving, how can you imply it is?"

* Doctors' fees were so low that they lived no better than other college-educated professionals.

* Union workers declined the job of digging an underground parking lot because it would destroy an ancient tree.

Source: Bernard Sloan, The Gainesville Sun, Gainesville, Florida, June 18, 1979, page 4A.

Attempts To Justify Different Standards For Business: Competitive business is a tough and demanding arena. When our competitors fail to "play by the rules" - or have entirely different rules of which we do not approve - can we afford to be ethically different or more demanding? Some even argue that the behavior of individuals in the business setting should not be

197

judged on the same basis as everyday behavior. Here are four attempts to explain why:

The Doctrine of Laissez Faire: Adam Smith, in <u>The Wealth of Nations</u>, published in 1776, provides a justification for self-centeredness in business, by arguing that the unashamed pursuit of self-interest - with minimal regulatory interference by government (the Doctrine of Laissez Faire) - is the economic mainspring of men and the basis for the greatest social good. But this is as far as many go in referring to Smith. They forget, or omit, the fact that he was quite aware of limitations to the doctrine, due to the various conditions he observed about him: irresponsible competitive practices, inhumane wages, the abuse of children, and the demeaning of people in the workplace. For example:

> Smith observes that the worker who does highly repetitive tasks and has no opportunity to engage in problem solving does so "at the expense of his intellectual, social, and martial virtues...
>
> "(that) this is the state into which the labouring poor, that is, the great body of the people must necessarily fall, unless government takes some pains to prevent it."[22]

And he warns that:

> "The proposal of any new law or regulation of commerce which comes from (the dealers) ought always to be listened to with great precaution, and ought never to be adopted till after having been long and carefully examined...(for) It comes from an order of men, whose interest is never exactly the same with that of the public, who have generally an interest to deceive and even to oppress the public, and who accordingly have, upon many occasions, both deceived and oppressed it."[23]

It is a significant fact that by 1800, when the Industrial Revolution began to pick up steam, Smith's qualifying reservations received little attention from the new crop of "laissez-faire" economists. They asserted that support of unregulated competition was the only way to avoid starvation for a rapidly expanding population. True, they conceded, the conditions for many working people were deplorable, but conditions would get even worse if government interfered. One simply could not apply high personal standards of social responsibility to the business arena. Regrettably, these pronouncements were accepted without question by many sincere "non-experts."

Milton Friedman, a modern proponent of laissez faire, asserts that:

> "there is one and only one social responsibility of business - to use its resources and engage in activities designed to increase its profits so long as it stays within the rules of the game, which is to say, engages in open and free competition without deception and fraud...

> "In an ideal free market resting on private property, no individual can coerce any other, all cooperation is voluntary, all parties to such cooperation benefit or they need not participate. There are no shared values, no 'social responsibilities' in any sense other than the shared values and responsibilities of individuals."[24]

But how many of Friedman's "ideal free markets" have ever existed? And is it reasonable to expect that unrestrained self-serving behavior today is less destructive than it was in Smith's time, or in the less-regulated earlier history of our country? In fact, aren't many of the ethical breaches that occur today due to too-much, short-term competition, rather than too little? In the short run, one can reap unwarranted profits by shifting from good to shoddy products and services, by making unwarranted price reductions that preclude the company's future viability, by exploiting employees in a buyer's labor market, and by getting out before one can be held financially accountable.

Moffett and Friedland provide an interesting update on the potential problems of inadequately regulated free enterprise:

"In Latin America's rollicking era of free-market economics and anything-goes ethics, scandal is one thing that comes cheap...

"It had long been an accepted article of faith that free-market economics, combined with greater democratization, would make the region's business and government activities more transparent. Instead, corruption may be more prevalent than ever. It is just that the players have changed, from bureaucrats and military dictators to a new class of closely allied entrepreneurs and politicians."[25]

Arthur Okun, Distinguished Economist

"...The market needs a place, and the market needs to be kept in its place...The tyranny of the dollar yard stick...given the chance...would sweep all other values, and establish a vending-machine society."

Source: Inequality and Efficiency, Washington, D.C.: Brookings Institution, 1975, page 119.

Friedman stresses an unyielding focus on making profit, legally. But at what cost to society? Legal behavior is not synonymous with ethical behavior. For example, should a business be permitted to handicap the futures of employees, customers, communities - and even our nation's security - in the service of short-term greed? Is it reasonable for us to expect business to enhance our quality-of-life, rather than debase it, if our only standard is: "Don't break the law"?

Would Friedman have agreed with President Hoover's position in 1932 - during the most severe economic depression in our history - that relatively little should be done by the government in the form of direct aid; that we would have to be

200

patient and let our unfettered system work its will until better times came along? Yet, 25 percent of the labor force was unemployed, there were no unemployment benefits, no social-security benefits, no food stamps, and millions in personal savings were lost in uninsured bank accounts. In addition, thousands of deserving farmers and homeowners were thrown into the street as the result of automatic foreclosures on their property.

Fortunately, Franklin Roosevelt, Hoover's successor, was not willing to simply sit back and let the system work its will. He and his top administrators laid the groundwork for many safeguards that we value and take for granted today, such as:

> Social security,
>
> minimum-wages,
>
> unemployment compensation,
>
> insured bank accounts,
>
> child labor, environmental, industrial accident, and working conditions regulations,
>
> constraints upon unfair competitive practices,
>
> and creation of the Securities and Exchange Commission to curb the unethical manipulations of many Wall-street operators.

From F.D.R.'s Second Inaugural Address, 1937

"The test of our progress is not whether we add more to the abundance of those who have much, it is whether we provide enough for those who have too little."

Source: Reported by Constance Bridges in Great Thoughts Of Great Americans. New York: Thomas Y. Crowell Company, 1951, page 247.

At the time, many big-business leaders, and other wealthy people, detested Roosevelt and labeled him a "traitor to his class." We can only wonder how many today - in their heart of hearts - would strongly reject these constructive modifications to our free-enterprise system. To do so, they would have to be blind or indifferent to the incidence of ruthlessly executed downsizings; the savings and loan debacle; the hypocritical support of corporate welfare in the face of denouncements of rank-and-file welfare; the open buying of political influence for personal gain; the exorbitant, unearned compensation of many CEOs; and the attempts to raid pension funds and dodge health, safety, and environmental regulations. Fortunately, as we will see, a promising basis for the transformation of heartless capitalism is the fact that the empowerment of lower-level personnel - coupled with higher-level ethical leadership - make modern companies *even more competitive*.

Social Darwinism: Around 1900, Herbert Spencer argued for a "no-holds-barred" philosophy of personal striving by invoking Darwin's "survival of the fittest" doctrine. He argued that the business arena is analogous to Darwin's jungle. Government should not intrude into natural processes. Just as animals in the jungle submit to the "survival of the fittest," we should let businesses fight it out. The best ones will win, and we will have stronger institutions as a result.

Key terms here are "fittest" and "stronger institutions." What do they mean: That might makes right? That the physically weak should be fair game for the morally weak? That quantity of life is more important than quality of life? That trust, harmony, and peace are less desirable than deceit, manipulation, and warfare? F. Neil Brady observes that societies succeed to the extent that they transcend animal-like behavior; not to the extent that they regress toward it.[26]

"The trouble with the rat race is that even if you win, you're still a rat."

Source: Attributed to Lily Tomlin by Donald Kanter and Philip Mirvis in The Cynical Americans. San Francisco: Jossey-Bass, 1989, page 118.

The Game Analogy: Another recent development is the emergence of the "game analogy": the idea that competitive business, like various sports, has its own special rules and requirements that are necessarily different from the rules of everyday, non-business living. We have popular books on "getting ahead in business" that often draw upon the lessons of poker, football, and other games. F.N. Brady, building upon the analyses of Carr, Kennedy, and Jackall,[27] points to the relevant characteristics of football, since it appears to be the game that most managers like to identify with:

> The rules permit behaviors that are generally unacceptable in a broader social context: behaviors similar to, but just short of open fighting.

> It is acceptable to fool or "work" the referees (enforcers of the law). There is no violation unless one is caught. An offending player is not expected to volunteer his guilt. There is no implication associated with doing this beyond success or failure. In fact, successful deception is often grudgingly admired by those not as adroit.

> Violations do not accumulate from one game to the next. One can exploit the present situation and not be accountable for the damage done at some future time.[28]

If one is guided by the game analogy, then lying and deception can cease to exist as antisocial behaviors in their own right. As one manager puts it: "We lie all the time, but if everyone knows that we're lying, is a lie really a lie?"[29]   The problem with this, of course, is that the "spectators" - employees, suppliers, customers, citizens, community officials, public enforcement officers, and generations to come - are not given a choice about playing a particular game.   Certainly, these spectators are *not* encouraged to believe that those "on the field" are untrustworthy, and they often suffer from consequences of the "playing" that go far beyond the win-loss records of the executive "teams" involved. In addition, we should observe that, more often than not, employees and other "spectators" tend to be alienated rather than entertained by the "game." The close kinship between the game analogy and Social Darwinism is obvious.

Jackall states that those who adopt this approach tend to turn "ethics into etiquette, values into tastes, personal responsibility into an adroitness at public relations, and notions of truth into credibility." He concludes that top-management proponents of the game analogy - given their pivotal institutional role in our time - help to create a society "where morality becomes indistinguishable from the quest for one's own survival and advantage."[30]   And Brady adds that "Our general distaste for game-analogy business behavior arises from more than an incompatibility with ethical theory; we *feel* the moral distance as well."[31]

Crafty (?) and Cruel

According to <u>Time</u>, Continental Can employed a secret computer program called BELL (reverse acronym for Let's Limit Employee Benefits) during the 1970's to avoid pension costs by laying off employees just before they became vested in the company's retirement plan.   However, the company was thwarted by a United Steel Workers class-action-suit settlement in early 1991 that forced it to pay $415 million to some 3000 people.

<u>Source</u>: <u>Time</u>, January 14, 1991, page 45.

Today, many companies can save a bundle by switching into Cash-Balance or Pension Equity pension plans, but their older employees can end up with their pensions reduced by more than 50 percent - so far, legally! For example, Ellen Schultz reports that Stephen Langlie retired from the Onan Corporation after 37 years with a pension of $424. per month, rather than the $1000 per month he calculates he would have received under his pre-conversion plan.

Source: Ellen Schultz, "Pension Protester: Fired For Complaining?" The Wall Street Journal, February 11, 1999, page C27.

Department Of Labor Links Big-Name Retailers To Sweatshops

Retailers to Secretary of Labor: "You had no *right* to tarnish our image like that."

"We had no way of knowing what was happening..."

"It's not *our* responsibility to crack down on sweatshops. It's *your* responsibility."

Source: Robert Reich, former Secretary of Labor, Locked In The Cabinet. New York: Alfred Knopf, 1997, page 269.

Cost/Benefit Analysis: Lastly, cost/benefit analysis - determining the "costs" of a particular action against its "gains" - is a widely used approach today for business decision-making. It has evolved from a formulation presented in 1789 by Jeremy Bentham in his book, An Introduction to the Principles of Morals and Legislation, in which he elaborates upon the pursuit of self-interest with his doctrine of "hedonistic utilitarianism." This entails the idea that actions should be determined by the twin goals of preventing pain and enhancing pleasure. Therefore, the purpose of all legislation should be the greatest happiness of the greatest number.

Among notable critics of this narrow formulation was John Stuart Mill. In his book, Utilitarianism (1861), he questions if happiness is simply the pursuit of pleasure and the avoidance of pain. If so, what about the higher emotions and demands associated with friendship, love, and honor? Should other people be nothing more than means to our selfish ends? Does it not demean cherished values - like the concept of liberty - to attempt to value them in terms of money? And what time frame are we to operate in - the virtues of remaining faithful to one's self and of discharging one's obligations are often associated with short-term pain or self-denial.

Though modern cost/benefit analysis is an important tool of decision making - when it reflects the interests of all affected parties - it cannot suffice ethically as the *only* tool. It is simply not up to the task of resolving such issues as the legalization of hard drugs, the betrayal of one's family or professional obligations, the adequate conservation of our planet, or the justification of slave labor. And its limitations for business decision making are made quite clear by Mark Dowie in his report on the tragedies caused by the 1971 Ford Pinto:[32]

> After assembly-line tooling had been completed, Ford discovered through pre-production tests that the Pinto's fuel system was quite vulnerable to rear-end crashes. Though Ford had the patent on a much safer system, top management decided that an additional $11 per car was not cost effective for society; nor, alternatively, was it considered cost effective to spend $5.08 per car to gain significant safety improvement through the installation of a rubber bladder in the gas tank. And, apparently, Ford thought that the idea of giving consumers the option of paying more for one of these features probably wouldn't pass the cost/benefit

test, due to the negative impact (cost) of a possibly diminished public image.

The company released the following cost/benefit analysis to justify an estimated loss of 500 lives: The benefits section estimated the value of 180 fewer burn deaths at $200,000 per death ($10,000 of this representing "pain and suffering"), the value of 180 fewer serious burn cases at $67,000 per case, and the value of 2100 fewer burned vehicles at $700 each. Total estimated "benefit" to the company: $49.5 million. But the cost of gaining this benefit (avoiding the losses) was far more: $11 per vehicle for 12.5 million vehicles = $137 million. However, the benefits calculations apparently omitted an estimate of the added money that would have to be spent on insurance premium increases and productivity losses, as well as the millions that would be required to settle damage suits out of court, as well as an estimate of the large lobbying costs that were subsequently incurred to buy an eight-year delay in the establishment of federal mandatory rear-impact standards.

Dowie quotes Dr. Leslie Ball, retired safety chief for the NASA manned space program, as asserting that "The release to production of the Pinto was the most reprehensible decision in the history of American engineering." And he quotes Byron Bloch, another safety expert who studied the case in depth, as saying that "Ford made an extremely irresponsible decision when they placed such a weak tank in such a ridiculous location in such a soft rear end. It's almost designed to blow up - premeditated."[33]

However, Ford was not the only company. According to Milo Geyelin, as early as 1971, rear-end-collision fuel fires had become a problem for General Motors. An engineering analyst had predicted that there would be some 60 fire-related suits over the next five years that would cost the company some $500,000 each. Consequently, GM began working on rear-end, safety-related refinements. But then the company suspended work on the project while awaiting final word on what federal regulators would require - advising GM engineers that any improvements beyond the minimum requirements would have to be justified by cost/benefit analysis.

Geyelin reports that, in a later court case, many jurors were amazed to learn that a 1979 Chevrolet Malibu had a more vulnerable fuel-tank location than the preceding model. In fact, it had been placed nine inches closer to the rear bumper than in the older model, and six inches closer than a 1969 GM design directive had claimed was safe! In addition, a tank-protection brace across the frame of the older model had been omitted in the newer one. General Motors had to pay $1.2 billion in one case and millions per case in others. As of September, 1999 there were still some 100 fuel-system-fire cases pending, and a judge blasted the company for "Conduct rising to the level of obstruction of justice" for its efforts to suppress damaging internal documents.[34]

An even more constrained application of cost/benefit analysis in practice is provided by the case of U.S. Steel. According to a 1983 California Newsreel, the company requested tax concessions in order to generate funds with which to upgrade its obsolete plants and equipment, so that it could maintain its competitive position in making steel. But, after appreciable amounts of money had accumulated, it failed to honor this implied commitment to invest in future steel production, and used the money for diversification into more profitable products and services. This prompted Ron Welch, President of Steelworkers' Local 1397, to observe that "We are still the most profitable steel industry in the world...we say they have a moral responsibility to the goddamn workers."[35]

In response to this type of criticism, David Roderick, Chairman of U.S. Steel, explained that "Many people don't fully appreciate that the primary role and duty of management really is to make money..."[36] But in what time frame? And with whose capital? And at what cost to society? Taxpayers had subsidized

208

the company to avoid slamming the door, economically, on many steelworker communities. Needless to say, the costs of placing the communities on welfare, both monetarily and psychologically, are difficult to calculate.

The idea of making decisions solely on the basis of their legality, and/or the results of cost/benefit analyses, appeals to those who argue that corporations can not, and should not, be held morally responsible in a broader sense of the term. They argue that corporate personnel are only agents of the stockholders who seek nothing other than the maximization of profits and the protection of their property. If this seems morally contemptible, they conclude, blame the system, not the hapless agents.

Yet, it is more the rule than the exception that, in practice, top managers - rather than stockholders - appoint and control the board of directors - the only organizational agency to which they are accountable.[37] This is clearly implied by the fact, pointed out earlier, that, typically, the pay of chief executive officers is unrelated to corporate performance. And isn't it strange how many dutiful "agents" spend so much effort and corporate money to block the solicitation and expression of the preferences of their "principals," the stockholders? For example, a coalition of public-interest groups obtained more than twice the number of proxy votes needed to seat a new director of their choice, but top management succeeded in dissuading (or confusing) enough of them to defeat the move. It did so by employing follow-up proxy solicitations - both a second and a third time - at considerable expense to the company.[38]

Some top managers seem to forget that formal managerial authority in the private sector is not God-given. It derives from the rights of contract and private property that are conferred by society. And society wants these rights, as it does any other rights, to be exercised in the interest of society. The public may not be aware of the complexities of ethical decision making in organizational settings, but it has become more definite about what it does not want: business behavior based upon only one of the four approaches discussed above.

Conclusion: Our experience with free enterprise has demonstrated a need to supplement the restraining effects of the market with specific regulations and oversight to:

Provide for those who cannot provide for themselves;

safeguard the health, safety, and individual rights of employees;

discourage collusion against consumer and industry interests;

prevent deceit in advertising, the mislabeling or adulteration of products, the misuse of pension funds, and the exploitative manipulation of stock; and

protect our environment.

<u>Workable Programs Are Attainable</u>: Despite conflicting claims on behavior, the "hardball" nature of much business competition, and the diversity of approaches we've just examined, it is quite possible to fashion and successfully implement a positive code of business ethics for domestic operations in America and, to a lesser degree, for operations in different cultures.

A boost to such efforts was provided by the release in 1991 by the United States Sentencing Commission (USSC) of guidelines for punishing organizations for illegal behavior and, particularly, by the provision for substantial reductions in penalties for those companies that have taken special, formal steps to control the behavior of their personnel. According to Weaver, Trevino, and Cochran, as of 1998, 51 percent of large, U.S. companies had ethical "hot lines" for reporting ethical concerns, and 30 percent had ethical/legal compliance offices. In addition, ethics officers had established their own professional association.[39] Robert Reich, a former Secretary of Labor, suggests a lowering of the income tax for those companies that meet certain minimum criteria in discharging their responsibilities toward employees and communities - while raising the tax for those who do not.[40]

Within An Organization: A successful code can be established and implemented within a given organization:

When the values are well-established and consistently supported by top managers of integrity, and

the factors of organizational selection and self-selection tend to attract and hold only those people who have - or are able to adopt - a congruent ethical orientation.

In addition, studies involving mutual trust and genuine influence sharing between labor and management suggest that a given organization can afford, financially, to be ethically different or more demanding in America. Study results show that quality-of-work-life improvements in various types of companies have been accompanied by significant gains in quality and productivity.* But these studies provide only indirect evidence: various other non-ethical factors - such as improved problem solving and teamwork - were usually involved also.

---

*Several of these studies are presented in Chapter 1 of my book, Effective Group Problem Solving (San Francisco: Jossey-Bass, 1987). Another is presented by Fasolo & Davis-LaMastro in the Journal Of Applied Psychology, 1990 (pp. 51-59); and others are presented in Teamwork: Joint Labor-Management Programs In America, edited by Jerome Rosow (New York: Pergamon Press, 1986). David Bollier reports the findings of a more recent study of 25 firms (Aiming Higher:25 Stories Of How Companies Prosper By Combining Sound Management And Social Vision. New York: AMACOM, 1996); and Edward Lawler presents additional case material, and emphasizes ethical aspects, in High Involvement Management (San Francisco: Jossey-Bass, 1986).

However, we do have more direct evidence. The supermarket-and-drugstore-chain employees of five high-cost stores - in comparison with the employees of five low-cost stores - reported organizational climates that were significantly lower in trust, truthfulness, integrity, and justice.

In addition, the poor-climate stores had higher net costs with regard to employee sickness and accident compensation claims.[41] And Sears Roebuck - based upon the findings of an 800-store study - found that employee attitudes about workload, supervisory treatment, and related matters had a significant effect upon employee turnover, customer satisfaction, and revenues: when attitudes on 10 factors improved by five percent, revenue went up one-half percent.[42]

We also have the example from 1982 of the Johnson and Johnson Tylenol case. Seven people in the Chicago area were killed by capsules that had been deliberately laced with cyanide. Though the company was never implicated in the poisoning, it immediately withdrew all Tylenol capsules from the U.S. market (at an estimated cost of $100 million) rather than attempt to disclaim any responsibility or focus its energies upon legal defenses. At the same time, the company undertook a comprehensive communications program with its employees and the pharmaceutical and medical communities. As a result, Johnson and Johnson was perceived as putting consumer welfare ahead of conserving profits. Its image was enhanced rather than tarnished, and the long-term effect was financial success rather than loss.[43]

Among Different Organizations: A significant contribution toward fashioning a positive code of ethics for organizations has been made by the American Bar Association and other sponsors: They have formulated some 300 uniform acts since 1914, and developed the Uniform Commercial Code in 1952. All states have adopted parts of the Uniform Commercial Code and many of the 300 uniform acts. Though the primary emphasis in all of these is upon the promulgation of technical definitions and rules, ethical aspects are presented both implicitly and explicitly. This

212

is illustrated by the following excerpts from the Uniform Commercial Code:

"The remedies provided by this act shall be liberally administered to the end that the aggrieved party may be put in as good a position as if the other party had fully performed..." (Section 1-106)

"'Agreement' means the bargain of the parties in fact as found in their language or by implication from other circumstances including course of dealing or usage of trade or course of performance as provided in this Act." (Section 1-201(3))

"'Buyer in ordinary course of business' means a person who in good faith and without knowledge that the sale to him is in violation of the ownership rights or security interest of a third party in the goods buys in ordinary course from a person in the business of selling goods of that kind but does not include a pawnbroker." (Section 1-201(9))

"If the court as a matter of law finds the contract or any clause of the contract to have been unconscionable at the time it was made the court may refuse to enforce the contract, or it may enforce the remainder of the contract without the unconscionable clause, or it may so limit the application of any unconscionable clause as to avoid any unconscionable result." (Section 2-302)

"When it is claimed or appears to the court that the contract or any clause thereof may be unconscionable the parties shall be afforded a reasonable opportunity to present evidence as to its commercial setting, purpose and effect to aid the court in making the determination." (Section 2-302(2))

"Unless excluded or modified, a warranty that the goods shall be merchantable is implied in a contract for their sale if the seller is a merchant with respect to goods of that kind." (Section 2-314)

And the court-decision-based comments on Section 2-314:

"If seller states that goods are 'guaranteed'... [This] ...has effect of limiting effect of fine-print disclaimer clauses where their effect would be inconsistent with large-print assertions of 'guarantee.'"

"...good faith is expressly defined as including in the case of a merchant observance of reasonable commercial standards of fair dealing in the trade."[44]

Listed below are some sample titles from the some 300 uniform codes that states can consider for adoption:

Adoption Act of 1994[45]
Interstate Family Support Act of 1996[46]
Health Care Consent Act[47]
Child Custody Jurisdiction Act[48]
Consumer Credit Code of 1974[49]
Deceptive Trade Practices Act of 1966[50]
Employment Termination Act of 1991[51]
Premarital Agreement Act[52]
Reciprocal Enforcement of Support Act of 1968[53]
Rights of the Terminally Ill Act of 1989[54]
Model Penal Code[55]
Crime Victims Reparations Act[56]

For a complete directory, see <u>Uniform Laws Annotated</u>. St. Paul, MN: West Publishing Company, 1995.

In addition to these uniform codes, many trade and professional associations have formulated their own codes, and have established means for enforcing them. It seems reasonable to assume that the use of the procedures for encouraging truthfulness and full disclosure in group problem solving (presented in Chapter 6) and the Search Conference (presented at the end of this chapter) with representatives from various firms, industries, and non-profit organizations would facilitate the further development of inter-organizational codes.

Across Cultures: Various cultures have certain strongly held values that can differ dramatically. This is illustrated by data collected in 40 countries from the employees of subsidiaries of a large multinational company. Each statement in the accompanying box was found to represent the dominant sentiment of the employees of one or more of the countries. Conflicting statements are placed opposite each other to dramatize the extent of cross-cultural differences.

Conflicting Values Across Cultures

The use of power should be legitimate	The legitimacy of power is irrelevant
All should have equal rights	Power-holders are entitled to privileges
Time is free	Time is money
The same value standards should apply to all	Value standards may differ for in-groups and out-groups
One's opinions should be determined by one's clans and organizations	Everyone has a right to a private life and opinion
One's involvement with organizations is moral	One's involvement with organizations is calculative
There should be equality between the sexes	Men should dominate in society
Interdependence is the ideal	Independence is the ideal
Conflict and competition can be constructive	Conflict and competition should be avoided
Deviant persons and ideas are not necessarily dangerous	Deviant persons and ideas are dangerous
Identity is based in the social system	Identity is based in the individual

Source: Based upon Gert Hofstede, "Motivation, Leadership, and Organization: Do American Theories Apply Abroad?" Organizational Dynamics, Summer 1980, pages 42-63, with permission from Elsevier Science.

Given these culturally-based differences, reports about varying behaviors across cultures are not surprising:

For a large group of Chinese employees, Lindsay and Dempsey found that participation in decision making meant having each person present a mini-speech, the complete absence of challenge or discussion, and the pronouncement of a decision by the leader.

They also observed that group members exhibited a strong need to avoid disagreement with the leader as well as with each other. In other words, to be "untruthful" in this context.[57]

*   *   *

Dorfman and Howell report that, in Mexico, a male manager who solicits inputs from subordinates is likely to be viewed as being weak. He is supposed to be a strong, unilateral decision maker.[58]

*   *   *

Traditionally, the Japanese have seen individuality and independence as evidence of immaturity, and autonomy as the freedom to comply with one's obligations.

They have regarded the logic of decisions as being less important than congruence with group sentiment; consequently, the "why" of the Westerner is threatening and irritating. Their ideal has been to jump into the group without leaving a trace.

They feel that one must give indiscriminate devotion to one's group members, for it is immature and divisive to like any given member more than another.

Historically, there was no Japanese counterpart for a Western judicial system, nor for the Western concept of individual rights, though there were many ways of expressing the ideals of duty, sacrifice, and obligation.

The traditional Japanese employer had less freedom to do as he pleased with employees than the early American employer. He was viewed somewhat as a father whom society would not let disown or unduly abuse his children.[59]

*   *   *

A majority of people in other parts of the world view what we regard as "bribery" and "conflict of interests" as being quite legitimate.

Given the evidence presented above, it seems unlikely that we will be able to obtain agreement about the usefulness of many business values and behaviors from representative spokespersons of diverse cultures. However, as we will see below, penalties for "sticking to one's ethical guns" in international operations are not as evident as opponents to the regulation of our foreign business practices would have us believe.

<u>What Needs To Be Done</u>: There are many measures that will nurture more ethical behavior at home, as well as help us to be both competitive and ethical (by our standards) abroad:

Reform Boards of Directors: There is agreement among many experts that most boards that do not have a founder or majority stockholder as chairman fail to function as they are supposed to. They charge that board members, typically, serve at the pleasure of the chief executive officer, and rarely arrange for an adequate check upon her or his performance or account of events. Therefore, they fail to relate the CEO's compensation to his or her contribution in any meaningful way, and they fail to detect and respond to serious warning signals in time.[60] In response to such complaints, the Securities and Exchange Commission started requiring U.S. businesses in 1993 to provide more complete top-executive-compensation information to their stockholders, including detailed explanations about pay practices from board compensation committees.

Critics also assert that it is against the public interest for the same person to serve on the boards of competing companies, and that this practice often spreads that person's time and talents too thin. In addition, they point to the further undercutting of potential for control when subordinates of the CEO serve as "inside" members. In fact, two studies have shown a significant relationship between the proportion of "outsiders" on a board and the reduction in the number of shareholder suits.[61] In view of such findings, a number of large companies have moved in the direction of weakening insider control. A 1990 study by the Investor Responsibility Center of some 800 large companies shows that 16 percent of them had barred inside members from serving on committees to nominate new board candidates. And, subsequently, a study in 1992 by Directorship magazine indicates that the number proscribing this practice had increased to 30 percent.[62]

Some people defend the appointment of inside members on the grounds that intimate knowledge of the business must be brought to the boardroom, and that few outside members have either the background needed, or the time, to satisfy this requirement. Additionally, they argue that the CEO must have board members with whom she or he can work effectively. Critics reply that properly qualified, half-time or full-time outside board members are the answer; that the concept of qualifications should be broadened to include ethical credentials, and that all members should be provided with full access to relevant data for auditing purposes. Also, they think that outside board members will learn what they need to know about the business through presentation and questioning sessions with non-voting top managers. And - of the greatest importance - outsiders will be able to check upon the strategic direction of the organization, rather than being captive to the unilateral direction of the CEO.

As for compatibility with the CEO, critics observe that it should be the other way around - the CEO should be compatible with the board's values and strategic direction or he or she should not be retained. And they add that it would be unrealistic to expect a board to operate as outlined above without giving it adequate legal and other staff personnel to assist it, along with greater compensation for the increased level of involvement that would be required.

A major barrier to this type of reform is the present "insiders' monopoly" on the nomination process. Some have suggested that any shareholder or shareholder group that represents at least one-thousandth of the voting stock (or comprises 100 or more individuals with no ties to the present board) should have the right to nominate up to three directors to stand for election. In addition, they would require that all nominees have equal opportunity to communicate their credentials and positions to the shareholders at company expense. And they feel that any faction that can muster ten percent of the total voting shares should be able to elect a director.[63]

Former GE Executive

"[GE's] directors were in every case selected by the officers...We had then, in effect, a huge economic state governed by non-elected, self-perpetuating officers and directors - the direct opposite of the democratic model."

Source: T. K. Quinn, Giant Business - Threat To Democracy. New York: Exposition Press, 1953, page 145.

Here are some additional proposals made by Nader, Green, and Seligman:

Prior to the cessation of local operations, boards should be required to oversee the preparation of "community impact statements" similar to the environmental impact statements presently required by environmental protection acts, to encourage consideration of this factor in decision making.

Upon a finding by three directors, or three percent of the shareholders, that a public health hazard exists, a corporate referendum should be held in the political jurisdiction affected by the health hazard. The affected citizens would decide by majority vote if the hazard is to continue in its present form.[64]

Harold Geneen, former chair and CEO of ITT Corporation, observes that directors tend to be more responsible overseers of an organization when they have a personal stake in it. Consequently, he suggests that directors be made more responsible through personal financial liability; say, for up to some multiple of their compensation.[65] And Christopher Stone of the USC Law School recommends provisions for the appointment of a "public director" in extreme cases of repeated delinquency.[66]

Following this line of thought, directors might be required to take a certain minimum amount of stock as part of their compensation and hold it for a minimum number of years. This is suggested by the fact that the Hay Consulting Group found that companies in which chief executives owned larger amounts of stock had typically provided greater returns to their stockholders.[67] And the results of a study conducted in 1999 suggest that those outside directors who own at least $100,000 of company stock will act more swiftly in removing weak management.[68]

Hopefully, more responsible directors would create more rational compensation systems for chief executive officers. According to Roger Lowenstein, several boards are already awarding stock options at prices above prevailing share prices, so that their CEOs gain only to the extent that their companies gain in the marketplace. Alternatively, Alfred Rappaport suggests that the price of options be indexed to the share-price gains of a company's competitors.[69]

Select The Right Leaders: The reforms discussed above are also designed to discourage the appointment, and maintenance, of unethical leaders. Hopefully, boards will require both internal and external candidates to satisfy certain ethical qualifications, in addition to the usual ones. There is no surer way to put the ethical integrity of an organization at risk than to leave this matter to chance. As Edgar Schein points out, among the most powerful mechanisms for the development and maintenance of an organizational culture are:

What leaders pay attention to, measure and control;

their reactions to critical incidents and crises;

their criteria for allocating rewards and status;

their criteria for recruitment, selection, promotion, retirement, and excommunication.[70]

Ethically Empower Lower-Level Personnel: Many non-perceptive managers are like the one in the cartoon who says "Give me your honest opinions, even if it costs you your job!" Such managers are likely to expect "real adults" to speak up publicly when they need to, and tend to construe silence as implying agreement. In the real world, however, few of us want to risk "self-destructing."

Since there is no simple ethical formula to apply across all complex organizational situations, top management should use a collaborative approach to hammer out realistic standards and guidelines. It can effectively involve other stakeholders - owners, employees, customers, community residents, and the public at large - by utilizing the guidelines presented in Chapter 6 to encourage truthfulness and full disclosure. In addition, the Search Conference (presented at the end of this chapter) can help to resolve many initial doubts and apparent obstacles through a process of non-defensive personal involvement. Not only will realistic involvement produce better codes of conduct, it will enhance understanding of the codes that are established, and improve individual commitment to them, and enforcement of them.

Two other steps that will strengthen the ethical resolve of lower-level personnel are:

Encouragement of legitimate "whistle blowing"-feedback from any level in the organization about ethical or legal violations that have received inadequate attention through the usual channels. A successful means for doing this is to provide and publicize a 24-hour, recorder-equipped "hotline" for anonymous calls.

Provision for effective, collaborative adjudication of the standards that are set.

The importance of adjudication cannot be overstressed. Despite the most honorable intentions of those at the top, there are always some below who will use their authority in an abusive manner. No one can be all-knowing and all-seeing. And what constitutes "fairness" varies with the perceptions of the participants and the complexities of the situation. A promising approach is the use of grievance mediation provided by a five-person, grievance-review panel (comprising three employee representatives and two management representatives). It communicates a genuine desire for fairness, and a high degree of trust, on the part of management.

And the approach is practical. Such panels have proven themselves at numerous General Electric facilities for more than 14 years. Leroy Brown of the employee-relations department at GE Appliance Park-East - where this approach was first used around 1982 - told me in a 1989 phone conversation that there had not been an instance in which the employee majority had abused its ability to outvote the management-panel members. And Ron Richardson, manager of human-resource programs in 1999, told me that this is still the case for the many facilities that now use the panels and fully believe in their effectiveness.

However, there are two key requirements for success: (1) employee volunteers who serve as panelists must take eight hours of training - on their own time - in the legal and ethical aspects of grievance handling, problem-solving techniques, and effective listening, and (2) each aggrieved person is allowed to choose the names of four panelist at random, and then put one name back.[71] The need for this type of collaboration is based upon a long-standing recognition of the negative effects of unchecked power. Aristotle wrote about this around 335 B.C., basing his evaluation upon his study of many forms of government. He observed that the unrestrained use of power corrupts reason; therefore, the rule of law must dominate the rule of men.[72]

"It is wiser to enthrone and follow principles
than it is to enthrone and follow people."

Source: Marilyn von Savant, <u>Parade Magazine</u>, March 10, 1996, page 8. Reprinted with permission from <u>Parade</u> and Marilyn von Savant, copyright (c) 1996.

Individual self-control and self-direction can be strengthened by the development and distribution of checklists such as the following:

> Whom could your action injure? In what ways?
> Do you plan to compensate those injured?
>
> Can you discuss the problem with those affected before you make the decision?
>
> Would it bother you for your boss, your CEO, your board, your spouse, your child, or society at large to know of your decision?
>
> Under what conditions would you allow exceptions to your position?[73]

There is no such thing as a perfect program for all time. Organizations are subject to never-ending dynamic processes that produce new demands and challenges. Yet, those who launch successful new innovations or programs are often the last to see any need for change or adjustment in their creations with the passage of time. Consequently, as a safeguard, top management should regularly take stock of the organization's standards and procedures for enforcement.

An effective means for doing this is to periodically solicit anonymously written and deposited contributions to encourage all levels of personnel to "tell it like it is." The question posed might be: "What keeps this organization from performing more ethically?" (See the detailed procedure for collecting and processing such inputs that was presented in Chapter 6 in the section on Encouraging Truthfulness and Full Disclosure in Group Problem Solving).

Use Communication, Modeling, and Discussion: It is not enough to collaboratively formulate an ethical code and make provisions for enforcing it. Employees come and go, and some are likely to remain unclear as to the implications of code language. One can often hear rationalizations, such as:

> Surely it isn't stealing to take some paper or pencils from the office for personal use at home? Anyway, wouldn't you have to get money for what you take to make it theft?

> Shouldn't the things we take be viewed as deserved fringe benefits that our employer can easily afford?

> If an employer steals from me via uncompensated overtime, what's wrong with me getting even? As a matter of fact, when it's alright to take from my employer, why is it wrong to overcharge the customers when we can?

Many employers are surprised to learn that what they regard as theft or improper conduct is not common knowledge among their employees, nor do they appreciate the important influence they have as positive (or negative) role models. Behavior standards must be formulated, actively presented, illustrated, and discussed - not once, but often. And desirable behavior must be consistently modeled by managers from the top down. Employees can become quite cynical about ethical pronouncements from "on high" when they witness the inappropriate use of company cars, planes, and expense accounts, and the distribution of excessive or unearned bonuses or other "perks."

In addition, regular training sessions are essential. Personnel at all levels need practice in applying the organization's ethical principles and guidelines. A good medium for such practice is the analysis of cases; especially, when case material is drawn from past organizational experience. In addition, role playing, aided by learning points and feedback, is quite helpful.

Another useful approach involves the exchange of anonymously contributed personal experiences. Thomas Dunfee, a business ethics researcher, reports the salutary effects of hearing individual accounts of those who have said "no" and have "survived," - often quite well - in the same organization. He points out that many subordinates submit to the unethical demands of a boss because they assume, erroneously, that resistance means certain self-destruction. However, some who have resisted claim to have received even greater respect, subsequently, from the very people who had propositioned them! It may be that many unscrupulous managers can obtain enough "self-selected" victims, that they do not have to risk exposure by punishing or further soliciting those who resist.[74]

Use The Principled Negotiations Approach in Bargaining: When we bargain with aggressive others, is it naive to assume that we can convert a hardball, "win-lose" game approach to something else? No, it is not-according to the results of research and development work done by the Harvard Negotiation Project. In addition to engaging in theory building and developing instructional materials, the project has experienced considerable success with its training programs and conflict clinics.

The rationale that underlies its work is presented in a 1983 best-selling book, <u>Getting To Yes</u>, by project members Roger Fisher and William Ury. In it, they present the detailed rules and procedures of "principled negotiations." It is a "win-win" approach that focuses upon the "interests" of the respective parties rather than their "positions," as is illustrated in the

226

accompanying box. It stresses the identification of options for mutual gain and means for strengthening mutual trust, as well as techniques for defusing and defending against "dirty-trick" attempts.

Focus Upon "Interests" Rather Than "Positions"

Positions

Jane: "I have a right to the last of the oranges you just took from the basket. You've had more of them this week than I."

Betty: "Don't make me laugh. You weren't even thinking about an orange until you saw me take it. No one kept you from eating more of them this week; you're just trying to make trouble."

Interests

Jane: "I can't wait to taste the delicious juice."

Betty: "I'd rather have something else to drink, I want the peeling so I can make some marmalade."

Source: This and accompanying comments based upon Getting To Yes by Roger Fisher, William Ury, and Bruce Patton. Copyright © 1981, 1991 by Roger Fisher and William Ury. Reprinted by permission of Houghton Mifflin Co. All rights reserved.

In the example above, Jane and Betty have conflicting "positions" (they both want the same orange) but complementary "interests": Jane only wants the non-peeling part of the orange to eat, and Betty only wants the peeling with which to make marmalade. Usually, we can find a number of mutually acceptable ways to accommodate interests; whereas, positions are more likely to be fixed and defended on a "win-lose" basis.

To defend against "dirty tricks," Fisher and Ury recommend that we first identify such tactics as are being used - get them out on the table - and then insist upon this as the first issue to be negotiated. For example, "If you insist upon misrepresenting the facts in the case - or in trying to intimidate me - is there any good reason why I shouldn't do the same with you?"

Downsize Intelligently: Earlier, we discussed the unexpected problems and poor profits that were associated with many "downsizings." Part of the problem results from the belief that resistance to change is just part of human nature, and you can't do anything about it. However, consider this question: Will most people resist an unexpected raise or desired promotion? Hardly. Actually, We only resist those changes that we perceive or experience as being threatening or inconveniencing.

How often have we seen or heard of a scenario like this: A manager exhorts his group to improve its innovativeness and productivity for the competitive well-being of the firm. After considerable improvement, he reaps a huge bonus and increased job security, while group members are praised for their great work and learn that many of them will no longer be needed! Layoffs occur, and the loyalty of the survivors goes out the window. They resent the generous bonuses given to those higher up, as they receive little compensation for the increased efforts required by increased work loads. In addition, they can't help but wonder how long it will be before the ax will fall again.

This is hardly the kind of environment that nurtures trust, creativity, and commitment. No wonder that downsizing often backfires. On the other hand, things can be quite different when an organization makes a genuine effort to assure that everyone affected will come out of a change better off than before or - at the minimum - at least as well off. The key lies in assuring employment security, not security in a specific job. This also helps to minimize anxiety about the unknown. For example, many years ago the Armour Automation Committee learned that, prior to a layoff in its Fort Worth plant, only three out of 1000 workers had exercised the "take-it-or-leave-it" option of moving to a company-job opening in another city. This, despite the fact that jobs in the Fort Worth area were hard to come by.

Fortunately, the company was receptive to the lesson this taught. Later, in Sioux City, it presented a significantly modified transfer program: To reduce the economic and personal-adjustment risks of going to a new town, each employee was given the option of returning to Sioux City any time within six months, at company expense, and without losing severance-pay rights. This approach was highly successful. The reduction of risk caused many to elect the option, and few asked to be returned.[75]

In addition, we have the example of what IBM did in the early 1980's with its installation of robotics:

> There was early communication with those affected about the benefits of the changes, how they would be made, and how each person would be affected (especially with regard to opportunities for improving or maintaining one's status).

> Retraining and job transfer programs were planned and publicized well in advance.

> Initial applications of robotics were made to the most hazardous and boring jobs.

> As far as possible, the new equipment was phased in during a plant growth mode to enhance the feasibility of employment security.[76]

When an organization does not have the in-house capability for accommodating all displaced personnel, it can form those who are willing into a support group, provide them with guidance, assist them with retraining, and carry them on the payroll - as long as they seek employment locally or elsewhere - with full assistance from the human-resource staff. The fact that they are employed at the time of application has a positive influence upon their self-esteem, as well as the reactions of prospective employers. In addition, such an upfront investment in money and effort has a strong, positive effect upon the employees who stay, the members of the community, and all future applicants. Companies have found that such an approach more than pays for itself in the long run.

Reduce The Conflict Between Job and Family Obligations: There are still organizations that take the position: "If you let family obligations interfere with an unqualified commitment to the organization, that's commendable...but we can't use you!" As with compassionless downsizing, this approach generates unnecessary stress and needlessly undermines genuine loyalty based upon mutual respect and accommodation. Lisa Miller tells us about several companies with a different approach:

> When employees at EDS have been on the road four days or more, their managers are encouraged to give them one or two days off to be with their families.

> Every weekend, Price Waterhouse flies its consultants home from wherever they are in the U.S..

> Traveling Hewlett-Packard executives can call an 800 number for help with family matters, including how to read to their children over the phone.

> For $5 per hour, the Atlanta office of Deloitte and Touche provides such concierge services as transporting family members, walking the dog, or watering the grass.[77]

And Laura Koss-Feder adds to the list:

> Shelley Cames, a quality consultant, felt it necessary to leave Hewlett-Packard in 1995 to care for her disabled mother who lived five hours away. However, the company accommodated her with a telecommuting arrangement, whereby she works one week per month from her regular office, and three weeks per month from the farm.

Mariott International maintains a 24-hour, toll-free hotline staffed by social workers, to provide employee assistance, advice, and referrals for almost any problem.

And CMP Media subsidizes a full-service, day-care center that permits a working mother to see a child, if needed, any time during the work day.[78]

And the payoff? Marriott International estimates that its hotline service saves the company some $4 million annually in reduced absenteeism and turnover. Hewlett-Packard estimates that such programs as telecommuting, flextime, and giving time off for volunteer work in K-12 school programs, have reduced staff turnover 25-33 percent below that of its competitors.[79]

Of course, perks, however appropriate, are never an adequate substitute for fair pay, when an employer can afford it. Sooner or later, such unfairness undermines trust and leaves employees with the conviction that they are "being had." However, we often lose sight of the motivating potential of the kinds of consideration mentioned above in situations where high pay and large bonuses are not within the discretion of an employer. For examples, think of conscientious and often heroic military personnel, law-enforcement officers, firefighters, teachers, and other public servants.

Use The Search Conference: Ideally, managers at all levels should put the welfare of the organization ahead of promoting the often-conflicting and self-serving interests of their own groups. However, when most group leaders are doing the latter, this ideal becomes an invitation to ridicule and self-destruction. The complying leader is perceived as a naive "traitor" to his or her own people. The Search Conference, developed by Fred Emery and Eric Trist, is a proven tool for realizing the ideal approach:

It provides specific procedures for a group of up to 35 to develop meaningful overall values and goals - along with compatible group goals, and it facilitates understanding and everyday cooperative behavior across different groups, organizational levels, and cultures.

More than 400 such conferences have been conducted in America, Australia, Canada, England, France, India, Holland, Honduras, New Zealand, Mexico, Norway, Turkey, and elsewhere.[80] Most of these have been successful because, as Russell Ackoff observes, "Awareness of consensus relative to ends usually brings about subsequent cooperation relative to means among those who would not otherwise be so inclined."[81]

The Search Conference

The underlying purpose of a Search Conference is to have participants *discover for themselves* common perceptions about the following issues (in the order presented):

(1) Relevant trends and concerns in the external environment that derive from the past and are likely to continue in the future, along with new concerns that are likely to develop in the next 5-15 years.

(2) The present state of the organization (or community), the origins of this state, and the projected future for the next 5-15 years (given the projected future of the external environment).

(3) The most desirable state for the organization (or community) in the next 5-15 years, in terms of such factors as basic activities; inter-unit relations; leadership style; organization structure, policies and procedures; relations with the larger community; or any other factors of interest to the participants - *without regard* to present internal and external constraints or projected trends.

(4) Present internal and external constraints that will have to be overcome - along with any strategic opportunities that will need to be exploited - to realize the ideal future state.

(5) The formation of various representative task groups to fashion action plans for submission to the entire group for debugging and refinement (since the purpose of the process through Issue 4 was to create participant openness and collaboration rather than finished solutions).

Upon the completion of each issue in small working groups, all participants meet as one to share and meld their outputs. This process is facilitated by having the output of each group displayed on wall-hung, flipchart pages and presented by a group representative.

After completing the first four issues, participants have a better understanding of their organization's (or community's) strengths, internal and external obstacles to change, and the fact that the future is not a "given"; that it can be constructively influenced. A complete Search Conference requires at least $2 \frac{1}{2}$ days, preferably in a "social island" setting away from distractions and competing demands. For more complete guidance, see The Search Conference by Emery and Purser. San Francisco: Jossey Bass, 1996.

Install Gainsharing: Gainsharing involves sharing with employees the fruits of productivity gains caused by them. When properly planned and implemented, it creates a kind of "win-win" partnership between management and labor that enhances mutual influence, trust, and commitment; yet, requires no money outlays by the employer. It has been used successfully by various types of large and small organizations, such as manufacturing firms, hospitals, restaurants, and stores. More than 2000 organizations now use it, and a 1992 survey found that human-resource managers mention it as the most important HR topic of the 1990's.[82]

There are three generic plans for gainsharing - the Scanlon Plan, the Rucker Plan, and Improshare. For all three, a basic formula is negotiated that incorporates a single standard (or multiple standards) of performance. In any month or quarter in which employees do better than standard, they get a bonus. In addition, they participate in planning, problem solving, and in making suggestions for improving operations. These activities comprise the most important aspect of gainsharing for creating and maintaining trust and commitment. Two excellent books provide detailed information for planning and implementing gainsharing: Gainsharing by Brian Graham-Moore and Timothy Ross. Washington, DC: The Bureau of National Affairs, 1990 (primarily for the technical aspects); and Gainsharing and Power: Lessons From Six Scanlon Plans by Denis Collins. Ithaca, NY: Cornell University Press, 1998 (primarily for behavioral and ethical aspects).

Adjust For International Operations: We should avoid overgeneralizations about adjusting to foreign realities. For example, critics say that the Foreign Corrupt Practices Act is an arrogant attempt to export U.S. morality and to enforce our laws in foreign jurisdictions. They argue that we are doing this at a particularly bad time, given the threatened loss of profits to U.S. stockholders and the loss of jobs to U.S. workers - not to mention our trade deficit. And they point out that other nations have failed to follow our lead in outlawing bribery abroad, and that members of the Organization of Economic Cooperation and Development have so far resisted our efforts to negotiate an agreement about acceptable business conduct.

However, there is evidence for challenging these criticisms. In 1980, our Foreign Service posts provided information about improper-payment activity in various countries and the presumed negative impact of the act upon our trade with them. John Graham found no clear-cut relationship between the two factors. In fact, he found bigger trade increases in some of the countries where we were supposed to be the most disadvantaged.[83] One might argue that this was due to widespread evasion of the act; however, the high level of industry complaints about it, and the fact that the Department of Justice undertook 83 investigations in the several years immediately following its passage, suggest otherwise.[84]

Kate Gillespie looked into post-FCPA scandals in the Middle East. She found that more host-country investigations had exposed non-U.S. multinational wrongdoing than had U.S. investigations, and that Asian and European expatriate managers faced increased likelihood of being sentenced to host-country prisons. "In the Middle East, alone," she observes, "numerous heads of state are scrambling to somehow deal with issues of corruption before revolutionary movements affect them. If multinational managers wish to remain cynical in the face of these evolving social changes, they may - but, in the meantime, they should be careful whom they bribe."[85]

Whatever the final resolution to the debate, it seems apparent that ethical firms can prosper in presumably hostile ethical environments. For example, Lane and Simpson surveyed executives and government officials about prospects for Canadian companies that wish to operate in developing countries without resorting to unethical practices. Many of their respondents stressed the presence of trustworthy people in these countries who know how to fight the system and are attracted by the prestige and informational access that association with a foreign company can provide. They observe, however, that most North American companies have been in too much of a hurry. Normally, time, effort, patience, and multiple visits are required to identify the right people, and to establish useful relationships with them. This is a long-term investment that can be quite rewarding.[86] As Ford Worthy notes: "blood" and "history" are the bonds that tie together many Asian families and extended families. "Westerners who link up with an Asian partner with the right family connections find doors opening that remain closed even to outsiders willing to pay off the doorman."[87]

Since increasing numbers of local regimes are beginning to appreciate what trustworthy firms can do for their economies and their political futures, they are moving toward the establishment of negotiating conditions that will attract and hold such firms. This, in turn, makes it likely that a climate more supportive of international anti-bribery agreements will emerge. Ethical firms should carefully monitor these trends and respond to opportunities when they arise. In pursuing this course, they are aided by the 1988 amendments to the Federal Corrupt Practices Act which charge our President with pursuing an anti-bribery agreement among OECD countries. Subsequently, after two years of negotiation, the first anti-bribery pact by the OECD was signed by 34 nations in 1999. It criminalizes bribes to government officials that are made outside of the home country, and disallows tax deductions for such payments.[88]

As opportunities for further collaboration develop, the Principled Negotiation Approach and the Search Conference may prove to be particularly useful in helping to bridge ethical differences. With regard to the role of top managers, there are various ways they can communicate and reinforce their commitment to ethical conduct abroad:

> They can initiate the collaborative development, dissemination, and enforcement of ethical standards for their foreign operations, as did the Caterpillar Tractor Company with its detailed <u>Code of Worldwide Business Conduct</u> (presented below).

> They can require selectees for foreign assignment to commit in writing that they will uphold the code, and will satisfy other formally developed ethical qualifications.

> They can regularly audit their foreign operations for compliance with ethical standards. For example, Caterpillar's code ends with the following statement:

> > "Before the close of each year, the company's General Counsel will prepare an appropriate listing of senior company managers... Those on the list will be required to complete a memorandum, by year-end: (1) affirming knowledge and understanding of the code; and, (2) reporting events or activities which might cause

236

an impartial observer to conclude that the code hasn't been followed. These reports should be sent directly to the General Counsel. Reports will be treated in confidence."[89]

They can conduct special recognition ceremonies for individuals and organizational units that productively adhere to ethical values in the face of difficult circumstances. And for deliberate infractions, when outright dismissal is not warranted, they can withhold bonuses or other special rewards.

Excerpts From Caterpillar's Code of Worldwide Business Conduct and Operating Principles

"We intend to hold to a single high standard of integrity everywhere. We will keep our word. We won't promise more than we can reasonably expect to deliver, nor will we make commitments we don't intend to keep. In our advertising and other public communications, we will avoid not only untruths, but also exaggeration and overstatement...Thus, we are all expected to adhere to high standards of personal integrity. For example, any illegal act ostensibly taken to 'protect' the company is wrong. The end doesn't justify the means.

"Fair competition is fundamental to the free enterprise system. We support laws prohibiting restraints of trade, unfair practices, or abuse of economic power. And we avoid such practices everywhere - including areas of the world where laws don't prohibit them...There must be no arrangements or understandings with competitors affecting prices, terms upon which products are sold, or the number and type of products manufactured or sold - or which might be construed as dividing customers or sales territories with a competitor...No supplier is required to buy Caterpillar products in order to compete for business, or continue as a supplier.

"The integrity of Caterpillar's financial reporting and accounting records is based on validity, accuracy, and completeness of basic information supporting entries to the company's books of account...There must be no concealment of information from (or by) management, or from the company's independent auditors...Employees who become aware of possible omissions, falsification, or inaccuracy of accounting and financial entries, or basic data supporting such entries, are held responsible for reporting such information. These reports are to be made as specified by corporate procedure.

"It isn't enough to successfully offer useful products and services. A business should, for example, employ and promote people fairly, see to their job safety and the safety of its products, conserve energy and other valuable resources, and help protect the quality of the environment.

"To the extent our resources permit - and a host country or community wishes - we will participate selectively in such matters [helping to solve community problems]. Each corporate facility is an integral part of the community in which it operates. Like an individual, it benefits from character building, health, welfare, educational, and cultural activities. And like an individual, it also has a citizen's responsibility to support such activities.

"Caterpillar...may, to the extent legally permissible, support committees aimed at encouraging political contributions by individuals. The company itself will not normally make political contributions, even when it is legally permissible and common practice.

"In dealing with public officials, as with private business associates, Caterpillar will utilize only ethical commercial practices. We won't seek to influence sales of our products (or other events impacting on the company) by payments of bribes, kickbacks, or other questionable inducements... Employees are required to make good faith efforts to avoid payment of gratuities or 'tips' to certain public officials, even when such practices are customary to expedite or secure performance of routine governmental actions, such as processing visas or obtaining permits or public services. Where these payments are as a practical matter unavoidable, they must be limited to customary amounts.

"Those who have 'material' inside information are expected to refrain from using it for personal gain or furnishing it to others...[This] pertains to: (1) all employees and their families; and (2) any consultants or other persons who, by reason of their relationship with Caterpillar, possess such information."

Source: Caterpillar Code Of Worldwide Business Conduct And Operating Principles. Peoria, Illinois: Caterpillar Tractor Company, August 1, 1992, pages 1-12.

Sir Adrian's Guidelines

Sir Adrian Cadbury, founder of the English chocolate company, discusses guidelines for giving gifts:

"...When do gifts to employees become bribes? I use two rules of thumb to test whether a payment is acceptable from the company's point of view: Is the payment on the face of the invoice? Would it embarrass the recipient to have the gift mentioned in the company newspaper?

"The first test ensures that all payments, however unusual they may seem, are recorded and go through the books. The second is aimed at distinguishing bribes from gifts, a definition which depends on the size of the gift and the influence it is likely to have on the recipient.

"Listing a payment on the face of the invoice may not be a sufficient ethical test, but it is a necessary one; payments outside the company's system are corrupt and corrupting."

Source: Adrian Cadbury, "Ethical Managers Make their Own Rules," Harvard Business Review, September-October, 1987, page 72.

From time to time, foreign managers can be reminded of various costs to the organization that can result from unethical behavior:

Permissible bribery abroad can erode integrity at home. It is hard to distinguish different degrees of honor; therefore, we tend to become the least of what our behavior represents. The loss of reputation and self-esteem may be slow and subtle, but the cumulative effects can be personally devastating.

A reputation for bribing can strengthen the need to bribe. It tends to attract unprincipled agents in the host country, while repelling those who prefer to deal on a different basis.

Bribery can serve as a substitute for constructive study, networking, and effort on the part of overseas personnel. When coupled with dishonest record keeping, it can serve as a cover-up for failure.[90]

Reduce The Conflict Between Domestic And Foreign Work-Environment Requirements: At the turn of the century, our states began to pass workman's compensation laws so that the cost of industrial accidents would be passed on to consumers and no individual company would be penalized, competitively, for investing in special equipment, or for looking after injured employees. Then, we added minimum-wage and environmental-protection regulations to curb the unprincipled exploitation of our human and natural resources.

But under the banner of unrestricted free trade, we permit foreign goods marketed here to be produced under the same conditions we forbid for our own workers. Thereby, we pressure our employers, cost-wise, to diminish the quality of work life for the very workers we say we are committed to protecting. For example, one of the arguments in favor of passing the North American Free Trade Agreement (NAFTA) was that it would help to create 200,000 new U.S. jobs by increasing our trade surplus with Mexico. Yet, the opposite has happened. We have gone from a pre-NAFTA surplus to a deficit of some $17 billion, and the Economic Policy Institute estimates that we have lost more that 600,000 jobs as a direct result of the agreement. Why have so many jobs moved away? U.S. Representative Allen Boyd reports that the average Mexican-border-plant wage is $5 *per day*, and these plants do not begin to meet our environmental and labor standards.[91]

The problem is illustrated by the experience of Nogales, Arizona. According to Jim Carlton, as companies such as G.E., Xerox, and Samsonite started operations across the border, the town's unemployment rate rose to 23 percent, almost half of the downtown stores closed, and sales tax receipts dropped some 20 percent. In addition, chemical spills from trains and trucks headed for Mexico forced the town to spend some $300,000 for a hazardous-materials response team.[92]

We should push for provisions in new trade agreements that help protect the hard-earned progress we have made. By removing the unwarranted cost advantages that many foreign producers enjoy, we will help to level the competitive playing field and provide support for the concept of "fair" free trade. In addition, we will encourage improvement in environmental and working-life conditions for everyone, everywhere. As a move in this direction, a growing number of U.S.-based multinational companies have backed conduct codes for contract manufacturers in low-wage countries.

For example, Pascal Zachary reports that Levi Strauss Associates, Reebok International, and Nike have threatened to cut off suppliers who tolerate substandard working conditions, and that a number of foreign companies in Germany, the Netherlands, and Britain have taken the lead with regard to agricultural suppliers: their coffee packages now have labels that purport to guarantee that the beans were picked by workers who earn a fair share of company profits. He indicates that U.S. importer Starbucks Coffee requires its overseas suppliers to pay wages and benefits that at least "address the basic needs of workers and their families," and utilize child labor only when it does not "interfere with mandated education." In addition,

Starbucks urges their suppliers to help workers "gain access to safe housing, clean water and health facilities and services" and to give them the right of free association - to work "because they want to or need to, but not because they are forced to do so."[93]

But intentions, alone, will not suffice. There must be adequate means for auditing actual behavior. Now, certain leading accounting firms are beginning to accommodate this need. Thomas Grose reports that Ernst and Young has an environmental services group staffed with non-accountant specialists, and that BP Amoco and other companies are now including audit reports of their environmental, social, and ethical behavior in their annual reports. Of course, audits must be made relative to standards, and various groups have formed to assist in developing these. For example, there are the Boston-based Coalition for Environmentally Responsible Economics (CERES), the European Federation of Accountants and Auditors in Brussels, Friends of the Earth (an environmental activist group), and SustainAbility (a consulting firm).[94]

Conclusion: We have explored why unrestrained competition tends to undermine the core values we have stressed in this book; why appropriate legislation and managerial restraint are essential for the nurture of a healthy society. We have seen that the demands of ethical behavior in business - especially international business - are often more difficult and complex than in everyday life. However, they are not beyond solution, as indicated by the promising remedies we have discussed. Indeed, it is encouraging that a 1989 survey of some 1500 executives in 20 nations found that "personal ethics" headed the list of characteristics needed by the ideal corporate leader in the year 2000.[95]

OVERVIEW

Like every society throughout history, we have had various "insider" groups looking with disapproval upon certain "outsider" groups, and - unlike most - we are a very big country. Yet, commitment to certain core values has been the "glue" that has held us together and made us one of the most dynamic and progressive societies on earth.

We have been able to tolerate significant diversity in secondary or peripheral beliefs - and provide certain rights, protections, and opportunities for all - because most "insiders" *and* "outsiders" of the past accepted personal responsibility for supporting themselves, supporting "their own," and obeying the law. And, as we have seen, a majority of Americans still agree that certain moral values are the proper foundation upon which we must build. They agree with Andrew Thomas's observation that a productive life must be something more than "a slow-motion, egoistic orgy"; that it must be:

"...A series of obligations to be fulfilled as honorably as possible, with occasional interludes for moderate self-indulgence. True, lasting happiness can come only from learning to deny oneself, if only because this lays the foundation for order and security. Self-discipline is therefore the most important lesson that we can teach our children, and we do them no favors by indulging their misbehavior."[1]

Walter Isaacson, Managing Editor of Time

"The ultimate goal of democracy and freedom, after all, is not to pursue material abundance but to nurture the dignity and values of each individual. This is the fundamental story of this century, and if we're lucky and wise, it will be the story of the next one."

Source: Walter Isaacson, "Our Century... And The Next One," Time, April 13, 1998, page 73.

For some time now, we have been confronted by growing negative forces that threaten to tear us apart. As Lance Morrow noted some 15 years ago:

"The U.S. has become an appallingly Balkanized, self-contradicting collection of tribes...

"Americans have used their immense endowment of natural wealth to buy the individual out of his social responsibilities...

"It will require quite a transformation for Americans to rediscover in peacetime the things they have known only fleetingly in war: whatever it is they have in common, and think is worth having."[2]

In 1994, he added:

"The American challenge now is not to pay homage to every cultural variation and appease every ethnic sensitivity, but rather to encourage universally acceptable ideals of behavior: self-discipline, compassion, responsibility, friendship, work, courage, perseverance, honesty, loyalty, and faith...

"Some of the most important virtues (self-discipline, courage, responsibility) require self-abnegation - and nothing is further from the spirit of an age that regards self-abnegation as an offense against self-fulfillment..."[3]

"A letdown in moral values is now considered the number one problem facing our country."

Source: An anonymous survey of a random sample of 2000 adult Americans, reported in James Patterson and Peter Kim, The Day America Told The Truth. New York: Prentice-Hall Press, 1991, page 237.

Unfortunately, many psychological therapists have contributed to this trend by defining the "good life" largely in terms of self-enhancement. W. J. Doherty observes that "therapists since the time of Freud have overemphasized individual self-interest, giving short shrift to family and community responsibilities."[4] Anecdotal support for this observation was provided by my uncle, Creed Bates of Chattanooga, Tennessee, who served as principal of a large city high-school for some forty years, starting in 1922. When I asked if he had noted any significant changes during those years, his answer was an emphatic "yes." He observed that:

> "During the Roaring 1920's, as well as the Depression of the 1930's, the primary concern of high-school seniors was to prepare adequately to go out and be on their own.
> "After World War II, this concern was displaced by new preoccupations: 'Am I happy?' (if not, it's someone else's fault); and 'Am I getting what's coming to me?'"

Sentiment of the Times?

Young daughter to a friend: "I hate all this responsibility ...I'm still a kid! I wanna LIVE like a kid - I just want to be TREATED like an adult! Is that so difficult to understand?"

Source: Lynn Johnson, "For Better or For Worse" comic strip, The Gainesville Sun, of Gainesville, Florida, February, 25, 1998, page 4D.

Tony Bouzas makes the cogent observation that "It is the subtle shift from a sense of common destiny, embodied in tribal ambitions, to the consensus that the society exists to gratify individual desires that spells the doom of a people."[5] In this same vein, Isac Prilleltensky notes that:

"Once people overcome the myth that existing social arrangements are immutable, they are in a position to question power structures that interfere with the pursuit of fundamental values for everyone, rather than just for those who benefit from privilege and comfort. A critical analysis of who benefits from current social conditions, and at whose expense, is the first step in overcoming oppression."[6]

Abraham Lincoln On Liberty

"We all declare for liberty; but in using the same *word* we do not all mean the same *thing*. With some the word liberty may mean for each man to do as he pleases with himself, and the product of his labor; while with others the same word may mean for some men to do as they please with other men, and the product of other men's labor."

Source: Carl Sandburg, Abraham Lincoln: The Prairie Years And The War Years. New York: Galahad Books, 1993, page 507.

Our system is now in danger. We need to be reminded of basic truths. We have become so caught up in the proliferation of innumerable "equal rights" - often without equal responsibilities - that we are losing sight of the requirements for a viable society. True, it is harder for some individuals to succeed than for others, but we are beginning to rediscover that: people - short of being insane - must be held responsible for the consequences of their behavior.

We have seen how values are acquired, how they and other factors influence our behavior, and what we can do to change for the better. We have seen that rather than giving sympathy and handouts to the disadvantaged, we need to create development and work opportunities for them and help them to nurture the will to exploit these opportunities. We have seen that many ethical judgments can be quite involved and debatable - that simplistic behavioral prescriptions can be just as dysfunctional as the absence of agreed-to direction.

We have discussed how we can use our analytical skills to estimate the gains and penalties - both materially and psychologically - for those who will be affected by a decision, and then strive to strike a balance between ethical imperatives (from a refined conscience) and the gains and penalties associated with them on the basis of ethical utilitarianism (cost/benefit analysis) - realizing that neither approach, alone, is sufficient for all occasions. And we can better appreciate the likelihood that representatives of different cultures may move collaboratively toward agreement about mutually acceptable core values.

Given the effectiveness of the many remedies presented in this book, we are hardly helpless in the face of our problems. We have seen that significant steps are being taken - or can be taken - to introduce and nurture core values in the areas of group problem solving, parenting, education, political leadership, the administration of justice, the administration of welfare, the rehabilitation of criminals and the chronically unemployed, and the management of domestic and international business.

Now, we need to become personally involved. Shall we have moral growth or further decline for our families, communities, and nation? We need only to act - the choice is ours.

Notes

INTRODUCTION

1 Bernard Wysocki, Jr., "Americans Decry Moral Decline," The Wall Street Journal, June 24, 1999, pages A9, A12.

2 J.K. Mahon, The War Of 1812, University of Florida Press, 1972, page 368.

3 "Separation Anxiety: 'New' Marines Illustrate Growing Gap Between Military And Society," The Wall Street Journal, July 27, 1995, pages A1, A4.

4 Susan Mayer, What Money Can't Buy. Harvard University Press, 1997, page 24.

5 John Dorfman, "Crash Courses: How The Two Great Stock-Market Crashes Compare," The Wall Street Journal, May 28, 1996, page R13.

6 George Will, The Morning After: American Successes And Excesses 1981-1986. Free Press, 1986, page 44.

7 William Buckley, Jr. column, The Wall Street Journal, January 11, 1993, page 6A.

8 Carol Kalish, "International Crime Rates." Washington: U.S. Department of Justice, Bureau Of Justice Statistics Special Report, 1984, Table 4, page 3.

9 "Three Big Reasons Drive American Youth To Drugs," adapted from a commencement address Father Byron delivered at St. Louis University, in The Gainesville Sun of Gainesville, Florida, May 24, 1989, page 13A.

10 Joshua Fischman, "Minds Of States," <u>Psychology Today</u>, October 1985, page 20.

11 Reported by Emily Harrison in "Where There's A Will," <u>Smart Money</u>, December, 1996, page 148.

12 See <u>Values And Violence In Auschwitz</u> by Anna Pawelczynska, University of California Press, 1979.

13 Lawrence Harrison, "The Cultural Roots Of Poverty," <u>The Wall Street Journal</u>, July 13, 1999, page A22.

14 Harrison, Ibid.

15 John Heilbrunn, "The Gruesome Consequences Of A Political Idea," <u>The Wall Street Journal</u>, October, 25, 1999, page A50.

16 <u>Time</u>, March 21, 1994, page 45.

17 Ibid.

18 Alan Cooperman, "No End In Sight To A Gruesome And Widespread Ritual," <u>U.S. News And World Report</u>, July 7, 1997, page 51.

19 Salman Rushdide, "India At Five-O," <u>Time</u>, August 11, 1997, page 41.

20 Lisa Beyer, "The Price Of Honor," <u>Time</u>, January 18, 1999, page 55.

21 Reported by authors Edward Eichel and J. Gordon Muir in <u>The Wall Street Journal</u>, March 18, 1994, "Letters To The Editors," page A11.

22 Edward Peters, <u>Torture</u>, New York: Basil Blackwell, 1985.

23   Associated Press, "Millions Of Children Said In Forced Labor," Asheville Citizen-Times, September, 19, 1995, page 1A.

24 Reported by Lisa Beyer, "The Religious Wars," Time, May 11, 1998, page 34.

25 Michael Horowitz, "New Intolerance Between Crescent And Cross," The Wall Street Journal, July 5, 1995, page A8.

26 Nina Shea, "A War On Religion," The Wall Street Journal, July 31, 1998, page W11.

27 Paul Liben, "Farrakhan Honors African Slavers," The Wall Street Journal, October 20, 1995, page A12.

28 Cover story: "The Bible: The Believers Gain," Time, December 30, 1974, pages 34-41.

29 "The Personal Values Of Alcoholics and Addicts," Journal Of Clinical Psychology, 1975, pages 554-557.

30 Milton Rokeach, The Nature Of Human Values. New York: Free Press, 1973.

31 Marianne Jennings, "Business Students Who Hate Business," The Wall Street Journal, May 3, 1999, page A22.

32 "Is It Posssible To Be Pro-Life And Pro-Choice?," Parade Magazine, April 22, 1990, pages 5, 6. Reprinted with permission from the authors and from Parade, copyright © 1990.

33 "When Is An Embryo Human?," Letters To The Editor, The Wall Street Journal, November 14, 1994, page A11.

Chapter 1: WHY CERTAIN CORE VALUES ARE ESSENTIAL TO OUR WELL BEING

1 Denise Rousseau, Sim Sitkin, Ronald Burt, and Colin Camerer, "Not So Different After All: A Cross-Discipline View Of Trust," The Academy Of Management Review, Vol. 23, No. 3, 1998, page 395.

2 Part 1, Chapter 4, in "The Descent Of Man," in Robert Hutchins, editor, Great Books Of The Western World. Chicago: Encyclopaedia Britannica, 1952, 49, pages 314-315.

3 Trust: The Social Virtues And The Creation of Prosperity. Free Press, 1995.

4 See Wray Herbert, "Morality's Bottom Line," U.S. News And World Report, August 21, 1995, pages 51-53.

5 "Psychology And The Naturalistic Ethics Of Social Policy," American Psychologist, November 1994, page 967.

6 Robert Hutchins, editor, Great Books Of The Western World. Chicago: Encyclopaedia Britannica, 1952, 43, page 31.

7 Ibid., page 174.

8 Ibid., page 272.

9 Chapter 1 of his essay "On Liberty," in Robert Hutchins, editor, Great Books of the Western World. Chicago: Encyclopaedia Britannica, 1952, 43, page 269.

10 Richard Brookhiser, Founding Father: Rediscovering George Washington. New York: The Free Press, 1996, page 193.

11   George Anastplo, "American Constitutionalism And The Virtue Of Prudence," in Leo Paul S. de Alvarez, editor, Abraham Lincoln, The Gettysburg Address, And American Constitutionalism. Irving, Texas: University of Dallas Press, 1976, pages 94-106; Gouverneur Morris, A Diary Of The French Revolution, edited by Beatrix Davenport.   Boston: Houghton Mifflin, 1939, 1:61 (to Washington, 29 April 1789).

12   Carl Sandburg, Abraham Lincoln: The Prairie Years And The War Years. New York: Galahad Books, 1993, pages 133, 134. Excerpts from Abraham Lincoln: The Prairie Years And The War Years, copyright 1939, 1926 by Harcourt, Inc., and renewed 1966, 1953 by Carl Sandburg, reprinted by permission of the publisher.

13 Letter from George Washington to Morris, 12 April 1786, in W. B. Allen, editor, George Washington: A Collection. Indianapolis: Library Classics, 1989, page 319.

14 Letter from John Adams to Evans, 8 June 1819, in Adrienne Koch and William Peden, editors, Selected Writings Of John And John Quincy Adams. New York: Knopf, 1946, page 209.

15   Benjamin Franklin, "An Address To The Public From The Pennsylvania Society For Promoting The Abolition Of Slavery," 1789, in J.A. Leo Lemay, editor, Writings. New York: Library of America, 1897, page 1154.

16 James Madison, speech at Constitutional Convention, 6 June 1787, in Max Farrand, editor, The Records Of The Federal Convention of 1787. New Haven: Yale University Press, 1937, 1:135.

17 Query 18 of his Notes On The State Of Virginia (1787) in Writings, Merrill Peterson, editor.   New York: Library of America, 1984, pages 288-289.

18   Thomas West, <u>Vindicating The Founders</u>. New York: Rowman and Littlefield Publishers, Inc., 1997, page 22.

19   Ibid., pages 11,12.

20   Ibid., page 7.

21   Arthur Zilversmit, <u>The First Emancipation: The Abolition Of Slavery In The North</u>. University of Chicago Press, 1967, pages 116-124, 131, 181, 193, 222; David Davis, <u>The Problem Of Slavery In The Age Of Revolution, 1770-1823</u>. Cornell University Press, 1975, page 319.

22   Thomas West, <u>Vindicating The Founders</u>, New York: Rowman and Littlefield Publishers, 1997, page 3.

23   Gary Nash, <u>Race And Revolution</u>. Madison, Wisconsin: Madison House, 1990, page 43;   James Kettner, <u>The Development Of American Citizenship, 1608 - 1870</u>. Chapel Hill: University of North Carolina Press, 1984, page 302; Ira Berlin, <u>Slaves Without Masters: The Free Negro In The Antebellum South</u>, 1974, reprint. New York: Oxford, 1981, pages 46-50, 396;   Benjamin Quarles, <u>The Negro And The American Revolution</u>.   Chapel Hill: University of North Carolina Press, 1961, chapters 4-6;   Paul Finkelman, editor, <u>Slavery, Revolutionary America, And The New Nation</u>. New York: Garland, 1989, page xii.

24   Matt Moffett, "Against Their Will," <u>The Wall Street Journal</u>, January 11, 1999, page R28.

25   Carl Sandburg, <u>Abraham Lincoln: The Prairie Years And The War Years</u>. New York: Galahad Books, 1993, page 197. Excerpts from <u>Abraham Lincoln: The Prairie Years And The War Years</u>, copyright 1939, 1926 by Harcourt, Inc., and renewed 1966, 1953 by Carl Sandburg, reprinted by permission of the publisher.

26 Carl Sandburg, <u>Abraham Lincoln: The Prairie Years And The War Years</u>. New York: Galahad Books, 1993, page 110. Excerpts from <u>Abraham Lincoln: The Prairie Years And The War Years</u>, copyright 1939, 1926 by Harcourt, Inc., and renewed 1966, 1953 by Carl Sandburg, reprinted by permission of the publisher.

27 Thomas West, <u>Vindicating The Founders</u>, New York: Rowman and Littlefield Publishers, Inc., 1997, page 29.

28 Carl Sandburg, <u>Abraham Lincoln: The Prairie Years And The War Years</u>. New York: Galahad Books, 1993, page 317. Excerpts from <u>Abraham Lincoln: The Prairie Years And The War Years</u>, copyright 1939, 1926 by Harcourt, Inc., and renewed 1966, 1953 by Carl Sandburg, reprinted by permission of the publisher.

29 Samuel Morrison and Henry Commager, <u>The Growth Of The American Republic</u>. New York: Oxford University Press, 1950, page 46.

30 Frederick Douglas, "What Are The Colored People Doing For Themselves?," in Herbert Storing, editor, <u>What Country Have I? Political Writings by Black Americans</u>. New York: St. Martin's, 1970, pages 45-46.

31 Alexander Stephens, "Corner-Stone Speech," March 21, 1861, in Henry Cleveland, <u>Alexander H. Stephens</u>. Philadelphia: National Publishing, 1866, page 721.

32 "The World Of Epictetus: Reflections On Survival And Leadership," <u>Atlantic Monthly</u>, April 1978, pages 99, 105.

33 Hans Kung and Karl-Josef Kuschel, editors, <u>A Global Ethic: The Declaration Of The Parliament Of The World's Religions</u>. London: SCM Press, Ltd., 1993, pages 14, 15, 33, 37-39.

34   Milton Rokeach and Sandra ball-Rokeach, "Stability And Change In American Value Priorities," <u>American Psychologist,</u> May, 1989, page 778.

35 James Perry, <u>The Wall Street Journal</u>, March 5, 1998, pages A10-A14.

36   <u>Child Maltreatment And Paternal Deprivation</u>. Lexington Books, 1986, page 221.

37   <u>Uniform Crime Reports</u>. Washington: Federal Bureau of Investigation, 1991, page 279.

38 Barbara Whitehead, "Dan Quayle Was Right," <u>The Atlantic,</u> April 1993, page 77.

39 Reported by William Buckley, Jr. in the <u>Asheville Citizen-Times</u>, October 16, 1995, page 4A.

40   "Family Values Gain Ground," <u>The Wall Street Journal,</u> December 28, 1995, page A6.

41 Tori DeAngelis, "When Children Don't Bond With Parents," <u>Monitor</u> [of the American Psychological Association], June 1997, page 10.

42   For example, see <u>The Secret Strength Of Depression</u> by Frederic F. Flach. New York: The Hatherleigh Company, 1995.

43   "What Do Families Do?"   <u>Family Affairs</u>, Winter/Spring 1991, page 4.

44 Betty Hart and Todd Risley, <u>Meaningful Differences In The Everyday Experience Of Young Children</u>. Baltimore: Paul H. Brooks Publishing Company, 1995, pages 2, 180, 183.

45 "The Costly Retreat From Marriage," <u>Public Interest,</u> Spring 1988, pages 60-62.

46 Myron Magnet, "The American Family,1992," <u>Fortune</u>, August 10, 1992, pages 42-47.

47 Andrew Thomas, <u>Crime And The Sacking Of America: The Roots of Chaos</u>. Washington, D.C.: Brassey's, 1994, pages 165-166.
48 Ibid., page 166.

49 Ibid., page 190.

50 <u>Time</u>, August, 15, 1994, page 51.

51 Tori DeAngelis, "When Children Don't Bond With Parents," <u>Monitor</u> [of the American Psychological Association], June 1997, page 10.

52 Quoted by William Raspberry in <u>The Gainesville Sun</u> of Gainesville, Florida, April 6, 1995, page 8A; the report is available from The Institute for American Values, 1841 Broadway, Suite 211, New York, N.Y. 10023.

53 "Sex Trumps Gender," <u>The Wall Street Journal</u>, March 6, 1996, page A19. See also the report of sociologist Melford Spiro in his 1979 book, <u>Gender And Culture: Kibbutz Women Revisited</u>.

54 "Public School Aggression Among Children With Varying Day Care Experience," <u>Child Development</u>, 1985, page 700.

55 Michael Rutter, "Social-Emotional Consequences Of Day Care for Preschool Children," <u>American Journal Of Ortho-psychiatryy</u>, 1981, page 4; Christopher Bagley, "Agression And Anxiety In Day-Care Graduates," <u>Psychological Reports</u>, 1989, page 250; Urie Bronfenbrenner, "Research On The Effects Of Day Care On Child Development." In National Research Council, <u>Toward A National Policy For Children And Families</u>. Washington: National Academy of Sciences, 1976, page 117.

56   Andrew Thomas, "A Dangerous Experiment In Child-Rearing," The Wall Street Journal, January 8, 1998, page A8.

57 Ibid.

58 Milton Rokeach and Sandra Ball-Rokeach, "Stability And Change In American Value Priorities", American Psychologist, May, 1989, page 778.   This finding is also supported by a Reader's Digest poll of 1053 Americans across four generations reported by Everett Ladd: "Exposing The Myths Of The Generation Gap," Reader's Digest, January 1995, page 50.

59 James Perry, The Wall Street Journal, March 5, 1998, pages A10-A14.

60 Materials obtained from PREP, The Network for Educational Development [a non-profit consortium], 13157 Olive Spur Road, ST. Louis, MO 63141.

61   John   Emshwiller,   "Riot   Fallout   Lingers   In   L.A.'s Koreatown," The Wall Street Journal, October 26, 1992.

62 Reported in William F. Buckley's column in The Gainesville Sun of Gainesville, Florida, December 2, 1981.

63 Crime And The Sacking Of America: The Roots Of Chaos. Washington: Brassey's, 1994, pages 268, 303.

64   Milton Rokeach and Sandra Ball-Rokeach, "Stability And Change In American Value Priorities", American Psychologist, May, 1989, page 778.   Also a scientific sampling of 1053 Americans across four generations conducted for the Reader's Digest, reported by Everett Ladd: "Exposing The Myths Of The Generation Gap," Reader's Digest, January 1995, page 50.

65 Steve Gelman, editor, "Americans Tell Us What The Nation Needs," in Rediscover America 1492-1992 (Special Advertising

Section presented by Chrysler Corporation), <u>Time</u>, July 20, 1992; Milton Rokeach and Sandra Ball-Rokeach, "Stability And Change In American Value Priorities", <u>American Psychologist</u>, May, 1989, page 778.

66 William Holstein, "The New Economy," <u>U.S. News And World Report</u>, May 26, 1997, page 48.

67 John Kasarda, "Why Asians Can Prosper Where Blacks Fail," <u>The Wall Street Journal</u>, May 28, 1992, page A20.

68 Raju Narisetti, "Manufacturers Decry A Shortage Of Workers While Rejecting Many," <u>The Wall Street Journal</u>, September 8, 1995, page A1.

69 Ibid., page A4.

70 "What's Become Of Research On The Cultural Basis Of Cognitive Development?" <u>American Psychologist</u>, 1995, 50 (10), pages 860, 861, 864.

71 Charles Morrison, "Officials Step Up Efforts To Keep Even More Kids In School," <u>Asheville Citizen-Times</u>, October 7, 1999, page A5.

72 Ibid.

73 Stephen Ceci and Wendy Williams, "Schooling, Intelligence, And Income," <u>American Psychologist</u>, October 1997, pages 1051-1054.

74 Milton Rokeach and Sandra Ball-Rokeach, "Stability And Change In American Value Priorities", <u>American Psychologist</u>, May, 1989, page 778. This finding is also supported by a <u>Reader's Digest</u> poll of 1053 Americans across four generations reported by Everett Ladd: "Exposing The Myths Of The Generation Gap," <u>Reader's Digest</u>, January 1995, page 50.

75 Materials obtained from PREP, The Network for Educational Development [a non-profit consortium], 13157 Olive Spur Road, ST. Louis, MO 63141.

76 Hans Kung and Jurgen Moltmann, editors, <u>A Global Ethic: The Declaration Of The Parliament Of The World's Religions</u>. London: SCM Press, Ltd., 1993, pages 14, 15, 33, 37-39.

77 David Horowitz, <u>Hating Whitey</u>. Dallas: Spence Publishing Company, 1999, page 91.

Chapter 2: THE COMPATIBILITY OF OUR CORE VALUES WITH THOSE OF VARIOUS RELIGIONS AND OTHER SOURCES

1 "Human Rights In The Context Of Global Problem-Solving: A Buddhist Perspective," by Sulak Sivaraksa. In Hans Kung and Jurgen Moltmann, editors, <u>The Ethics Of World Religions and Human Rights</u>. Philadelphia: Trinity Press International, 1990, page 89.

2 <u>Small Is Beautiful</u>. New York: Harper and Row, 1975, page 51.

3 <u>How To Live Well</u>. Belmont, CA: Wadsworth Publishing Company, 1988, page 123.

4 See "Confucianism" in the <u>Encyclopaedia Britannica</u>.

5 Denise and John Carmody, <u>How To Live Well</u>. Belmont, CA: Wadsworth Publishing Company, 1988, page 110.

6 See "Islam" in the <u>Encyclopaedia Britannica</u>.

7 Ibid., See "Decalogue."

8 Ibid., See "Judaism."

9   Quoted by Hans Kung in "Towards World Ethic Of World Religions." In Hans Kung and Jurgen Moltmann, editors, The Ethics Of World Religions And Human Rights. Philadelphia: Trinity Press International, 1990, pages 118-119. Translated by Gordon Wood and reprinted in Concilium, 1990, No. 2. (Stichting, Concilium and SCM Press copyright c 1990).

10 Hans Kung and Karl-Josef Kuschel, editors, A Global Ethic: The Declaration Of The Parliament Of The World's Religions. London: SCM Press, Ltd., 1993, pages 14, 15, 33, 37-39.

11 Rushworth Kidder, Shared Values For A Troubled World. San Francisco, Jossey-Bass, 1994, pages xi-xiii, 17, 312-320.

12 Robert Hutchins, editor, Great Books Of The Western World. Chicago: Encyclopaedia Britannica, 1952, 12, page 261.

13 Robert Hutchins, editor, Great Books Of The Western World. Chicago: Encyclopaedia Britannica, 1952, 42, page 275.

14 Richard Brookhiser, Founding Father: Rediscovering George Washington. New York: The Free Press, 1996, pages 48-49, 56, 73, 85, 100, 179-184.

15 Richard Harwell, Lee [an abridgement]. Charles Scribner's Sons, 1961, pages 585, 588.

16 Carl Sandburg, Abraham Lincoln: The Prairie Years And The War Years. New York: Galahad Books, 1993, pages 403-404. Excerpts from Abraham Lincoln: The Prairie Years And The War Years, copyright 1939, 1926 by Harcourt, Inc., and renewed 1966, 1953 by Carl Sandburg, reprinted by permission of the publisher.

17 Ibid., page 149.

18 Ibid., pages 635, 701-702.

Chapter 3: OUR CORE VALUES ARE BEING SUBVERTED

1   Carl Sandburg, <u>Abraham Lincoln: The Prairie Years And The War Years</u>. New York: Galahad Books, 1993, page 594. Excerpts from <u>Abraham Lincoln: The Prairie Years And The War Years</u>, copyright 1939, 1926 by Harcourt, Inc., and renewed 1966, 1953 by Carl Sandburg, reprinted by permission of the publisher.

2 Ibid., page 445.

3 Ibid., page 259.

4 Ibid., page 356.

5 Ibid., pages 299, 538.

6 Ibid., pages 416-420.

7 Ibid., page 481.

8 Ibid., page 278.

9 Ibid., page 201.

10   Samuel Morrison and Henry Commanger, <u>The Growth Of The American Republic</u>. New York: Oxford University Press, 1950, pages 46, 48.

11 "The Year 2000: Is It The End - Or Just The Beginning?," <u>Time</u>, March 30, 1992, page 76.

12 Dividends, "Youth Gone To Seed," Time, October 12, 1981, page 86.

13 A Tribe Apart: A Journey Into The Heart Of American Adolescence. New York: Fawcett Columbine, 1998, page 100.

14 Rushworth KIdder, Shared Values For A Troubled World. San Francisco, Jossey-Bass, 1994, page 13.

15 Tony Bouza, The Decline And Fall Of The American Empire. New York: Plenum Press, 1996, page 4. Copyright (c) 1996 by Tony Bouza. Reprinted by permission of Perseus Books Publishers, a member of Perseus Books, L.L.C..

16 Reported by Amitai Etzioni in The Wall Street Journal, November 13, 1995, page A14.

17 D. Kanter and P. Mirvis, The Cynical Americans. San Francisco: Jossey-Bass, 1989, pages 5-6.

18 Editorial, "Bankruptcy Policies," The Gainesville Sun of Gainesville, Florida, October 25, 1997, page 8A.

19 The Wall Street Journal, January 29, 1997, page A11.

20 "'Me' Decades Generate Depression," Monitor [of the American Psychological Association], October 1988, page 18.

21 "No Wonder Medicare And Medicaid Are Out Of Control," Reader's Digest, September, 1995, pages 78-100.

22 Jason West, W. Cohen and M. Tharp, "Road Rage," U.S. News And World Report, June 2, 1997, pages 24-25.

23 Asra Nomani, The Wall Street Journal, June 10, 1998, page A1.

24 John Marks, "The American Uncivil Wars," U.S. News And World Report, April 22, 1996, pages 67-68.

25 "Computer Massacre, Our Warning," The Wall Street Journal, December, 10, 1993, page A14.

26 H.N. Snyder and M. Sickmund, Juvenile Offenders And Victims: A National Report. Washington, DC: U.S. Department of Justice, Office of Juvenile Justice and Delinquency Prevention, No. NCJ-153569, 1995.

27 Editorial, "Lack Of Discipline Haunts A New Generation," Asheville Citizen-Times, September 22, 1997, page A4

28 J.E. Richters and P. Martinez, "Children As Victims Of And Witnesses To Violence," the NIMHI Community Violence Project: Volume 1. Psychiatry, 1993, pages 7-21.

29 Crime And The Sacking Of America: The Roots Of Chaos. Washington: Brassey's, 1994, pages 255, 256.

30 Tori DeAngelis, "Senate Seeks Answers To Rising Tide Of Violence," Monitor [of the American Psychological Association], May 1992, page 11.

31 George Will of the Washington Post writers group, "TV Is Leaving A Violent Legacy," in The Gainesville Sun of Gainesville, Florida, April 8, 1993, page 8A.

32 Ibid.

33 "The Influence Of Suggestion On Suicide: Substantive And Theoretical Implications Of The Werther Effect," American Sociological Review, 1974, page 340.

34 Investigative Reports,"Copycat Crimes," aired February 1, 1999.

35 Reported by Nathan Seppa, "TV Producers Neglect To Show The Consequences Of Violent Acts, A New Study Shows," Monitor [of the American Psychological Association], April, 1996, page 8.

36 Randy Fitzgerald, "History Hollywood Style," Reader's Digest, October 1996, pages 89-93.

37 Reported by Peter Freiberg in Monitor [of the American Psychological Association], April 1991, page 31.

38 Reported by Peter Freiberg, "Research Identifies Kids At Risk For Problem Gambling," Monitor [of the American Psychological Association], December, 1995, page 36.

39 David Wilson, "Is Marriage Obsolete?" The Boston Globe, August 6, 1989, page A31.

40 "The Parents Agree," Report of the National Parenting Association Task Force in The Wall Street Journal, July 7, 1995, page A10.

41 Frank Furstenburg and Andrew Cherlin, Divided Families: What Happens To Children When Parents Part. Cambridge: Harvard University Press, 1991, page 35.

42 William Bennett, "Quantifying America's Decline," The Wall Street Journal, March 15, 1993, page A12.

43 Douglas Besharov, "The Other Clinton Promise - Ending Welfare As We Know It," The Wall Street Journal, January 18, 1993, page A10.

44 Reported by Maggie Gallagher, "Fatherless Boys Grow Up Into Dangerous Men," The Wall Street Journal, December 1, 1998, page A22.

45 Nadya Labi, "A Bad Start?" Time, February 15, 1999, page 61.

46 Bernard Wysocki, Jr., "Most Turn To Family, More The State, For Answers," The Wall Street Journal, June 24, 1999, page A9.

47 The Index Of Leading Cultural Indicators. New York: Touchstone, 1994, page 103.

48 A Tribe Apart: A Journey Into The Heart Of American Adolescence. New York: Fawcett Columbine, 1998, pages 19-20.

49 Aaron Hoover, "English Teacher's Assignment Sheds Light On Problem," The Gainesville Sun of Gainesville, Florida, March 25, 1995, pages 1A, 4A.

50 Reported by Sara Martin and Bridget Murray, "Social Toxicity Undermines Youngsters In Inner Cities," Monitor [of the American Psychological Association], October, 1996, page 27.

51 "Now For The Bad News: A Teenage Time Bomb," Time, January 15, 1996, page 52.

52 Kay Hyonowitz, "Kids Today Are Growing Up Way Too Fast," The Wall Street Journal, October 28, 1998, page A22.

53 A Tribe Apart: A Journey Into The Heart Of American Adolescence. New York: Fawcett Columbine, 1998, page 12.

54 "Pop Culture And Drugs," The Wall Street Journal, July 26, 1995, page A12.

55 Associated Press, "Marijuana Use By Teens Up," Asheville Citizen-Times, September 13, 1995, page 1A.

56 "Kids and Pot," Time, December 9, 1996, page 30.

57 Ibid.

58 Walter Billings, "Crank," Time, June 22, 1998, page 25.

59 "Pop Culture And Drugs," The Wall Street Journal, July 26, 1995, page A12.

60 Quoted from Department of Health and Human Services Report in USA Today, November 16, 1994.

61 Quoted by Hosea Martin in "Don't Wait For Role Models," The Wall Street Journal, June 28, 1996, page A8.

62 Elijah Anderson, Code Of The Streets. New York: W. W. Norton and Company, 1999, Chapter 2.

63 J.D. Osofsky, S. Wewers, D.M. Hann, and A.C. Ficks, "Chronic Community Violence: What is Happening To Our Children," Psychiatry, 1993, pages 36-45.

64 "An Exploratory Study Of Values And Attitudes Of Black Delinquents In Custody," Journal Of Crime and Justice, 1990, pages 66-85.

65 John Emshwiller, "Riot Fallout Lingers In LA's Koreatown," The Wall Street Journal, October 26, 1992, page B6.

66 David Van Biema, "Marching To Farrakhan's Tune," Time, October 16, 1995, page 74.

67 Morgan Reynolds, "Europe Surpasses America - In Crime," The Wall Street Journal, October 16, 1998, page A14.

68 S.J. Ventura, J.A. Martin, S.C. Curtin, and T.J. Mathews, "Report Of Final Natality Statistics, 1995," Monthly Vital

<u>Statistics Report 45</u> (Volume 11, Supplement 2). Hyattsville, MD: National Center for Health Statistics, 1997.

69 "The Parents Agree," Report of the National Parenting Association Task Force in <u>The Wall Street Journal</u>, July 7, 1995, page A10.

70 <u>Paved With Good Intentions: The Failure Of Race Relations In Contemporary America</u>. New York: Carroll and Braf, 1992, page 82.

71 "To Be Young, Male, And Black," <u>The Washington Post</u>, December 28, 1989, page A1.

72 Douglas Besharov, "The Other Clinton Promise - Ending Welfare As We Know It," <u>The Wall Street Journal</u>, January 18, 1993, page A10.

73 Reported by Bill Schackner of the <u>Pittsburg Post Gazette</u>, "Higher Education, A Gender Gap, More Black Women In College," in <u>The Gainesville Sun</u> of Gainesville, Florida, February 18, 1998, page 6A.

74 "The Roots Of Black Poverty," <u>The Wall Street Journal</u>, October 30, 1995, page A18.

75 <u>The Gainesville Sun</u> of Gainesville, Florida, February 6, 1993, page A10.

76 "The Hidden Hurdle," <u>Time</u>, March 16, 1992, page 44.

77 Associated Press, "Black Teacher Group Opposes Test Plans," <u>The Gainesville Sun</u> of Gainesville, Florida, November 19, 1982, page 8B.

78 See his book: <u>Up From Slavery</u>. Doubleday, Page, and Company, 1901.

79 The Gainesville Sun of Gainesville, Florida, June 2, 1990, page 9A.

80 Newsweek, August 15, 1994, page 57.

81 Reported by John Kasarda, "Why Asians Can Prosper Where Blacks Fail," The Wall Street Journal, May 28, 1992, page A20.

82 John Wilke, "Power Struggle," The Wall Street Journal, November 13, 1995, page A1.

83 John Kasarda, "Why Asians Can Prosper Where Blacks Fail," The Wall Street Journal, May 28, 1992, page A20.

84 Jane Mayer and Jill Abramson, Strange Justice. New York: Houghton-Mifflin, 1994, pages 45,46.

85 Maxwell columns of The Gainesville Sun of Gainesville, Florida, December 8, 1990 and April 25, 1991.

Chapter 4: HOW WE ACQUIRE VALUES

1 Betty Hart and Todd Risley, Meaningful Differences In The Everyday Experience Of Young Children. Baltimore: Paul H. Brooks Publishing Company, 1995, pages 180, 182.

2 See Jean Piaget, The Psychology Of The Child, Inhelder, Basic Books, 1969.

3 George Colt, "Were You Born That Way?," Life, April 1998, pages 40-50.

4 The Tangled Wing: Biological Constraints On The Human Spirit. New York: Holt, Rineharrt, and Winston, 1982.

5 Ibid., page 273.

6 Ibid., page 118.

7 Ibid., pages 313-314.

8 Ibid., pages 109, 111, 348.

9 Ibid., pages 112, 274-275.

10 John Lang, "Happiness Is A Reunited Set Of Twins," U.S. News and World Report, April 13, 1987, pages 63-66; Stanley Wellborn, "How Genes Shape Personality," U.S. News And World Report, April 13, 1987, pages 58-62.

11 Dan Hurley, "Arresting Delinquency," Psychology Today, March 1985, page 64.

12 Reported by Sarnoff Mednick, "Crime In The Family Tree," Psychology Today, March, 1985, page 60.

13 Jerry E. Bishop, "Probing The Cell: Researchers Close in On Some Genetic Bases Of Antisocial Behavior," The Wall Street Journal, February 12, 1986, page 19.

14 Newsweek, February 27, 1978, page 91.

15 Samuel Yochelson and Stanton Samenow, The Criminal Personality Volume II: The Change Process. New York: Jason Aronson, 1977; and a presentation by Dr. Yochelson at the American Psychological Association Meetings in Washington, August, 1976.

Chapter 5: THE ROLE OF VALUES IN CAUSING
BEHAVIOR

1 Stanley Milgram, "Some Conditions Of Obedience And Disobedience To Authority," Human Relations, 1965, 18, pages 57-76.

2 Ibid., page 74.

3 Ron Jones, "Based On A True Story," Whole Earth Review (now Whole Earth), Summer, 1993, pages 70, 74, 81.

4 Leslie Weinfield, "The Third Wave," Peninsula, September, 1991, page 50.

5 Craig Haney, Curtis Banks, and Philip Zimbardo, "A Study Of Prisoners And Guards In A Simulated Prison," Naval Research Reviews, September 1973, 1-17.

6 John Lancaster, "The Sex Life Of The Navy," The Washington Post, May 17, 1992, page C2.

7 Paula Caproni and Joycelyn Finley, "Crises Of Moral Awareness In Organizations: The Tailhook Case," in Dorothy Moore, editor, Aacademy of Management Best Papers Proceedings 1994. Papers presented at the Fifty-Fourth Annual Meeting of the Academy of Management, Dallas, Texas, August 14-17, 1994.

8 See Values And Violence in Auschwitz by Anna Pawelczynska, University of California Press, 1979.

9 Albert Bandura, "Self-Regulation Of Motivation Through Anticipatory And Self-Reactive Mechanisms," in R. A. Dienstbier, editor, Perspectives On Motivation: Nebraska Symposium On Motivation, 1990. Lincoln: University of Nebraska Press, 1991, pages 69-164; also see Bandura, Social Foundations Of Thought And Action: A Social Cognitive Theory. Englewood Cliffs, NJ: Prentice-Hall, 1986.

10 Overcoming Reorganizational Defenses. Boston: Allyn and Bacon, 1990, page 10.

Chapter 6: HOW TO NURTURE CORE VALUES IN
OURSELVES AND OTHERS

1 Based upon material from two books by Camilla Anderson:
<u>Saints, Sinners, And Psychiatry</u>. The Durham Press, 1962;
<u>Beyond Freud</u>. Harper and Brothers, 1957.

2 For a good reference on RET, see: Albert Ellis and Windy
Dryden, <u>The Practice Of Rational Emotive Therapy</u>. New York:
Springer Publishing Company, 1987.

3 Dennis McCafferty, "Can Teen Drinking Be Curbed?" <u>USA
Weekend</u>, June 12-14, 1998, page 24.

4 For a good reference on behavior management, see: Garry
Martin and Joseph Pear, <u>Behavior Modification: What It Is and
How To Do It</u>. Prentice-Hall, 1991.

5 Michael Lemonick, "Spare The Rod? Maybe," <u>Time</u>, August
25, 1997, page 65

6 "Spanking Makes A Comeback," <u>The Wall Street Journal</u>,
June 9, 2000, page W16.

7 David Reiss, with Jenae Neiderhiser, E. Mavis Hetherington,
and Robert Plomin, <u>The Relationship Code</u>. Cambridge, MA:
Harvard University Press, 2000, pages 4, 14, 29, 34, 36, 92-93,
99, 196, 236, 353, 365.

8 Robert Eisenberger and Judy Cameron, "Detrimental Effects
Of Rewards: Reality Or Myth?," <u>American Psychologist</u>, Vol
51, No.11, 1996, pages 1153-1166.

9 Bridget Murray, "Rewards Should Be Given When Defined
Goals Are Met," <u>Monitor</u> [of the American Psychological
Association], June 1997, page 26)

10 William M. Fox, "Group Reaction To Two Types Of Conference Leadership, <u>Human Relations</u>, 1957, 10, pages 279-289.

11 Mark W. Merrill, "Soaring Divorce Rates Are Wrecking Our Communities And Our Nation," <u>Asheville Citizen-Times</u>, September 8, 1997, page A5. For further information, Mark Merrill may be reached at the following address: Florida Family Council, P.O. Box 2882, Tampa, Florida 33602.

12 Reported in the Medicine section of <u>Popular Science</u>, July 1997, page 32.

13 "A Nonbearing Account," <u>Newsweek</u>, April 2, 1990, page 9.

14 J.B. Hardy and L.S. Zabin, <u>Adolescent Pregnancy In An Urban Environment: Issues, Programs, And Evaluation.</u> Baltimore: Urban and Schwarzenberg, 1991.

15 J.P. Allen, S. Philliber, S. Herling, and G.P. Kupermine, "Preventing Teen Pregnancy And Academic Failure: Experimental Evaluation of A Developmentally Based Approach," <u>Child Development</u>, 1997, pages 729-742)

16 "'Baby Think It Over' Program Helps Deter Teen Pregnancy," <u>The Gainesville Sun</u> of Gainesville, Florida, November 4, 1999, page 10A.

17 Al Santoli, "They Turn Young Men With Children Into Fathers," <u>Parade Magazine</u>, May 29, 1994, pages 16-19; quote on page 16. Reprinted with permission from <u>Parade</u>, copyright © 1994.

18 "Some Universals Of Social Behavior." Presidential address to the Division of Personality and Social Psychology of the American Psychological Association at its annual meetings in San Francisco, August 28, 1977.

19   Review And Outlook, "White Fright," <u>The Wall Street Journal</u>, June 19, 1995, page A10.

20 Review And Outlook, "Pop Culture And Drugs," <u>The Wall Street Journal</u>, July 26, 1995, page A12.

21 "The Effects Of Exposure To Violence On Young Children," <u>American Psychologist</u>, September, 1995, pages 782, 784.

22 Betty Hart and Todd Risley, <u>Meaningful Differences In The Everyday Experience Of Young Children</u>. Baltimore: Paul H. Brooks Publishing Company, 1995, pages 77-92; 112-114.

23 Bridget Murray, "Teach Your Children Well," <u>Monitor</u> [of the American Psychological Association], June 1997, page 24.

24 Amy Dickinson, "Must-See TV," <u>Time</u>, November 29, 1999, Personal Time: Your Family Section.

25 Sue Shellenbarger, "Work And Family," <u>The Wall Street Journal</u>, February 25, 1998, page B1.

26 "What Matters? What Does Not?," <u>American Psychologist</u>, February 1998, Number 2, pages 174-175.

27 Mark Merrill, "Soaring Divorce Rates Are Wrecking Our Communities And Our Nation," <u>Asheville Citizen-Times</u>, September 8, 1997, page A5.

28 Margaret Jacobs, "In Oregon, A Novel Way To Rescue Violent Kids," <u>The Wall Street Journal</u>, October 23, 1998, page B1.

29 Sam Allis, "How To Start A Cease-Fire: Learning From Boston," <u>Time</u>, July 21, 1997, pages 28-29.

30 "Community Approach Shows Results In Michigan City," <u>The Boston Globe</u>, December 3, 1990, page A1.

31 Timonthy Noah and David Wessel, "Urban Solutions: Inner-City Remedies Offer Novel Plans - And Hope, Experts Say," The Wall Street Journal, May 4 1992, page A1.

32 Peter Maas, "What We're Learning From New York City," Parade Magazine, May 10, 1998, pages 4-6. Reprinted with permission of the author and with permission from Parade, copyright © 1998.

33 Susan Warren, "Parents Are On A Kick For Tae Kwon Do As a Disciplinary Art," The Wall Street Journal, October 3, 1997, pages A1, A5.

34 Editorial, "Lack Of Discipline Haunts A New Generation," Asheville Citizen-Times, Septemvber 22, 1997, page A4.

35 Bridget Murray, "Why Aren't Antidrug Programs Working?," Monitor [of the American Psychological Association, September 1997, page 30.

36 The New York Times, "Twins Of The Street: Homelessness And Addiction," May 22, 1989, pages A1, A13; (Editorial) Cuomo Commission, The New York Times, "Addiction In The Homeless Shelters," February 20, 1992, page A24.

37 James Willwerth, "Working Their Way Back," Time, November 22, 1999, page 70.

38 Jonathan Dahl, "Street Triage: A San Diego Shelter Feeds The Homeless With An Uneven Hand," The Wall Street Journal, February 18, 1992, page A1.

39 "The Poor? I Hire Them," The Wall Street Journal, May 24, 1995, page A14.

40 Beth Rogers, "Expanding The Talent Search: From Welfare To Work Force," HRM Magazine, July 1991, page 36.

Reprinted by permission of John Wiley & Sons, Inc., Copyright © 1991.

41 Dana Milbank, "Hiring Welfare People, Hotel Chain Finds, Is Tough But Rewarding," The Wall Street Journal, October 31, 1996, page A1.

42 John Greenwal, "Off The Dole And On The Job," Time, August 18, 1997, page 43.

43 Dana Milbank, "Hiring Welfare People, Hotel Chain Finds, Is Tough But Rewarding," The Wall Street Journal, October 31, 1996, page A10.

44 Kay Hymowitz, "Job Training That Works," The Wall Street Journal, February 13, 1997, page A18

45 Ellen Graham, "Marriott's Bid To Patch The Child-Care Gap Gets A Reality Check," The Wall Street Journal, February 2, 2000, page B1.

46 Kay Hymowitz, "Job Training That Works," The Wall Street Journal, February 13, 1997, page A18

47 John Greenwald, "Off The Dole And On the Job," Time, August 18, 1997, page 43-44.

48 Jeffrey Tannenbaum, "Making Risky Hires Into Valued Workers," The Wall Street Journal, June 19, 1997, pages B1-B2.

49 Peter Freiberg, "Unemployment Lines Cut By Prevention Program," Monitor [of the American Psychological Association], February, 1991, page 35.

50 John Greenwald, "Off The Dole And On The Job," Time, August 18, 1997, pages 42, 44.

51 Paulette Thomas, "With A 'Microloan' For A Truck, Family Leaves Welfare," The Wall Street Journal, October 14, 1997, page B1.

52 Hank Whittemore, "Hitting Bottom Can Be The Beginning," Parade Magazine, March 15, 1992, pages 4-6. Reprinted with permission of the author and with permission from Parade, copyright © 1992.

53 Holman Jenkins, Jr., "What Happened When New York Got Businesslike About Crime," The Wall Street Journal, April 28, 1999. page A19; Heather MacDonald, "How To Fight And Win," The Wall Street Journal, July 20, 1999, page A20.

54 Hugh Thomas, The Slave Trade. New York: Simon and Schuster, 1997.

55 Philip Porter, "Liberia," Encyclopaedia Britannica, 1965, 13, page 1026; Foreign News, "Liberia: The Old Pro," Time May 18, 1959, page 30.

56 Matt Moffett, "Against Their Will," The Wall Street Journal, January 11, 1999, page R28.

57 "South African Justice: Bloodthirsty Ways To Fight Carjackers," The Wall Street Journal, January 11, 1999, page A1.

58 George Ayittey, "African Thugs Keep Their Continent Poor," The Wall Street Journal, Jaunary 2, 1998, page 8. See his book: Africa in Chaos. New York: St. Martin's Press, 1998.

59 Geofrey Wheatcroft, "The End Of The Old Regime," The Wall Street Journal, September 10, 1997, page A20.

60 Gerald O'Driscoll, Jr., Kim Holmes, and Melanie Kirkpatrick, "Economic Freedom Marches On," The Wall Street Journal, November 30, 1999, page A26.

61   Thomas Sowell, "Race, Culture, And Equality," Forbes Magazine, October 5, 1998, page 144.   Reprinted by Permission of Forbes Magazine © 2000 Forbes 1998.

Chapter 7: THE NEED FOR NURTURING CORE VALUES IN OUR SCHOOLS AND HOW WE CAN DO IT

1   Ted Forstmann, "School Choice By Popular Demand," The Wall Street Journal, April 21, 1999, page A22; Universal Press Syndicate, William Buckley, Jr., "In A Head-To-Toe Examination, America 1999 Is In A Sorry State," in The Gainesville Sun of Gainesville, Florida, November 4, 1999, page 9A.

2   Associated Press, Anjetta McQueen, "Students Ignorant Of Civics," The Gainesville Sun of Gainesville, Florida, November 19, 1999, page 4A.

3   "Be Careful What You Wish For," The Wall Street Journal, November 14, 1996, page A22.

4   Aaron Hoover, "Freshmen Give GHS Teachers Hard Time," The Gainesville Sun of Gainesville, Florida, March 25, 1995 page 1A.

5   Earl Carlson, "To Improve Our Schools, It Must Start At Home," The Gainesville Sun of Gainesville, Florida, April 4, 1995, page 11A.

6   June Kronholz, "Here's Y The Teaching Of Algebra In The U.S. Has Been Such A Flop," The Wall Street Journal, June 16, 1998, page A1.

7 Raju Narisetti, "Manufacturers Decry A Shortage Of Workers While Rejecting Many," The Wall Street Journal, September 8, 1995, pages A1, A4.

8 Gail Heriot, "Doctored Affirmative-Action Data," The Wall Street Journal, October 15, 1997, page A22.

9 Ibid.

10 Nina Youngstrom, "Inner City Youth Tell Of Life In A `War Zone,'" Monitor [of the American Psychological Association], January 1992, page 36.

11 A Tribe Apart: A Journey Into The Heart Of American Adolescence. New York: Fawcett Columbine, 1998, pages 64, 90.

12 Kay Hymowitz, Ready Or Not. New York: The Free Press, 1999, pages 153, 154, 156.

13 Frank Bruni, "Students' Violent Prose Pits Free Speech against Safety," New York Times, May 8, 1998, page A10.

14 Steve Wulf, "A New Lesson Plan," Time, May 26, 1997, page 75.

15 Romesh Ratnesar, "The Bite On Teachers," Time, July 20, 1998, page 24.

16 Los Angeles Times article, "Poll: Education Goals In Conflict," reported in The Gainesville Sun of Gainesville, Florida, October 22, 1997, page 3A.

17 Jay Greene, W. Howell and Paul Peterson, "Cleveland Shatters Myths About School Choice," The Wall Street Journal, September 18, 1997, page A14.

18 Albert Hunt, "Education Becomes Top Issue, And Consensus May Emerge For Significant Change," <u>The Wall Street Journal</u>, March 14, 1997, page R4

19 "Failure Outside The Classroom," <u>The Wall Street Journal</u>, July 11, 1996, page A14.

20 John Fialka, "Math Scores Rising In U.S. Public Schools, With Minorities And Texas Leading," <u>The Wall Street Journal</u>, July 26, 2000, page A28.

21 Steve Wulf, "A New Lesson Plan," <u>Time</u>, May 26, 1997, pages 76, 78.

22 "Who Should Teach?" <u>The Wall Street Journal</u>, July 15, 1998, page A14.

23 Reported by Tori DeAngelis, "Minority Performance Is Hampered By Stereotypes," <u>Monitor</u> [of the American Psychological Association], October, 1996, page 38.

24 Susan Tifft, "Diamonds In The Rough," <u>Time</u>, August 6, 1990, page 58); Charles Kuralt, "CBS Sunday Morning," August 23, 1992; also my conversation with Brenda Tapia, director of the program at Davidson.

25 Ibid.

26 Lynne Cheney, "Effective Education Squelched," <u>The Wall Street Journal</u>, May 12, 1999, page A22.

27 William Bulkeley, "Now Johnny Can Read If Teacher Just Keeps Doing What He's Told," <u>The Wall Street Journal</u>, July 19, 1999, pages A1, A9.

28 From paper, "A Behaviorist Looks At The Moynihan Report," presented at a Seminar on the Moynihan Report (<u>The Negro Family: The Case For National Action</u>, 1965) and the

Negro, at the Driftwood Inn, Vero Beach, Florida, June 9-12, 1968.

29 Editor of the National Review, "Roadblocks Against U.S. Illiteracy," in The Gainesville Sun of Gainesville, Florida, September 14, 1988, page 8A. Taken from the On The Right column by William Buckley, Jr. (c) Dist. by Universal Press Syndicate. Reprinted with permission. All rights reserved.

30 Suzanne Johnson, "Reformed School," Tulanian, Spring 1998, pages 29-33.

31 "Vouching For A Religious Education," The Wall Street Journal, December 28, 1995, page A6.

32 Ibid.

33 "School Choice Data Rescued From Bad Science," The Wall Street Journal, August 14, 1996, page A12.

34 Reported by Howard Fuller, "New Research Bolsters Case For School Choice," The Wall Street Journal, January 21, 1997, page A18.

35 Jay Greene, W. Howell and Paul Peterson, "Cleveland Shatters Myths About School Choice," The Wall Street Journal, September 18, 1997, page A14.

36 William Bennett, "School Reform: What Remains To Be Done," The Wall Street Journal, September 2, 1997, page A18.

37 Amity Shlaes, "Voucher Program Passes A Test," The Wall Street Journal, October 30, 1998, page A18.

38 June Kronholz, "Texas' Student Exams Face Political And Judicial Tests," The Wall Street Journal, December 23, 1999, page A20.

39 "Shaking Up Schools,"   The Wall Street Journal, May 4, 1998, page A22.

40 June Kronholz, "Charter Schools Begin To Prod Public Schools Toward Competition,"   The Wall Street Journal, February 12, 1999, page A1.

41 Review and Outlook, "Turning Schools Right Side Up," The Wall Street Journal, November 16, 1999, page A30.

42 Thomas Toch, "Whittling Away The Public School Monopoly," The Wall Street Journal, November 15, 1999, page A50.
43 Review And Outlook, "Vouchers Work," The Wall Street Journal, November 28, 1997, page A10.

44 CHARACTERplus™ [a nonprofit consortium], 8225 Florissant Road, St. Louis, MO 63121. Phone: (800) 478 5684.

45 Brochures for the other six districts were obtained from the CHARACTERplus™ office at the address given above.

46 Rochelle Sharpe, "Efforts To Promote Teaching Of Values In Schools Are Sparking Heated Debate Among Lawmakers," The Wall Street Journal, May 10, 1994, page A20.

47 Report of the Los Angeles Times, "Instilling Character: One School's Approach," in The Gainesville Sun of Gainesville, Florida, June 2, 1996, page 4G.

48 Lisa Miller, "Morality Play," The Wall Street Journal, October 25, 1999, page A8.

49 Reported by Michael Ryan in Parade Magazine, May 2000, pages 22-23. For more information, write to: Lesson One Foundation, 245 Newbury Street, Department P, Boston, MA 02116, or call 1-617-247-2787.

50 Report of the <u>Los Angeles Times</u>, "Teaching Values: The Movement Afoot," in <u>The Gainesville Sun</u> of Gainesville, Florida, June 2, 1996, page 4G.

51 Lisa Miller, "Morality Play," <u>The Wall Street Journal</u>, October 25, 1999, page A8.

52 Steve Wulf, "A New Lesson Plan," <u>Time</u>, May 26, 1997, page 75.

53 Jefferson Center For Character Education, 2700 East Foothill Blvd., Suite 302, Pasadena, CA 91107.

54 Linda S. Gottfredson, "Societal Consequences Of The g Factor In Employment," <u>Journal Of Vocational Behavior</u>, 1986, 29, page 403.

55 Frank L. Schmidt, John Hunter, Alice Outerbridge, and Stephen Goff, "Joint Relation Of Experience And Ability With Job Performance: Test Of Three Hypotheses," <u>Journal Of Applied Psychology</u>, 1988, 73 (1), page 56.

56 See Arthur R. Jensen, "q: Artifact Or Reality?," <u>Journal Of Vocational Behavior</u>, 1986, 29 (3), pages 301-331.

57 Paul R. Sackett and Steffanie Wilk, "Within Group Norming And Other Forms Of Score Adjustment In Preemployment Testing," <u>American Psychologist</u>, 1994, 49 (11), page 942.

58 Charles Krauthammer, "Lies, Damn Lies And Racial Statistics," <u>Time</u>, April 20, 1998, page 32.

59 Ibid.

60 C. Capron and M. Duyme, "Assessment Of Effects Of Socio-economic status On IQ In A Full Cross-fostering Study," <u>Nature</u>, 1989, pages 552-554.

283

61 McNeil-Lehrer Television Report of October 2, 1995.

62 Children Of The Boat People: A Study Of Educational Success. University of Michigan Press, 1992.

63 "Failure Outside The Classroom," The Wall Street Journal, July 11, 1996, page A14.

64 "Why They Excel," Parade Magazine, January 21, 1990, pages 4-6. Reprinted with permission from the author and from Parade, copyright © 1990.

65 Associated Press, Paul Raeburn, "Immigrants Outperform Classmates," The Gainesville Sun of Gainesville, Florida, February 23, 1994, page A1.

Chapter 8: THE NEED FOR NURTURING CORE VALUES IN POLITICAL LEADERSHIP AND HOW WE CAN DO IT

1 Horance G. Davis, "Pentagon Lemons Are On A Roll," The Gainesville Sun of Gainesville, Florida, July 18, 1985, page 10A.

2 Ed Magnuson, "Government Is Run Horribly," Time, January 23, 1984, page 16; Mobil ad, Time, January 28, 1985, page 17).

3 "Alaskans Beware: Clean Water!" Asheville Citizen Times, August 3, 1991, page 4A.

4 Editorial, "Ready For World War I," The Gainesville Sun of Gainesville, Florida, March 11, 1992.

5 Kevin Phillips, Arrogant Capital: Washington, Wall Street And The Frustration of American Politics. Boston: Little, Brown, 1994.

6 Reported by Charles Murray, "Americans Remain Wary Of Washington," The Wall Street Journal, December 23, 1997, page A14.

7 Kevin Phillips, "Fat City," Time, September 26, 1994, pages 49-56).

8 Tony Bouza, The Decline And Fall Of The American Empire. New York: Plenum Praess, 1996, page 86. Copyright © 1996 by Tony Bouza. Reprinted by permission of Perseus Books Publishers, a member of Perseus Boqks, L.L.C..

9 Karen Tumulty, "Why Subsidies Survive," Time, March 25, 1996, pages 46, 47; Jackie Calmes, "Bold Talk On 'Corporate Welfare' Cuts Fades As Political Campaigns Heat Up," The Wall Street Journal, March 20, 1996, page A2.

10 "We Can't Afford Corporate Welfare," Reader's Digest, August, 1996, page 70.

11 Tom Schatz and Scott Denman, "But Pork Barreling Isn't Dead Yet," The Wall Street Journal, July 31, 1996, page A14.

12 Donald Barlett and James Steele, "The Empire Of The Pigs," Time, November 30, 1998, pages 52-60.

13 Donald Barlett and James Steele, "Fantasy Islands," Time, November 16, 1998, pages 79-80.

14 Ibid., page 83.

15 Albert Hunt, "Political Insiders To Public: Drop Dead," The Wall Street Journal, November 21, 1996, page A23.

16 David Broder, "No One Has To Answer To Voters These Days," Asheville Citizen-Times, July 9, 1998, page A10.

17 Donald Barlett and James Steele, "The Empire Of The Pigs," Time, November 30, 1998, page 66.

18 Peter Waldman, "Prosperity Is Good For Living-Wage Drive," The Wall Street Journal, December 20, 1999, page A1.

19 "Re-Moralizing America," The Wall Street Journal, February 7, 1995, page A22.

20 Letter from Lincoln to John Johnston dated December 24, 1848. In William Bennett, editor, The Book Of Virtues. Simon Schuster, 1993, page 403.

21 S.J. Ventura, J.A. Martin, S.C. Curtin, and T.J. Mathews, "Report Of Final Natality Statistics, 1995," Monthly Vital Statistics Report 45 (Volume 11, Supplement 24). Hyattsville, MD: National Center for Health Statistics, 1997.

22 Mickey Kaus, "The Welfare Mess - How It Got That Way," The Wall Street Journal, September 12, 1994, page A16.

23 S.J. Ventura, J.A. Martin, S.C. Curtin, and T.J. Mathews, "Report Of Final Natality Statistics, 1995," Monthly Vital Statistics Report 45 (Volume 11, Supplement 2). Hyattsville, MD: National Center for Health Statistics, 1997.

24 James G. Wilson, "A New Approach To Welfare Reform: Humility," The Wall Street Journal, December 29, 1994, page A10.

25 "Why Murphy Brown Is Winning," The Wall Street Journal, June 3, 1996, page A14.

26 Rebekah Coley and P. Lindsay Chase-Lansdale, "Adolescent Pregnancy And Parenthoold," American Psychologist, February 1998, pages 153, 158.

27 Robert Ellickson, "The Homeless Muddle," Public Interest, Spring 1990, pages 45-47, 54-55.

28 Universal Press Syndicate, Reported by William Buckley, Jr., "Shedding Light On A Problem," in The Gainesville Sun of Gainesville, Florida, February 13, 1997, page 12A.

29 Gertrude Himmelfarb, "Re-Moralizing America," The Wall Street Journal, February 7, 1995, page A22.

30 Washington Post writers group, "Law Threatens Fabric Of Society," The Gainesville Sun of Gainesville, Florida, April 11, 1996, page 10A.

31 Daniel Kennedy and August Kerber, Resocialization: An American Experiment. New York: Behavioral Publications, 1973, pages 119, 127.

32 Ibid., pages 50, 63, 65.

33 Susan Mayer, What Money Can't Buy. Harvard University Press, 1997. See Introduction; pages 97-99,137, 150-152.

34 Albert Hunt, "One Government Program That Really Works," The Wall Street Journal, October 28, 1999, page A27.

35 Robert Rector, "Wisconsin Beats The Feds On Welfare Reform," The Wall Street Journal, March 6, 1997, page A14.

36 Review and Outlook, "Baby Talk," The Wall Street Journal, June 14, 1999, page A20.

37 Michael Barone, "Why Michigan Works," Reader's Digest, June 1997, pages 108-110.

38 Ron Stodghill, "Off The Dole," Time, June 12, 2000, page 65.

39 Nancy Johnson, "The Results Are In: Welfare Reform Works," The Wall Street Journal, August 24, 1999, page A18.

40 Joe Klein, "The Predator Problem," Newsweek, April 29, 1996, page 32.

41 Information from the Bureau of Labor Statistics by phone November 25, 1996.

42 Mark Weisbrot, "What Will Raising The Minimum Wage Rate To $6.15 Per Hour Do To The Economy?" Asheville Citizen-Times, June 14, 1998, page A11.

43 Robert Murphy, "No Jobless Rise From Minimum Wage," The Wall Street Journal, June 15, 1998, page A29.

44 Bruce Bartlett, "Minimum Wage Hikes Help Politicians, Not The Poor," The Wall Street Journal, May 27, 1999, page A26.

45 "Be Careful What You Wish For," The Wall Street Journal, November 14, 1996, page A22.

46 "Welfare Reformers vs. Public-Sector Unions," The Wall Street Journal, November 21, 1996, page A22.

47 Edmund Phelps, Rewarding Work. Harvard University Press, 1997, Chapter 9.

48 John Harwood, "Welfare Test Suggests Combining Work With Fiscal Incentives for Long-Termers," The Wall Street Journal, August 28, 1997, page A16.

49 Associated Press, "Welfare Rolls At 30-Year Low; Declining Slowly," The Gainesville Sun of Gainesville, Florida, January 25, 1999, page 1A.

50 "From Boys Town to Oliver Twist," American Psychologist, August 1995, pages 574-575.

51   See S. Coppersmith, <u>Antecedents Of Self Esteem</u>.   San Francisco: Fremont and Company, 1967.

52   "A New Approach to Welfare Reform: Humility," <u>The Wall Street Journal</u>, December 29, 1994, page A10.

53   Richard Berman, "Be Careful What You Wish For,"   <u>The Wall Street Journal</u>, November 14, 1996, page A22.

54   Associated Press, "Hometown Filled With Hope: Troubled Kids Have Village Behind Them," in <u>The Gainesville Sun</u> of Gainesville, Florida, February 13, 1996, page 1B.

55   Otto Friedrich, "Seven Who Succeeded," <u>Time</u>, January 7, 1985, page 45; Dorothy Gaiter, "Tending Their Own: Public Housing Gets Residents To Work - And Off Welfare Roles," <u>The Wall Street Journal</u>, December 7, 1995, page A1.

56   William Bennett, "The Moral Origins Of The Urban Crisis," <u>The Wall Street Journal</u>, May 8, 1992, page A8.

Chapter 9: THE NEED FOR NURTURING CORE VALUES IN THE ADMINISTRATION OF JUSTICE AND HOW WE CAN DO IT

1 United States vs Wade, 388 U.S. 218, 256-257[1967] [White, J. dissenting].

2   "Lawyers As Professionals: Some Moral Issues," <u>Human Rights</u>, Volume 5, 1975-76, page 6.

3 John Miller, <u>The Unmaking Of Americans</u>. New York: Free Press, 1998, pages 126-127, 221.

4 Bernard Gavzer, "We're In The Fight Of Our Lives," <u>Parade Magazine</u>, July 28, 1996, page 4.

5 <u>The Wall Street Journal</u>, January 29, 1997, page A11.

6 "Bill's Prospects For Passage Appear Good," <u>Nation's Business</u>, November, 1998, page 9.

7 March Galanter, "The Day After The Litigation Explosion," <u>Maryland Law Reivew</u>, Volume 46, 1986, page 5.

8 Patrick Atiyah, "Tort Law And The Alternatives," 1987 <u>Duke Law Journal</u>, pages 1002-1044.

9 Douglas Smith, "The Plea Bargaining Controversy," <u>Journal Of Criminal Law And Criminology</u>, Volume 77, 1986, page 949.

10 "What Works? - Questions And Answers About Prison Reform," <u>Public Interest</u>, Spring, 1974, pages 22-54.

11 See Walter Olson, "How Employers Are Forced To Hire Murderers And Other Felons," <u>The Wall Street Journal</u>, June 18, 1997, page A23.

12 Quoted by Bernard Gavzer in "We're In The Fight Of Our Lives," <u>Parade Magazine</u>, July 28, 1996, page 4.

13 Diana Bork, <u>The Wall Street Journal</u>, January 29, 1997, page A11.

14 <u>Crime And The Sacking Of America: The Roots Of Chaos</u>. Washington: Brassey's, 1994, page 83.

15 Benjamin Civiletti, "Zeroing In On The Real Litigation Crisis: Irrational Justice, Needless Delays, Excessive Costs," <u>Maryland Law Review</u>, Volume 46, 1986, pages 45-46.

16 Reported by Steve Hanke, "Incarceration Is A Bargain," <u>The Wall Street Journal</u>, September 23, 1996, page A20.

17 Morgan Reynolds, "Europe Surpasses America in Crime,"

The Wall Street Journal, October 16, 1998, page A14.

18   Editorial, "'Invest In Kids' A Welcome Voice," Asheville Citizen-Times, August 11, 1996, page A14. Copyright 1997, Asheville (N.C.) Citizen-Times, reprinted with permission.

19   Stuart Adams, "Evaluating Correctional Treatments: After Martinson, What?," paper presented at the 1976 meetings of the American Psychological Association, September 3-7 in Washington.

20   Peter Freiberg, "Rehabilitation Is Effective If Done Well, Studies Say," Monitor [of the American Psychological Association], September 1990, page 17.

21   Crime And The Sacking Of America: The Roots Of Chaos. Washington: Brassey's, 1994, page 118.

22   Science And Society, "Factories Behind Bars," U.S. News And World Report, December 30, 1991/January 6, 1992, page 30.

23   Dan Sewell, "Many Companies Finding Skilled Employees Behind Bars," Asheville Citizen-Times, August 30, 1998, page A4.

24   Ibid.

25   Crime And The Sacking Of America: The Roots Of Chaos. Washington: Brassey's, 1994, page 296.

Chapter 10: THE NEED FOR NURTURING CORE VALUES IN BUSINESS AND HOW WE CAN DO IT

1   "Elementary Conditions Of Business Morals," California Management Review, Fall, 1958, pages 4, 6, 12.

2   Rebecca Clay, "Downsizing Backfires On Corporate America," <u>Monitor</u> [of the American Psychological Association], Jaunary 1998, page 24.

3   Joann Lublin, "Walking Wounded: "Survivors Of Layoffs Battle Angst, Anger, Hurting Productivity," <u>The Wall Street Journal</u>, December 6, 1993, page A1.

4   D. Kanter and P. Mirvis, <u>The Cynical Americans</u>. Jossey-Bass, 1989, pages 5,6.

5   "Will A Few Bad Apples Spoil the Core of Big Business?," <u>Business And Society Review</u>, Fall 1985, pages 4-5.

6   <u>Corporate Corruption: The Abuse Of Power</u>. Praeger, 1990, page 15.

7   Rushworth Kidder, <u>Shared Values For A Troubled World</u>. San Francisco: Jossey-Bass, 1994, page 13.

8   James Patterson and Peter Kim, <u>The Day America Told The Truth</u>. New York: Prentice-Hall Press, 1991, page 159.

9   "What CEOs Really Make," <u>Fortune</u>, June 15, 1992, pages 95-98.

10   Christine Gorman, "Listen Here, Mr. Big!," <u>Time</u>, July 3, 1989, page 40.

11   "Raising The Bar" And "Less Is More," <u>The Wall Street Journal</u>, April 10, 1997, pages R1, R4.

12   See G Ungson and R. Steers, "Motivation And Politics In Executive Compensation," <u>Academy of Management Review</u>, 1984 pages 313-323;   and J. Kerr and R. Bettis, "Boards Of Directors, Top Management Compensation, And Shareholder Returns," <u>Academy Of Management Journal</u>, 1987, pages 645-664.

13 Joann Lublin, "Executive Pay, The Great Divide," The Wall Street Journal, April 11, 1996, pages R1, R4.

14 Gary Strauss, "Study: Some CEO Salaries Don't Compute," USA Today, September 29, 1999, page 9A.

15 Interview on "Sixty Minutes" TV program, aired Sunday February 4, 1996.

16 J. Madeline Nash, "Medicine," Time, May 5, 1997, page 69.

17 Tony Bouza, The Decline And Fall Of The American Empire. New York: Plenum Press, 1996, pages 131, 134. Copyright © 1996 by Tony Bouza. Reprinted by permission of Perseus Books Publishers, a member of Perseus Books, L.L.C..

18 D. Kanter and P. Mirvis, The Cynical Americans. Jossey-Bass, 1989, page 84.

19 Vital Statistics, "Hey Ma, Get Me A Lawyer," Newsweek, October 30, 1989, page 10.

20 R. Kreitner, Management. Houghton Mifflin, 1989, page 773.

21 W. M. Hoffman & J. Moore, Business Ethics. McGraw-Hill, 1990, page 564.

22 The Wealth of Nations (1776). Random House, 1937, footnote 1, pages 734, 735.

23 Ibid., page 250.

24 Cited in W. Hoffman and J. Moore, Business Ethics. McGraw-Hill, 1990, page 157. Reproduced with permission of the McGraw-Hill Companies © 1990.

25 Matt Moffett and Jonathan Friedland, "A New Latin America Faces A Devil Of Old: Rampant Corruption," <u>The Wall Street Journal</u>, July 1, 1996, page A1.

26 F.N. Brady, <u>Ethical Managing: Rules And Results</u>. MacMillan Publishing Company, 1990, pages 190-193.

27 See A. Carr, "Is Business Bluffing Ethical?," <u>Harvard Business Review</u>, 1968; M. Kennedy, <u>Office Warfare: Strategies For Getting Ahead In The Aggressive 80's</u>. MacMillan, 1985; R. Jackall, <u>Moral Maze: The World Of Corporate Managers</u>. Oxford University Press, 1988.

28 <u>Ethical Managing: Rules And Results</u>. MacMillan Publishing Company, 1990, pages 178-187.

29 R. Jackall, <u>Moral Maze: The World Of Corporate Managers</u>. Oxford University Press, 1988, page 121.

30 Ibid., page 204.

31 F.N. Brady, <u>Ethical Meaning: Rules And Results</u>. MacMillan Publishing Company, 1990, page 194.

32 M. Dowie, "Pinto Madness," <u>Mother Jones</u>, September-October, 1977.

33 Ibid., pages 22-23.

34 Milo Geyelin, "Lasting Impact," <u>The Wall Street Journal</u>, September 29, 1999, pages A1, A6.

35 California Newsreel, 1983.

36 Ibid.

37 For supporting evidence, see: M. Mace, <u>Directors - Myth And Reality</u>. Harvard Business School Press, 1986.

38 E. Aranow and H. Einhorn, <u>Proxy Contests For Corporate Control</u>. Columbia University Press, 1968.

39 Gary Weaver, Linda Trevino, and Philip Cochran, "Corporate Ethics Programs As Control Systems: Influences Of Executive Commitment And Environmental Factors," <u>Academy Of Management Journal</u>, Vol. 42, No. 1, 1999, page 41.

40 Robert Reich, <u>Locked In The Cabinet</u>. New York: Alfred Knopf, 1997, page 293.

41 Paper by Marshall Sashkin about his study, "Does Fairness Make A Difference?," 1990.

42 Sue Shellenbarger, "Work And Family," <u>The Wall Street Journal</u>, July 22, 1998, page B1.

43 Reported by Charles Hill and Gareth Jones in <u>Strategic Management Theory</u>. Houghton Mifflin Company, 1992, page 44.

44 <u>Uniform Commercial Code</u>. © 1999. The American Law Institute and the National Conference of Commissioners on Uniform State Laws; reprinted with permission. (These selections from <u>Uniform Commercial Code</u>, West Publishing Company, 1987, page 42).

45 From <u>Uniform Laws Annotated, Supplementary</u> Pamphlet, Vol. 9, Part 1. St. Paul, MN: West Publishing Company, 1998.

46 Ibid.

47 Ibid.

48 Ibid.

49 <u>Uniform Laws Annotated</u>, Vol. 7A, Part 1. St. Paul, MN: West Publishing Company, 1999.

50 Ibid.

51 Ibid.

52 <u>Uniform Laws Annotated</u>, Vol. 9B, St. Paul, MN: West Publishing Company, 1987.

53 Ibid.

54 <u>Uniform Laws Annotated, Cumulative Annual Pocket Part</u>, Vol. 9B. St. Paul, MN: West Publishing Company, 1998.

55 From <u>Uniform Laws Annotated</u>, Vol. 10, St. Paul, MN: West Publishing Company, 1974. (The Model Penal Code was developed by The American Law Institute and approved by it in 1962, and was published by it in 1985, along with a multi-volume set of commentaries to the Code).

56 <u>Uniform Laws Annotated, Cumulative Annual Pocket Part</u>, Vol. 11. St. Paul, MN: West Publishing Company, 1998.

57 C. Lindsay and B. Dempsey, "Experience In Training Chinese Business People To Use U.S. Management Techniques," <u>The Journal Of Applied Behavioral Science</u>, 1985, No. 1.

58 P. Dorfman and J. Howell, "Production Sharing In The Mexican Maquiladora Industry: A Challenge For I/O Psychology," <u>The Industrial-Organizational Psychologist</u>, 1984, No. 1.

59 William Fox, "Japanese Management: Tradition Under Strain," <u>Business Horizons</u>, August, 1977.

60 See R. Nader, M. Green and J. Seligman, "Who Rules The Corporation?," and H. Geneen, "Why Directors Can't Protect The Shareholders." In W. M. Hoffman and J. M. Moore, <u>Business Ethics</u>. McGraw-Hill, 1990.

61 T. M. Jones, "Corporate Board Structure And Performance Variations In The Incidence Of Shareholder Suits," in James Post and L. Preston, editors, <u>Research In Corporate Social Performance And Policy</u>, Volume 8. Greenwich, Connecticut: Jai Press, 1986, pages 345-359; I. F. Kenner and R. B. Johnson, "An Investigation Of The Relationship Between Board Composition And Stockholder Suits," <u>Strategic Management Journal</u>, 1990, pages 327-336.

62   Stuart Mieher, "Firms Restrict CEOs In Picking Board Members," <u>The Wall Street Journal</u>, March 15, 1993, page B1.

63   R. Nader, M. Green and J. Seligman, "Who Rules The Corporation?" In W. M. Hoffman and J. M. Moore, <u>Business Ethics</u>. McGraw-Hill, 1990. Copyright © 1976 with Ralph Nader.

64 Ibid.

65   Harold Geneen, "Why Directors Can't Protect The Shareholders." In W. M. Hoffman and J. M. Moore, <u>Business Ethics</u>. McGraw-Hill, 1990.

66 R. Nader, M. Green and J. Seligman, op. cit.

67 Joann Lublin, "Buy Or Bye," <u>The Wall Street Journal</u>, April 21, 1993, page R9.

68   Timothy Schellhardt, "More Directors Are Raking In Six-Figure Pay," <u>The Wall Street Journal</u>, October 29, 1999, page B4.

69 Roger Lowenstein, "Is Greed Good?," <u>Smart Money</u>, June, 1999, page 73.

70 <u>Organization Culture And Leadership</u>. Jossey Bass, 1986.

71   Robert Boisseau and Harvey Caras, "A Radical Experiment Cuts Deep Into The Attractiveness Of Unions," Personnel Administrator, October, 1983, pages 76-78. Also personal phone conversation with Leroy Brown, January 26, 1989, and with Ron Richardson, February 24, 1999.

72   Aristotle, "Politics" [circa 335 B.C.]. In The Works Of Aristotle, Volume II, as part of Robert Hutchins, editor, Great Books of the Western World, Volume 9: Book 2, Chapter 10, Paragraph 5;   Book 3, Chapter 16, Paragraph 30;   Book 6, Chapter 4, Paragraph 40.

73   From L. Nash, "Ethics Without the Sermon," Harvard Business Review, November-December, 1981.

74   From presentation made while a Visiting Professor of Business and Law at the University of Florida in 1989.

75   Statement before the Subcommittee on Employment and Manpower of the Committee on Labor and Public Welfare, U.S. Senate, on behalf of the Automation Fund Committee, established by contracts between Armour and Company and others, February 6, 1964, page 7.

76   Michael Campion, "Human Resource Implications Of Robotics: A Survey Study At IBM," paper presented at Academy of Management Meetings, San Diego, August 13, 1985.

77 The Wall Street Journal, November 1, 1996, page B7.

78 Laura Koss-Feder, "Perks That Work," Time, November 9, 1998.

79 Ibid.

80 Merrelyn Emery and Ronald Purser, The Search Conference. San Francisco: Jossey-Bass, 1996, pages xix, 299-305.

81 Redesigning the Future: A Systems Approach To Societal Problems. John Wiley and Sons, 1974, page 30.

82 Thresa Welbourne and Luis Gomez-Mejia, "Gainsharing: A Critical Review And A Future Research Agenda," Journal Of Management, Vol. 21, No. 3, 1995, pages 559-609.

83 "The Foreign Corrupt Practices Act: A New Perspective," Journal Of International Business Studies, Volume 15, NO. 3, 1984, pages 107-121.

84 Foreign Corrupt Practices Act Reporter, 1979, page 700.

85 "Middle East Response To The U.S. Foreign Corrupt Practices Act," California Management Review, 1987, No. 4, page 30.

86 H. Lane and D. Simpson, "Bribery In International Business: Whose Problem Is It?," The Journal Of Business Ethics, 1984, No. 1, 35-43.

87 "When Somebody Wants A Payoff," Fortune, Fall, 1989, page 43.

88 Pascal Zachary, "Industrialized Countries Agree To Adopt Rules To Curb Bribery," The Wall Street Journal, February 16, 1999, page A18.

89 Caterpillar Code Of Worldwide Business Conduct And Operating Principles. Peoria, Illinois: Caterpillar Tractor Company, August 1, 1992, page 13.

90 Based upon H. Lane and D. Simpson, "Bribery In International Business: Whose Problem Is It?," The Journal Of Business Ethics, 1984, No. 3, 35-43.

91 U.S. Representative Allen Boyd, "Congress Can't Be On The Fast Track To OK Trade Deal," The Gainesville Sun of Gainesville, Florida, October 18, 1997, page 9A.

92 Jim Carlton, "U.S. Border Towns Suffer From Post-NAFTA Syndrome," The Wall Street Journal, August 28, 1998, pages B1, B4.

93 G. Pascal Zachary, "Starbucks Asks Foreign Suppliers To Improve Working Conditions," The Wall Street Journal, October 23, 1995, page B4.

94 Thomas Grose, "Called To Account," Time Select Business Section, Time, October 4, 1999.

95 Results of a survey conducted by Korn/Ferry International and the Columbia University School of Business reported in Rushworth Kidder, Shared Values For A Troubled World. San Francisco: Jossey-Bass, 1994, page 12.

OVERVIEW

1 Crime And The Sacking Of America: The Roots Of Chaos. Washington: Brassey's, 1994, page 299.

2 "On Being Citizens And Soldiers," Time, June 9, 1980, pages 86, 87.

3 "The Search For Virtues," Time, March 7, 1994, page 78.

4 Soul Searching: Why Psychotherapy Must Promote Moral Responsibility. New York: Basic Books, 1995, page 7.

5 Tony Bouza, The Decline And Fall Of The American Empire. New York: Plenum Press, 1996, page 191.

6 "Values, Assumptions, And Practices," American Psychologist, May 1997, page 530.

INDEX

Abortion, questions about, xxviii-xxix

Academic achievement, factors that affect, 93-94, 121-146

Adams, John, on slavery, 8

Addictive behavior, and value orientation, xxvii

Africa:

    absence of democracy in, 118-119

    causes of unrest in, xxii

    corruption in, 118-119

    fantasies about life in, 117-120

    Sub-Sahara, world's poorest region in, 119

Aggression:

    air rage, 45

    effects of child abuse upon, 49

    encouraged by television, 47-48

    negative change in level of, 45-46

    on school buses, 45

    road rage, 45

Air rage, 45

America Works, successful rehabilitation employment, 112

American Colonization Society, support of Liberia by, 118

American Seed Company, youth program dropped due to cheating, 42

Americans With Disabilities Act of 1990, being used inappropriately, 162-163

Anti-Social Personality Disorder, being used to impose dysfunctional workers upon others, 162-163

Armour, successful employee-transfer program of, 228-229

Asian-Americans, superior academic performance of, 144-145

Aurelius, Marcus, value orientation of, 35

Authority:

    avoiding abuses of, 222-242

    indiscriminate submission to, 77-79

    ultimate source of, in business, 209

"Baby Think It Over" Program, successful approach for discouraging premature motherhood, 101

Bankruptcies:
   Chapter 7 for, too easily awarded, 176-177, 179-180
   dilution of personal accountability with regard to, 176-177
   frequency, trend of, 43, 176-177
   needed remedial action for, 179-180

Barclay Enterprises, successful rehabilitation employment by, 111

Behavior:
   conscious analysis as a causal factor of, 66-67, 74, 76, 82
   conscious analysis as a factor in the development of a conscience, 66
   feelings of self-efficacy as a causal factor of, 82-83
   genetic inheritance as a causal factor of, 64-65
   interaction of causal factors of, 82, 167
   situational factors as a causal factor of, 76-83
   values as a causal factor of, 75-83

Behavior Management, 85-95
   B.F. Skinner on, 94
   consequence control in, 90-94
   cue control in, 88-90
   dealing with excessively charged values, 85-88
   dealing with the urge toward immediate gratification, 88-94
   in the Monitor Program, 106
   misuse of, in welfare programs, 159
   objections to, 93-94
   Pizza Hut "Book It" program, that successfully encourages reading, 94
   to improve academic performance, 129-130

BELL computer program, to lower pension costs via pre-vesting layoffs, 204

Birth control, 99-101
   "Baby Think It Over" Program, 101
   John Hopkins Pregnancy Prevention Program, 101
   need for, 14, 50, 53, 57, 159-160
   Teen Outreach Program, 101

Via Selective Tubal Occlusion, 99-100
Black negative sub-culture:
    black-on-black discrimination in, 61-62
    crime and delinquency in, 55-57
    disregard for academic attainment in, 57-59
    illegitimacy and broken families in, 57
    lack of mutual economic support in, 60-61
    negative changes in, 55-62
    rejection of positive role models in, 59-60
Boards of directors:
    need for reform of, 218-220
        require community-impact statements from, 220-221
        require equity stake in company from, 221
    value of outside members on, 219-220
Bribery in business abroad, dealing with, 196, 234-240
Buddhism, core values of, 25-26
Business leadership:
    ethical qualifications for, 221-222
    in international operations, 188-194, 235-242
    lack of trust and confidence in, 189-191, 198, 231
    reactions of managers to the Depression-Era policies of
        F.D.R., 202
    social responsibility and, 198-209
    sweatshops and, 205,240-242
    unwarranted compensation of, 191-193, 221
"Can Do" feelings (see Self-Efficacy)
Campaign Financing:
    avoiding problems with, 155-156
    need for reform of, 150-151, 153, 155-156
    possible solutions for problems associated with, 156
Cash-Balance pension plans, can penalize long-term
    employees, 205
Cathexis (emotional charging), dealing with the undesirable
    effects of, 64-66, 85-88
Censorship by the Hollywood Hays Office, 48-49
Chapter 7 for bankruptcy, too easily awarded, 176-177
Character Education, 54, 63-67, 136-141
    beneficial effects of, 141

Character First program for, 140
Character Plus program (formerly PREP): 137-139
    appreciation of learning in, 138-139
    civic values in, 138
    personal values in, 137
    social values in, 138
Character First program, for successfully teaching values in school, 140
Character Plus program (formerly PREP), for successfully teaching values in school, 137-139
    appreciation of learning in, 138-139
    civic values in, 138
    personal values in, 137
    social values in, 138
Charter Schools:
    experience with, 134-135
    response to, 134-135
Cheating, survey results of, 42-43, 189, 195-196
Child labor, xxiv, xxvi
Civic values, teaching of, 138
Code of Business Ethics:
    can be viable, 210-218, 234-240
    Code of Worldwide Business Conduct of the CaterpillarTractor Company, 236-239
Cognitive-ability scores:
    as assessed by GATB, 141-143
    influence of education upon, 22
    influence of rearing circumstances upon, 143
    warranted discrimination based upon, 141-143,
    yield different valid scores for different groups, 141-143
Compstat Computer-based Program, for processing timely crime data, 117
Conflicts of interest:
    created by the Equal Employment Opportunity Commission, 118, 179
    in government, 151, 153
Confucianism, core values of, 26-27
Conscience:

cathexis (emotional charging) as part of, 64-66
conscious analysis in relation to, 65-66
development of, 63-67, 67-74
influence of genetic inheritance upon, 64-65, 67-74
Conscious analysis, 65-67
    role of, in causing behavior, 76
    role of, in value acquisition, 66
Consequence control for improved compliance with
    conscious goals, 90-94
"Copycat" crimes, 48
Core values:
    across cultures, xv-xvi, xxii-xxvi, 25-35, 79-80, 215-218
    America's founding fathers on, 1, 4-7, 20
    Charles Darwin on, 1-2
    decline in adherence to, 41-62, 121-126, 148-154, 157-
        165, 175-179, 191-196, 244-246
    evidence in support of:
        being ambitious, hardworking, and aspiring, 18-20
        emphasis on learning, 20-22
        intact families, 13-17, 50-51
    George Washington on, 1
    how acquired, 4, 63-74
    importance of, 1-2, 4-7, 162, 243-244
    make a culture viable when shared, 1-2, 4-7
    nature of, xxx, 1-7
    of the world's religions, 25-33
    public-school practices that are inconsistent with, 121-122
    public support for today, 12-14, 18, 20, 22
    required to support intelligent inquiry and planning, 2
    school programs for teaching, 136-141
    successful teaching of, 54, 63-66, 136-141
Corporate welfare, abuses of, 149-155
Corruption:
    discouragement of, in business, 222-228, 233-242
    during and after the Civil War, 40-41
    idea of penalty reductions for companies that take
        meaningful corrective-action steps, 210-211
    in Africa, 118-119

in form of foreign payoffs by U.S. companies, 196
in government, 148-155
in Liberia, 118
in U.S. companies, 153-155, 187, 191, 193, 196, 204-205
in U.S. unions, 195
Cost/Benefit Analysis:
    applied to business, 205-209
    Ford Pinto example of, 206-207
    General Motors fuel fires example of, 207-208
Counselors, should be on piecework, 183
Court-case overload, the problem and remedial action, 177, 180
"Crank," effects of, 55
Crime:
    causes of, xix-xx, 47-62, 64-65, 69-74, 157-158
    "copycat," 48
    effective measures for reducing, 106-109
    homicide rates in 11 developed countries, xx
    impact of, upon the young, 46-48
    in Africa, 118-119
    juvenile rates of, 46, 50-51, 53, 55-56
    rates of, for 1933 versus 1994, xviii
    recent rate changes of, 46
Criminal justice:
    hampered by defense tactics, 175
    hampered by "legal blackmail," 177,180
    hampered by diminished personal accountability, 175-178
    need for panels of judges, 180
    need for punitive-damages caps, 180
    undermined by the Equal Employment Opportunity Commission, 179
Criminal Personality:
    defining elements of, 71-72
    individuals of this type should have their freedom constrained, 180-181
    influence of genetic inheritance upon, 73
    resistance of, to change, 73, 177-178

Cue control, for improved compliance with conscious goals, 88-90
Curfews, success of, with youthful drug offenders, 106

Darwin, Charles, on essential role of core values, 1-2
Declaration of the United Nations (see Universal Declaration of Human Rights of the United Nations)
Declaration of the World Conference of Religions For Peace, 30-31
Declaration Toward A Global Ethic, 13, 31-33
Delancey Street Foundation, successful rehabilitation of former criminals, 115-117
Democracy:
    absence of in Africa, 117-119
    requirements of, for success, 4-7, 18-20, 243-247
Depression rates, 44
Depression Era:
    crime rates during, xviii
    morality during, xvii-xviii
    reactions of Herbert Hoover to, 200-201
    remedial efforts of Franklin Roosevelt for, 201
Direct Instruction, for enhancing academic performance and self-esteem, 128
Discrimination, 119-120
    black-on-black, 61-62
    effects of, on ethnic groups, 120
    valid when based upon group-score differences, 141-143
Discussion leadership:
    for defining and gaining acceptance of organizational goals or action plans, 231-233
    for identifying problems or opportunities, solving a problem, and reviewing proposed solutions or programs, 95-97
DIVAD project, as example of misdirected effort, 147
"Don'ts," dysfunctional ones, 87
    dealing effectively with, 87-88
Douglas, Frederick, on importance of education, 11
Downsizing:

done intelligently, 228-230
and "layoff-survivor syndrome," 189-190
why it backfires, 189-190
Drugs:
and our youth, effectively dealing with, 54-55
use of curfews, 106
STAR program for dealing with, 108-109
poor prospects for rehabilitation, 55
subtle effects of marijuana, 54-55
use of, among the homeless, 109-110
Edison Schools, a management-of-schools company, 135-136
Education:
disadvantages of social promotions, 122-123, 134
effective encouragement of reading, 94, 144
expenditures per student, 121
experience with vouchers, 131-133
erosion of standards, 122-125
feasibility of higher standards, 134
growing importance of, 21-22
impact of charter schools, 134-135
impact of Edison Schools, 135-136
measures for improving school discipline, 131
need for parental involvement, 144-145
nonproductive public-school practices, 121-124
school violence, 45, 123
Educational improvement through:
Direct Instruction, 128
Love of Learning, 127-128
school choice, 131-136
parental involvement, 22, 103-105, 144-145
Success For All, 128-129
the teaching of values, 136-141
Educational standards, 122-125
beneficial effects of raising, 134
subverted by parental behavior, 123-124, 144-145
subverted by "the philosophy of the whole child," 122-123
Energy to act, role in causing behavior, 75-76, 82

"Entitlements", dysfunctional ones, 86
  effectively dealing with, 87-88
Environmental Protection Agency, an irrational act of, 148
Epictetus's Manual For the Roman Field Soldier, 13
Equal Employment Opportunity Commission, unrealistic requirements of, 176, 179
Ethical Behavior:
  audits of, 242
  benefits to business of, 2111-212, 234-236
  in international business operations, 234-242
  legal-compliance offices to enforce compliance with, 210-211
  strengthening of, 85-98, 210-211, 222-242
Ethical/Legal compliance office, 210-211
Ethics:
  absolutism versus excessive permissiveness, xxvii-xxix
  and abortion, xxviii-xxix
  and Cost/Benefit Analysis, 205-209
  and Social Darwinism, 202
  and the "game analogy" in business, 203-204
  based upon cross-cultural interviews, 34-35
  can be complex, xxvii-xxix
  core values versus less-essential ones, 3
  declaration of the United Nations about, 33-34
  Declaration of the World Conference of Religions For Peace, 30-31
  Declaration Toward A Global Ethic, 31-33
  decline of, in government, 149-154
  Epictetus's Manual For the Roman Field Soldier, 13
  in business, 185-191, 202-242
  in international business operations, 215-218, 234-242
  nature of, 63
  selection of leaders with regard to, 221-222
  strengthening ethical behavior, 218-242
Exclusionary Rule, misuse of, 176
  need to make it discretionary, 79
Executive Compensation, often excessive, 191-193, 221

Export-Import Bank, provides help to non-needy companies, 155

Family life:
    back-to-back work shifts to improve, 105
    program for encouraging fathers to be responsible for, 102
    impact of, upon cognitive-ability skills, 143
    impact of parental conflict upon, 105
    importance of, 13-17, 50-54, 63-66, 165
    importance of marriage to, 50
    improving the quality of, 103-105
    reducing conflict of, with the job, 230-231
    Retrouvaille Program for troubled marriages, 105
    value of pre-marriage counseling to, 98
Fathers, importance of, 14-16, 50, 126
"Featherbedding," by U.S. government, 149, 153-154
Federal Light Water Reactor Program, costly and unwarranted, 153-154
Federalist Paper No. 2, notes from, about shared values, 4-5
Federalist Paper No. 55, notes from, about virtue and self-government, 5
Fetus, changing characteristics of, xxix
Foster parents:
    in the Hope Meadows Project, 172-173
    in the Monitor Program, 106
    need to maintain extended-family influence in addition to, 171-172
4-H Club youngsters who have violated exhibition rules, 43
Franklin, Benjamin, on slavery, 8
Free enterprise:
    limitations to, 185-188, 198-201
    Milton Friedman on, 199-201
Free trade, disadvantages of, 240-242
Friedman, Milton, on free enterprise, 199-201
Foreign Corrupt Practices Act of 1977, 196, 234-235

Gainsharing for equitably sharing the fruits of employee-generated productivity gains, 233-234

Gambling, impact upon children of, 49

General Aptitude Test Battery (GATB), different scores for different groups, 142

Genetics, influence of, 67-74
heritability of certain attributes, 67-70

Ghetto housing, successful program for, 173

Girl Scouts, percentage willing to cheat on tests, 42-43

Morris, Governor, about France in the 1790's, 6-7

Government (U.S.), irresponsibility of, 147-154,162
DIVAD Project, 147
EPA 148
ethanol production, 153
Grace Report, and aftermath, 147-150
Jones Act of 1920, 149
measures to reverse, 155-173
Mining Law of 1872, 152
sugar subsidies, 152

Grace Report on government inefficiency, 147-148

Gratification, immediate, urge toward, 88
dealing with it via consequence control, 90-94
dealing with it via cue control, 88-90

Greed,
in Australia, 197
in the U.S., 191-193, 204-205, 208-209

Grievance mediation, to avoid the abuse of power, 223-224

Game analogy, applied to business ethics, 203-204

Grievance panels (see grievance mediation)

Group problem solving:
encouraging truthfulness and full disclosure in, 95-97
Improved Nominal Group Technique, for improvement of, 96-97
problems with conventional procedures for, 95
The Search Conference, for improvement of, 231-233

Hamilton, Alexander, on qualities for successful republicanism, 5

Happiness:
causes of, xx-xxii

and inherited wealth, xxi-xxii
and materialism, xx-xxii
Hard-core unemployed:
   characteristics of, 163
   vagrancy as a Constitutional right, 163-164
Hays Office of movie censorship, 48-49
Hinduism, core values of, 27-28
Histrionic Personality Disorder, being used to impose
   dysfunctional workers upon others, 162-163
Homeless and unemployed persons:
   constructive assistance for, 109-115
   need for "hand-holding" with, 112-113
   problems with, 109-113
Honesty, evidence of negative change in level of, 42-43
Hoover, Herbert, on Depression-Era policy, 200-201
Human rights, declaration of the United Nations about, 33-34
Hyperactivity, significant genetic basis for, 69-70
IBM's successful installation-of-Robotics program, 229
Illegitimacy:
   changing attitudes toward, 159-160
   in part of the black culture, 57
   means for discouraging, 99-101, 168
   problems associated with, 50, 159-160
   rate of, for non-poverty-level high-school seniors in Tipton
      County, IN, 160
Immigrants:
   importance of congruent values, on the part of, 41, 243-244
   need for the revision of admission requirements for, 243-244
Incarceration, an economically feasible means for reducing
   crime, 180-181
Incivility:
   air rage, 45
   in the military, 81-82
   negative trend toward, 45
   on school buses, 45

road rage, 45

Influence peddling in government, 150-155

International business:

Caterpillar Tractor's Code of Worldwide Business Conduct, 236-242

relevant cross-cultural value differences, 215-218

reducing the conflict between domestic and foreign working-conditions standards, 240-242

I.Q. scores (see cognitive-ability scores)

Islamism, core values of, 28

Jay, John:

on slavery, 8

on the importance of shared values, 4-5

Jefferson, Thomas:

on emancipation, 10-11

on relationship between ignorance and freedom, 20

on slavery, 8

Job-family conflict, reduction of, 230-231

John Hopkins Pregnancy Prevention Program, 101

Judaism, core values of, 29

Juvenile crime, 42, 46, 56, 73

in schools, 123

reduction of, via the Monitor Program, 106

Juvenile delinquency, 46, 50, 53-56

impact of, on youth, 46

need for early intervention to deal with effectively, 181-183

reduction of, via military-type program, 108

reduction of, via Project STAR, 108-109

reduction of, via Tae Kwon Do classes, 108

Kant, Immanuel, on an overriding core value, 35

Kibbutzim, lessons from, 17

Labor-management relations, when there is lack of trust, 188-191, 194

Laissez faire (see free enterprise)

Lama, Dalai:
  on materialism and happiness, xxii
  on the nature of all religions, 30
  on the purpose of religion, xxv
"Layoff survivor syndrome," as a result of dysfunctional downsizing, 188-190
Lee, Robert E.:
  on slavery, 36
  on the proper use of power, 36
"Legal blackmail" via requiring defendants in groundless lawsuits to pay for their defense, 177, 180
Liberia, failure of democracy in, 118
Lincoln, Abraham:
  about avoiding the appearance of a conflict of interest, 36
  about rehabilitation of the post-Civil War South, 37
  about slavery, 9, 37
  advice of, to a debt-ridden brother, 159
  disrespect toward, 39-40
  on liberty, 246
Lincoln Electric Company, higher skill levels now required of entering workers, 21, 122
Literacy level:
  decline in, 122
  reversing the decline of, 128-130, 144-145
Litigation:
  current problems with, 177
  possible remedies for problems with, 179
Lombardi, Vince, on the need for personal caring to accompany discipline, 109
Louisiana Alliance for Educational Reform, success of, 130-131
Love Of Learning, minority, educational enrichment program, 127-128
Lying, survey results of extent of, 43,191

Madison, James:
  on assumed requirements for successful republicanism, 5
  on emancipation, 10-11

on slavery, 8
Management of change:
  for others, 228-230
  for ourselves, 85-97
Marijuana, subtle effects of, 54-55
Market Promotion Program as example of unnecessary corporate welfare, 153
Marriage, importance of, 50-51
Marriott Corporation, successful rehabilitation employment program of, 112-113
Mathematics instruction:
  results of the Third International Math and Science Survey, 122
  value of changing female expectations, 127
McClelland, General George, disrespect of President Lincoln, 39-40
Medicare fraud, 44
Melville, Herman, on freedom, 85
Methamphetamine (meth), effects of, 55
Microboard Processing Company, successful employment rehabilitation of high-risk people by, 114
Microenterprise Centers, for would-be entrepreneurs, 115
Mill, John Stuart:
  on Cost/Benefit Analysis, 205-206
  on requirements for the exercise of productive individual liberty, 5
Minimum wage, needed changes in, 168-170
Monitor Program, successfully changes the behavior of violent juveniles, 106
Moral decline:
  evidence of, xv, 42-62, 150-154, 191-196
  in business, 191-196
  in government, 150-154
  in part of the black culture, 55-59
  reversal of, through values education, 63-66, 136-141
Movies, negative influence of, 48
Murphy Village, home of the exploitative "travelers," 79-80
"Musts," dealing with typical dysfunctional ones, 86

Narcissistic Personality Disorder, being used to impose dysfunctional workers upon others, 162-163

National Commission on Governing America's Schools, recommendations of, 135

National Institute for Responsible Fatherhood and Family Development, success of, 102

New York City's Model Block Program:
has reduced drug trafficking, 107-108
Nuisance Abatement Act, as used in, 107-108
Trespass Affidavit Program, as used in, 107-108

Nominal Group Technique (Improved), for identifying problems and opportunities and for reviewing proposed programs and solutions, 95-97

Nuisance Abatement Act, permits the transfer of improperly used apartments to legitimate families, 107-108

Operation Cul-de-Sac, for successful reduction of crime and drug dealing, 173

Oppositional Defiant Disorder, being used to impose dysfunctional workers upon others, 162-163

Parachutes, pack, World War I value that opposed use of, xv

Parental involvement with children:
as a vehicle for the encouragement of reading, 93-94, 144
importance of, 51-54, 63-66, 144-145, 165

Partners in Care, successful support for the mentally ill, 110

"Pay After Performance" rule, as part of Wisconsin's welfare reform program, 166-167

Perfect competition, why a fiction, 185-188

Peripheral values, nature of, 3

Personal values, teaching of, 137

Phi Delta Kappa/Gallup Poll, survey of values that should be taught in public schools, 139-140

Philosophy of the Whole Child, dysfunctional effects of, 122-123

Physical abuse, effects of, on the young, 49

Piaget, Jean, on stages of human development, 67

Pizza Hut "Book It" Program, to encourage reading, 94

Popular music, changes in character of, 47
"Pot," subtle effects of, 54-55
Poverty:
    negative effects of, 51
    not a major cause of crime, xix-xx, 157-158, 165
    used to excuse irresponsible behavior, 162-163
Power of values, xv-xxxvii, 75-82
    during the Depression Era, xvii-xviii
    in Africa, xxii-xxiii
    in Nazi death camps, xxii
    in the American-Indian subculture, xxiii
    in the Battle of New Orleans, xv-xvi
    in the U.S. Marine Corps, xvi
    in World War I, xv
    in World War II, xvi
    to depress economies, xxii-xxiii
    to encourage the mistreatment of individuals and groups,
        xxiii-xxvi, 77-82
    with the Mormons, xvi-xvii
Pre-marriage counseling, beneficial effects of, 98
PREP (see Character Plus program)
Principled Negotiations Approach, for "win-win"
    negotiations, 226-228
Prison environment, simulated effects of, 79
Prison labor:
    a productive and feasible idea today, 183-184
    Florida's PRIDE Enterprises, 183-184
Probation officers, should be on piecework, 183
Psychopathic Personality (see Criminal Personality)

Racial preference:
    impact of, on academic performance, 142-143
    impact of, on medical practice, 123
Rational Emotive Therapy, for dealing with dysfunctional
    values, 87-88
Rationality, dealing with limits to, 64-74, 76-83, 85-98
Reform needed:

of the administration of the Americans With Disabilities
  Act of 1990, 162-163
of bankruptcy procedure, 176-177, 179-180
of campaign financing, 155-156
of corporate welfare, 149-155
of Equal Opportunity requirements, 176, 179
of our schools, 45, 121-125, 130-136
of rehabilitation programs, 164-166, 177-178, 181-184
of the criminal-justice system, 175-179
of vagrancy laws, 160-161, 163-164, 166
of welfare programs, 157-161, 164-168
Regulation of business, need for, 185-188, 191-193, 240-242
Rehabilitation:
  basic requirements for the success of, 109, 117, 164, 181-
    184
  need to segregate criminals for success of, 180-182
  of drug addicts, 55
  of former convicts, 115-117, 177-178, 180-184
  regulatory obstacles to, 111
  via special employment programs, 110-117
  via subsidies to private-sector employers, 112-113, 169-
    170
Rehabilitation success via employment:
  America Works, 112
  Barclay Enterprises, 111
  Center for Employment Training, 115
  Chicago Manufacturing Institute, 115
  GAIN, 114
  Marriott Corporation, 112-113
  Microboard Processing Company, 114
  Microenterprise Centers, 115
  St. Vincent de Paul Village, 110-11
  South Bronx Overall Development Corporation, 114
  Strive Program, 113-114
  Wildcat Services, 114
Reich, Robert:
  linking by, of big-name retailers to sweat shops, 205
  on the need to reward responsible managements, 210-211

Reinforcement:
  negative, use of, 91-93
  positive, use of, 90-91
Religion:
  and abortion, xxix
  core values of various denominations, 25-33
  Declaration of the World Conference of Religions For
    Peace, 30-31
  Declaration Toward A Global Ethic, 13, 31-33
  oppression of Christians in the name of, xxv-xxvi
  theology of, versus unifying core values, xxiv-xxvii
Retrouvaille Program, successful intervention for troubled
  marriages, 105
Road rage, 45
Roosevelt, Franklin, Depression-Era policies of, 201

St. Vincent de Paul Village:
  assistance of, to the homeless, 110-111
  orientation program of, for shelter operators, 111
Savings and loan scandal, 191
School-bus violence, 45
School choice, experience with, 131-136
School reforms, successful programs of, 130-131, 134-135
School vouchers, experience with, 131-133
SCORE, aid to would-be entrepreneurs, 115
Scott Paper Company, higher skill levels now required for
  entering employees, 21
Search Conference:
  as a tool for voter and organizational-member input, 157,
    231-233
  for defining and gaining acceptance of organizational
    goals and action plans, 231-233
Segregation of criminals, need for, 177-178, 180-184
Selective Tubal Occlusion, to prevent pregnancy, 99-100
Self-discipline:
  enhancement of, 88-91, 108-109, 131
  need for, among the chronically unemployed, 113
Self-efficacy:

enhancing feelings of, 95
influence of, 82-83
Self-esteem:
enhancement of, via supportive, affectionate parents, 103-104
improvement of, via Direct Instruction, 128
improvement of, via enhanced self-efficacy, 95
inappropriate attempts at enhancement of, 121-123
lowered by sex without commitment, 14
Self-Sufficiency First, successful Wisconsin welfare-reform program, 166-167
Shared rights, values, and responsibilities, the bedrock of viable, self-government, 1-7, 85, 162, 164, 168, 173, 200, 243-244
Short-run versus long-run in business, consequences of, 199-200, 208-209
Single parenting:
Hope Meadows Project, an alternative to, 172-173
possible constructive alternative via the coordinated efforts of several agencies, 171-172
problems arising from, 14-17, 50-51
Situational factors:
as a cause of behavior, 77-82
effects of a simulated prison environment, 79
effects of indiscriminate submission to authority, 77-79
Murphy Village, effects of a negative subculture, 79-80
Tailhook, effects of a negative subculture, 81-82
The Wave, effects of a simulated, authoritarian environment, 78-79
Skinner, B.F., on our failure to use appropriate behavior management, 94
Slavery:
Abraham Lincoln on, 7, 9, 37
abolition of, in Northern states, 9
African wars as supporters of, 117-118
Alexander Hamilton on, 8
Benjamin Franklin on, 8
current practice of, xxvi

free Negro slave owners in the U.S., 9
George Washington on, 8
in Asia and Africa, 117-119
in Ethiopia, 118
issue of, in America, 7-12
in Liberia, 118
James Madison on, 8
John Adams on, 8
John Jay on, 8
monetary value of, in America, 9,10
Northwest Ordinance about, 9
Southern government's position on, 11-12
Thomas Jefferson on, 8
transitional period from, argument for, 10-11
Smith, Adam, on limitations to laissez faire, 198
Social Darwinism, "survival of the fittest" in business, 202
Social promotions, disadvantages of, 122-123, 134
Social values, teaching of, 138
Social workers, should be on piecework, 183
Socialization, process of, 63-74
Sociopath (see Criminal Personality)
"Speed," effects of, 55
Stages of human development:
    according to Piaget, 67
    cortical development and, 103-104
    impact of marijuana upon, 54
Standards, erosion of:
    for granting bankruptcies, 176-177
    in education, 58-59, 122-125
    in granting welfare support, 157-161
    in literacy level, 122
    in parental supervision, 51-54, 123-125
    in morality, xv, 42-59
    in popular-music lyrics, 47
    in respect for government, 150
    in respect for the law, xvii-xviii, 44-46, 50, 56
    in the quality of family life, 51-54
    of civility, 45-46, 81-82

of honesty, 42-45

of responsible sexual behavior, 53, 57

of self-control, 45-46

STAR Program, successful approach for reducing adolescent drinking, smoking, and drug abuse, 108-109

Stephens, Alexander, on South's position about slavery, 11-12

Strive Program, successful rehabilitation employment, 113-114

Subsidies to private-sector employers, 112-113, 169-170

Substance abusers:

being classified with the physically handicapped, 162

proportion of, among the homeless, 109-110

Success For All Program, successful approach for improving reading skill, 128-129

Sugar subsidies, detrimental effects of, 152

Suicide rate of young people, 1990 versus 1960, 50

Support Groups, 110

Awakenings, support for the mentally ill, 110

Fast Track to Employment, 110

INcube, helping the recovering mentally ill to start businesses, 110

Partners In Care, support for the mentally ill, 110

Schizophrenics Anonymous, 110

Sweatshops:

reactions of certain retailers to the problem of, 205

reducing the conflict between domestic and foreign regulation of, 20-242

Tae Kwon Do, for enhancing self-discipline in young people, 108

Tailhook scandal, influence of a negative subculture, 81-82

Teachers:

better preparation of, through productive workshops, 130

broader recruitment of, through the AmeriCorps Teach For America Program, 127

better preparation of, through the CITE Program, 126-127

need for better preparation of, 124-125

Teen Father Program, success of, 102

Teen Outreach Program, success in encouraging personal responsibility, 101

Television violence:

effects of, on behavior, 47-48

control of viewing of, 104

The Wave, simulation of an authoritarian environment, 78-79

Third International Math and Science Survey, results of, 122

"Tough love," success in dealing with juvenile delinquency:

military-style, 108

via Tae Kwon Do, 108

"Travelers," community of exploiters of others, 79-80

Trespass Affidavit Program, by which police can challenge non-residents, 107-108

Trust:

essential role of, 1-2

evidence of negative change in level of, 43-44

Tylenol Case, of Johnson and Johnson, 212

Unemployed (see homeless and unemployed)

Uniform Commercial Codes, provide ethical guidelines, 212-214

United States Sentencing Commission 1991 Guidelines, for punishing organizations for illegal behavior, 210-211

Universal Declaration of Human Rights of the United Nations, 33-34

Vagrancy:

as a Constitutional right, 163-164

need for the reform of laws pertaining to, 163-164, 166

Values:

about group decision-making in China, 216-217

about individuality and independence in Japan, 217-218

about participative management in Mexico, 217

cross-cultural differences in, xxii-xxvi

power of, xv-xxvii, 75-82

Values education (see character education)

Violence:
  air rage, 45
  as the result of early physical abuse, 49
  influence of, in the movies, 48
  influence of, on television, 47-48
  in popular music, 47
  on school buses, 45
  rates of, 46
  road rage, 45
Vouchers, experience with for school attendance, 131-133

Washington, Booker T., a former slave on the need for
  blacks to embrace positive core values, 59
Washington, George:
  on avoiding the appearance of a conflict-of-interest, 35-36
  on self-government as a prerequisite for viable democracy,
    6
  on slavery, 8
  on the required values for the prosperity and happiness of a
    people, 1
  on the abuse of power, 35-36
Welfare:
  decline in the quality of recipients of, 163-164
  erosion of standards for the granting of, 157-161
  Poor Law Reform of 1834 "principle of less-eligibility,"
    158-159
  state of, prior to recent reform efforts, 159-160
  undesirable behaviors encouraged by, 159, 162-164
Welfare reform:
  exploited teen mothers versus non-exploited ones, 168
  minimum wage issues, 168-170
  Minnesota's successful Subsidy to Private-Sector
    Employers Plan, 170
  Michigan's successful program, 167
  need for, 157-161
  New York City's effective Work Experience Plan, 169-170
  success nationally, 167-168

Wisconsin's successful Self-Sufficiency First Program, 166-167
"Whistle Blowing," encouragement of, 222-223
Willpower:
    enhancement of, 85-94, 97-98
    nature of, 70
Work Experience Plan, of New York City, for welfare reform, 169-170
Workshops, for improving teaching effectiveness, 130

Young people:
    age of first sexual experience by, 53
    delinquency rates for, 42-43, 45-46, 53-57
    effectiveness of curfews for drug offenders, 106
    dishonesty trends for, 42-43
    enhancement of self-discipline for, 108-109
    reducing violent behavior by, 106

About The Author

Dr. Fox received his bachelor's and master's degrees from the University of Michigan and his doctorate from Ohio State. He is a consultant in the areas of motivation, group problem solving, performance appraisal, and supervisory skills training, and is Professor Emeritus of organizational behavior and management at the Graduate School of Business Administration of the University of Florida. He is a member of the Society For Organizational And Industrial Psychology and a Fellow in the Academy of Management.

He was a Fulbright Lecturer in management and organization theory at the Finnish School of Economics and the Swedish School of Economics in Helsinki, he studied Japanese management as a Fulbright Senior Research Scholar at Kyoto University, and was a Principal Investigator for leadership research that was supported by the Office of Naval Research. In addition to having published several books, he has published numerous articles and has been a consultant to many organizations.